The Assassination of Julius Caesar

Also by Michael Parenti

The Terrorism Trap (2002)
Democracy for the Few (7th edition, 2001)
To Kill a Nation: The Attack on Yugoslavia (2000)
History as Mystery (1999)
America Besieged (1998)
Blackshirts and Reds (1997)
Dirty Truths (1996)
Against Empire (1995)
Land of Idols: Political Mythology in America (1994)
Inventing Reality: The Politics of News Media (1986, 1993)
Make-Believe Media: The Politics of Entertainment (1992)
The Sword and the Dollar (1989)
Power and the Powerless (1978)
Ethnic and Political Attitudes (1975)
Trends and Tragedies in American Foreign Policy (1971)
The Anti-Communist Impulse (1969)

The Assassination of Julius Caesar
A People's History of Ancient Rome

MICHAEL PARENTI

THE NEW PRESS

NEW YORK
LONDON

Published in the United States by The New Press, New York, 2003
Distributed by Two Rivers Distribution

ISBN 978-1-56584-942-6 (pbk.)
ISBN 978-1-59558-556-1 (e-book)

Library of Congress Cataloging-in-Publication Data
Parenti, Michael, 1933–
The assassination of Julius Caesar : a people's history of ancient
Rome / Michael Parenti.
p. cm.
Includes bibliographical references and index.
ISBN 978-1-56584-797-2 (hc.)
1. Caesar, Julius—Assassination. 2. Rome—Politics and
government—265–30 B.C. I. Title.
DG267 .P37 2003
937'.05'092—dc21
2002041060

The New Press publishes books that promote and enrich public discussion and
understanding of the issues vital to our democracy and to a more equitable
world. These books are made possible by the enthusiasm of our readers; the
support of a committed group of donors, large and small; the collaboration
of our many partners in the independent media and the not-for-profit sector;
booksellers, who often hand-sell New Press books; librarians; and above all
by our authors.

www.thenewpress.com

Printed in the United States of America

29 28 27 26 25 24 23 22 21 20 19

To Marina Anttila

Contents

Acknowledgments   ix

Introduction: Tyrannicide or Treason?   1

1. Gentlemen's History: Empire, Class, and Patriarchy   13

2. Slaves, Proletarians, and Masters   27

3. A Republic for the Few   45

4. "Demagogues" and Death Squads   59

5. Cicero's Witch-hunt   85

6. The Face of Caesar   113

7. "You All Did Love Him Once"   131

8. The *Popularis*   149

9. The Assassination   167

10. The Liberties of Power   187

11. Bread and Circuses   205

Appendix: A Note on
Pedantic Citations and Vexatious Names   223

Notes   229

Index   261

Acknowledgments

O ver the years Charles Briody tried to improve upon my childhood altar boy's Latin with ad hoc lessons, mostly on the telephone now that we live at opposite ends of North America. I must confess that all his best efforts never got me much beyond the *Gallĭa est omnis divisa in partes tres* level. For this I have only myself to blame. Luckily, all the major (and most minor) ancient sources are available in various English translations. Briody also generously provided me with some crucial literature and notes of his own, and did a most helpful reading of the manuscript. So too did Iain Boal and Daniel Shoup who, like Briody, gave me the benefit of their substantive criticisms and their classical education.

Peggy Karp did a close and especially valuable reading of the manuscript. Jane Scantlebury helped me locate sources, and tendered advice and encouragement over the long duration of the writing. She also contributed a useful critique of the manuscript. Susan McAllister went over an early version of the opening chapter for me, and provided other needed assistance.

Peter Livingston saved the day—and the book—laboring hard to snatch from the jaws of my treacherous computer precious text and endnotes that had been mysteriously devoured. He thereby saved me many impossible months of reconstructive effort. Willa

Madden, my webmeister, also conducted helpful operations against the wanton vicissitudes of electronic storage. Richard Wiebe and Andrea Segall brought several useful sources to my attention. And Sheeda Jamsheed helped me navigate my way through the University of California library to dig up some materials. My editor at The New Press, Colin Robinson, was enthusiastic and supportive all the way. His assistant, Abby Aguirre, was most helpful. Production editor Sarah Fan walked the book through its various phases with reassuring proficiency. And Holly Knowles provided an excellent index.

To all these fine people I extend my heartfelt thanks.

Introduction: Tyrannicide or Treason?

> O, what a fall was there, my countrymen!
> Then I, and you, and all of us fell down,
> Whilst bloody treason flourish'd over us.
> —*JULIUS CAESAR* ACT III, SCENE 2

O n the fifteenth of March, 44 B.C., in a meeting hall adjacent to Pompey's theater, the Roman Senate awaited the arrival of the Republic's supreme commander, Julius Caesar. This particular session did not promise to be an eventful one for most of the senators. But others among them were fully alive to what was in the offing. They stood about trying to maintain a calm and casual pose—with daggers concealed beneath their togas.

Finally Caesar entered the chamber. He had an imposing presence, augmented by an air of command that came with being at the height of his power. Moving quickly to the front of the hall, he sat himself in the place of honor. First to approach him was a senator who pretended to enter a personal plea on behalf of a relative. Close behind came a group of others who crowded around the ceremonial chair. At a given signal, they began to slash at their prey with their knives, delivering fatal wounds. By this act, the assailants believed they had saved the Roman Republic. In fact, they had set the stage for its complete undoing.

The question that informs this book is, why did a coterie of Roman senators assassinate their fellow aristocrat and celebrated ruler, Julius Caesar? An inquiry into this incident reveals something important about the nature of political rule, class power, and a people's struggle for democracy and social justice—issues that are still very much with us. The assassination also marked a turning point in the history of Rome. It set in motion a civil war, and put an end to whatever democracy there had been, ushering in an absolutist rule that would prevail over Western Europe for centuries to come.

The prevailing opinion among historians, ancient and modern alike, is that the senatorial assassins were intent upon restoring republican liberties by doing away with a despotic usurper. This is the justification proffered by the assassins themselves. In this book I present an alternative explanation: The Senate aristocrats killed Caesar because they perceived him to be a popular leader who threatened their privileged interests. By this view, the deed was more an act of treason than tyrannicide, one incident in a line of political murders dating back across the better part of a century, a dramatic manifestation of a long-standing struggle between opulent conservatives and popularly supported reformers. This struggle and these earlier assassinations will be treated in the pages ahead.

This book is not only about the history of the Late Republic but about how that history has been distorted by those writers who regularly downplay the importance of material interests, those whose ideological taboos about class realities dim their perception of the past. This distortion is also manifested in the way many historians, both ancient and modern, have portrayed the common people of Rome as being little better than a noisome rabble and riotous mob.

In word and action, wealthy Romans made no secret of their fear and hatred of the common people and of anyone else who infringed upon their class prerogatives. History is full of examples of politico-economic elites who equate any challenge to their privileged social order as a challenge to *all* social order, an invitation to chaos and perdition.

The oligarchs of Rome were no exception. Steeped in utter opulence and luxury, they remained forever inhospitable to Rome's democratic element. They valued the Republic only as long as it served their way of life. They dismissed as "demagogues" and "usurpers" the dedicated leaders who took up the popular cause. The historians of that day, often wealthy slaveholders themselves, usually agreed with this assessment. So too classical historians of the modern era, many of whom adopt a viewpoint not too different from the one held by the Roman aristocracy.

Caesar's sin, I shall argue, was not that he was subverting the Roman constitution—which was an unwritten one—but that he was loosening the oligarchy's overbearing grip on it. Worse still, he used state power to effect some limited benefits for small farmers, debtors, and urban proletariat, at the expense of the wealthy few. No matter how limited these reforms proved to be, the oligarchs never forgave him. And so Caesar met the same fate as other Roman reformers before him.

My primary interest is not in Julius Caesar as an individual but in the issues of popular struggle and oligarchic power that were being played out decades before he was born, continuing into his life and leading to his death. Well into my adulthood, most of what I knew about ancient Rome was learned from Hollywood and television. In my head were images of men in togas, striding about marbled palaces, mouthing lapidary phrases in stage-mannered accents, and of course images of chariot races and frenzied arena crowds giving thumbs-down to hapless victims.

In my woeful ignorance I was no different from many other educated Americans who have passed from grade school to the postdoctoral level without ever learning anything sensible about Roman history. Aside from the tableaux furnished by Hollywood and television, all that I knew of Julius Caesar I owed to two playwrights, William Shakespeare and George Bernard Shaw. If one has to be misinformed about a subject, it might as well be from the wonderful pens of Shakespeare and Shaw.[1] Fictional representations of history do not usually strive for accuracy, their primary goal being to entertain rather than educate. Still they often are more literal than literary in the way they impact upon our minds. And we had best monitor our tendency to treat the fictional as factual.

Shakespeare's *Julius Caesar* is a powerful play that draws heavily from Plutarch, in an imaginative yet surprisingly faithful way. Literary critics do not agree on whether Shakespeare wants us to consider the assassination as execrable or laudable. We are left to wonder whether Caesar is to be admired or denounced, whether Brutus is noble or loathsome, and whether he or Caesar or Antony or anyone is the hero of the play.[2] For all its ambiguities, Shakespeare's treatment is a politically safe rendition. He focuses on the immediate questions of tyranny versus republican freedom. Those are exactly the parameters within which the senatorial assassins confined the debate.

Likewise, Shakespeare shares the Roman elite's view of the common crowd as a mindless aggregation easily led hither and thither, first adulating Pompey, then bowing to Caesar, later hailing Brutus for saving them from tyranny, only in the next breath to be swayed by Antony. In Julius Caesar, the common people seemingly are capable only of mindless violence and degraded disportment. All this is in keeping with the dominant stereotype of the Roman proletariat that has come down to us.

George Bernard Shaw's Caesar and Cleopatra is charmingly written and highly engaging. Shaw's Caesar is a benign aging fellow, who reluctantly settles for an avuncular relationship with Cleopatra. Upon their first encounter, when she has yet to discover his identity, she repeatedly calls him "old gentleman." It is clear from the outset that there can be no romantic interest between them because of Caesar's age and the young queen's immaturity. At the end of the play, as Caesar departs for Rome, he voices his doubts that he will ever see Cleopatra again, but he promises to send her the young handsome Mark Antony, much to her delight.

In real life, when she was still in her teens, well before she met Caesar, Cleopatra already had slept with Antony. It happened in 55 B.C. when a Roman expeditionary force was in Egypt to restore Ptolemy to the throne. Antony was serving as commander of the cavalry.[3] Some time later, still predating Caesar's arrival, Cleopatra bestowed her favors upon a second Roman lover, Pompey's son Cnaeus, who was in Africa raising troops for his father. And Shaw notwithstanding, in late 48 B.C., though Caesar was fifty-three and she but twenty-three or so, she proved ready enough to bed her third Roman. It is said that Cleopatra was a woman of lively turn and enticing talents. She also had a keen sense of the political. That this Roman conqueror had the power to secure the Egyptian throne for her must have added to the attraction she felt for him. It developed into a protracted love affair. Eventually, she bore Caesar a son and moved to Rome in order to be closer to him, thereby demonstrating that some things never change.

Although he was engaged in other sexual liaisons and possessed of a wife, Caesar found time to give Cleopatra a lavish welcome befitting a queen, erecting a gold effigy of her in a consecrated area. He established her in a sumptuous villa across the Tiber, from which she held court, while political leaders, financiers, and men of letters, including the renowned Cicero, danced in attendance.

To his credit, Shaw does insert an iconoclastic sentiment not found in Shakespeare or among regiments of historians who have written about the Late Republic. In a prologue to *Caesar and Cleopatra* that is almost never performed, the god Ra tells the audience how Rome discovered that "the road to riches and greatness is through robbery of the poor and slaughter of the weak." In conformity with that dictum, the Romans "robbed their own poor until they became great masters of that art, and knew by what laws it could be made to appear seemly and honest." And after squeezing their own people dry, they stripped the poor throughout the many other lands they conquered. "And I, Ra, laughed; for the minds of the Romans remained the same size whilst their dominion spread over the earth." Very likely Shaw was inviting his audience to draw a parallel to the small colonialist minds that held sway over the vast British empire of his own day.

There is another instance of Shaw's iconoclasm. In Act II of *Caesar and Cleopatra*, Lucius Septimus refuses Caesar's invitation to join his ranks and prepares to depart. Caesar's loyal comrade in arms, Rufus, angrily observes: "That means he is a Republican." Lucius turns defiantly and asks, "And what are you?" To which Rufus responds, "A Caesarian, like all Caesar's soldiers." Left at that, we have the standard view espoused by Shakespeare and most historians: The struggle is between those fighting to preserve the Republic and those who make themselves an instrument of Caesar's power. But Shaw goes a step further, hinting that Republicanism vs. Caesarism is not really the issue. So he has Caesar interjecting: "Lucius: believe me, Caesar is no Caesarian. Were Rome a true republic, then were Caesar the first of Republicans."

That response invites the dissident query pursued in this book: how republican was the Late Republic? More than 2,000 years after

Caesar, most students of that period have yet to bid farewell to the misapprehensions about the republicanism embraced by Lucius and most others of his social set. They have yet to consider that republicanism might largely be a cloak for oligarchic privilege— as it often is to this day—worn grudgingly by the elites as long as it proved serviceable to their interests. At the same time, as we shall see, ordinary Roman citizens had been able to win limited but important rights under the Republic, and did at times make important democratic gains, including occasional successes around land redistribution, rent control, debt cancellation, and other reforms. As far as the Senate oligarchs were concerned, such agitation and popular victories were *the* major problem, perceived by them as the first steps down the path of class revolution.

To this day, dubious film representations about ancient Rome continue to be mass-marketed. In 2000, while I was working on this book, Hollywood brought forth *Gladiator,* a swashbuckling epic about revenge and heroism, offering endless episodes of arena bloodletting. Unencumbered by any trace of artistic merit, *Gladiator* played before packed houses in the United States and abroad, winning a Golden Globe Award and an Academy Award. The story takes place during the reign of the venal Emperor Commodus, more than two centuries after Julius Caesar's death. Worth noting is how the Roman Senate is depicted. We are asked to believe that the Senate was populated by public-spirited men devoted to the people's welfare. But the people themselves are portrayed as little more than a rabble. In one scene, two Senate leaders are seated in the Coliseum. When one of them complains of the unsavory proceedings below, the other opines that the crowd is interested only in bread and circuses, war and violence: "Rome is the mob. . . . The beating heart of Rome is not the marble of the Senate. It is the sands of the Coliseum. [The emperor] will bring them death and they will love him for it." This view of the Roman populace as mindless bloodthirsty riffraff unfortunately remains the *anti*-people's history purveyed by both the entertainment media and many classical scholars.

I cannot recall exactly when I moved beyond the stage and screen images of Rome and Caesar and became seriously interested in the Late Republic as a subject of intensive study. It was years ago, by way of my self-directed readings in ancient Greek history and political philosophy. At first, it appeared to me that the Romans could never be as compelling and absorbing as their Mediterranean cousins. But indeed they are, at least from 133 B.C. to about 40 B.C., the years covered in this book, most of which fall in that period designated the Late Republic.[4]

To assist the many readers who might be unfamiliar with ancient Rome, the first three chapters deal with Rome's history and sociopolitical life. Chapter Four treats the plutocracy's bloody repression of popular reformers and their followers from Tiberius Gracchus (133 B.C.) down to Caesar's early days. Chapter Five offers a critical portrait of the historians' hero, Cicero, with a narrative of how he mobilized the forces of political repression on behalf of elite interests. The next five chapters deal with Caesar's life and related political issues, his death and its aftermath. The final chapter caps the whole subject of ancient Rome, taking to task the stereotype of the Roman people as a "rabble" and "mob."

When the editors of The New Press told me they wanted to include this book in their People's History Series, I agreed. By my view, any history that deals with the efforts of the populace to defend itself from the abuses of wealth and tyranny is people's history. Such history has been written over the past century by such notables as W.E.B. Du Bois, Philip Foner, Herbert Aptheker, Albert Mathiez, A.L. Morton, George Rudé, Richard Boyer, Herbert Morais, Jesse Lemisch, Howard Zinn, G.E.M. de Ste. Croix, and others.

But writing "history from the bottom up" is not an easy task when it comes to the Roman Republic, for there exists no trove of ordinary people's letters, diaries, and memoirs; no back issues of labor publications and newspapers; no court, police, and government documents of the kind that compose the historical record of more recent centuries. Most of Rome's written histories, libraries, and archives were lost over time or were deliberately destroyed by the fanatical proselytizers of Christianity who conducted a systematic war of eradication against pagan scholarship and culture after they came to power in the fifth century A.D. In any case, as far as we know, the small farmers, proletarians, and slaves of Rome left no written record to speak of.

So one must read against the grain, looking for evidence of the Roman people's struggle in the self-serving words and repressive deeds of the wealthy oligarchs. A people's history should be not only an account of popular struggle against oppression but an exposé of the *anti*-people's history that has prevailed among generations of mainstream historians. It should be a critical history about a people's *oppressors*, those who propagated an elitist ideology and a loathing of the common people that distorts the historical record down to this day.

Here is a story of latifundia and death squads, masters and slaves, patriarchs and subordinated women, self-enriching capitalists and plundered provinces, profiteering slumlords and urban rioters. Here is a struggle between the plutocratic few and the indigent many, the privileged versus the proletariat, featuring corrupt politicians, money-driven elections, and the political assassination of popular leaders. I leave it to the reader to decide whether any of this might resonate with the temper of our own times.

1

Gentlemen's History: Empire, Class, and Patriarchy

Rome, thou hast lost the breed of noble bloods!
—*Julius Caesar* Act I, scene 2

The writing of history has long been a privileged calling undertaken within the church, royal court, landed estate, affluent town house, government agency, university, and corporate-funded foundation. The social and ideological context in which historians labor greatly influences the kind of history produced. While this does not tell us everything there is to know about historiography, it is certainly worth some attention.

Historians are fond of saying, as did Benedetto Croce, that history reflects the age in which it is written. The history of seemingly remote events vibrate "to present needs and present situations." Collingwood made a similar point: "St. Augustine looked at Roman history from the point of view of an early Christian; Tillemont, from that of a seventeenth-century Frenchman; Gibbon, from that of an eighteenth-century Englishman. . . ."[1]

Something is left unsaid here, for there is no unanimity in how the people of any epoch view the past, let alone the events of their own day. The differences in perception range not only across the ages and between civilizations but within any one society at any one time. Gibbon was not just "an eighteenth-century Englishman," but an eighteenth-century English *gentleman*; in his own words, a "youth of family and fortune," enjoying "the luxury and freedom of a wealthy house." As heir to "a considerable estate," he attended Oxford where he wore the velvet cap and silk gown of a gentleman. While serving as an officer in the militia, he soured in the company of "rustic officers, who were alike deficient in the knowledge of scholars and the manners of gentlemen."[2]

To say that Gibbon and his Oxford peers were "gentlemen" is not to imply that they were graciously practiced in the etiquette of fair play toward all persons regardless of social standing, or that they were endowed with compassion for the more vulnerable of their fellow humans, taking pains to save them from hurtful indignities, as real gentlemen might do. If anything, they were likely to be unencumbered by such sentiments, uncomprehending of any social need beyond their own select circle. For them, a "gentleman" was one who sported an uncommonly polished manner and affluent lifestyle, and who presented himself as prosperous, politically conservative, and properly schooled in the art of ethnoclass supremacism.

Like most other people, Gibbon tended to perceive reality in accordance with the position he occupied in the social structure.

As a gentleman scholar, he produced what elsewhere I have called "gentlemen's history," a genre heavily indebted to an upper-class ideological perspective.[3] In 1773, we find him beginning work on his magnum opus, *A History of the Decline and Fall of the Roman Empire*, while settled in a comfortable town house tended by half-a-dozen servants. Being immersed in what he called the "decent luxuries," and saturated with his own upper-class prepossession, Edward Gibbon was able to look kindly upon ancient Rome's violently acquisitive aristocracy. He might have produced a much different history had he been a self-educated cobbler, sitting in a cold shed, writing into the wee hours after a long day of unrewarding toil. No accident that the impoverished laborer, even if literate, seldom had the agency to produce scholarly tomes. Gibbon himself was aware of the class realities behind the writing of history: "A gentleman possessed of leisure and independence, of books and talents, may be encouraged to write by the distant prospect of honor and reward: but wretched is the author, and wretched will be the work, where daily diligence is stimulated by daily hunger."[4]

As one who hobnobbed with nobility, Gibbon abhorred the "wild theories of equal and boundless freedom" of the French Revolution.[5] He was a firm supporter of the British empire. While serving as a member of Parliament he voted against extending liberties to the American colonies. Unsurprisingly he had no difficulty conjuring a glowing pastoral image of the Roman empire: "Domestic peace and union were the natural consequences of the moderate and comprehensive policy embraced by the Romans. . . . The obedience of the Roman world was uniform, voluntary, and permanent. The vanquished nations, blended into one great people, resigned the hope, nay even the wish, of resuming their independence. . . . The vast extent of the Roman empire was governed by absolute power, under the guidance of virtue and wisdom."[6] Not a word here about an empire built upon sacked towns, shattered armies, slaughtered villagers, raped women, enslaved prisoners, plundered lands, burned crops, and mercilessly overtaxed populations.

The gentlemen historians who lived during antiquity painted much the same idyllic picture, especially of Rome's earlier epoch. The theme they repeatedly visited was of olden times as golden times, when men were more given to duty than luxury, women were chaste and unsparingly devoted to their family patriarchs, youth were ever respectful of their elders, and the common people were modest in their expectations and served valiantly in Rome's army.[7] Writing during the Late Republic, Sallust offers this fairy tale of Roman times earlier than his own: "In peace and war . . . virtus [valor, manliness, virtue] was held in high esteem . . . and avarice was a thing almost unknown. Justice and righteousness were upheld not so much by law as by natural instinct. . . . They governed by conferring benefits on their subjects, not by intimidation."[8]

A more realistic picture of Roman imperialism comes from some of its victims. In the first century B.C., King Mithridates, driven from his land in northern Anatolia, wrote, "The Romans have constantly had the same cause, a cause of the greatest antiquity, for making war upon all nations, peoples, and kings, the insatiable desire for empire and wealth."[9] Likewise, the Caledonian

chief Calgacus, speaking toward the end of the first century A.D.,
observed:

> [Y]ou find in [the Romans] an arrogance which no reasonable
> submission can elude. Brigands of the world, they have ex-
> hausted the land by their indiscriminate plunder, and now
> they ransack the sea. The wealth of an enemy excites their cu-
> pidity, his poverty their lust of power. . . . Robbery, butchery,
> rapine, the liars call Empire; they create a desolation and call
> it peace. . . . [Our loved ones] are now being torn from us by
> conscription to slave in other lands. Our wives and sisters,
> even if they are not raped by enemy soldiers, are seduced by
> men who are supposed to be our friends and guests. Our
> goods and money are consumed by taxation; our land is
> stripped of its harvest to fill their granaries; our hands and
> limbs are crippled by building roads through forests and
> swamps under the lash of our oppressors. . . . We Britons
> are sold into slavery anew every day; we have to pay the
> purchase-price ourselves and feed our masters in addition.[10]

For centuries, written history was considered a patrician literary
genre, much like epic and tragedy, concerned with the monumental deeds of great personages, a world in which ordinary men
played no role other than nameless spear-carriers, and ordinary
women not even that. Antiquity gives us numerous gentlemen
chroniclers—Homer, Herodotus, Thucydides, Polybius, Cicero,
Livy, Plutarch, Suetonius, Appian, Dio Cassius, Valerius Maximus,
Velleius Paterculus, Josephus, and Tacitus—just about all of

whom had a pronouncedly low opinion of the common people. Dio Cassius, for one, assures us that "many monarchs are the source of blessings to their subjects . . . whereas many who live under a democracy work innumerable evils to themselves."[11]

The political biases of ancient historians were not interred with their bones. Our historical perceptions are shaped not only by our present socioeconomic status but by the ideological and class biases of the past historians upon whom we rely. As John Gager notes, it is difficult to alter our habitual ways of thinking about history because "without knowing it, we perceive the past according to paradigms first created many centuries ago."[12] And the creators of those ancient paradigms usually spoke with decidedly upper-class accents.

In sum, Gibbon's view of history was not only that of an eighteenth-century English gentleman but of a whole line of gentlemen historians from bygone times, similarly situated in the upper strata of their respective societies. What would have made it so difficult for Gibbon to gain a critical perspective of his own ideological limitations—had he ever thought of doing so—was the fact that he kept intellectual company with like-minded scholars of yore, in that centuries-old unanimity of bias that is often mistaken for objectivity.

To be sure, there were some few observers in ancient Rome, such as the satirist Juvenal, who offer a glimpse of the empire as it really was, a system of rapacious expropriation. Addressing the proconsuls, Juvenal says: "When at last you leave to go out to govern your province, limit your anger and greed. Pity our destitute allies, whose poor bones you see sucked dry of their pith and their marrow."[13]

In 1919, noted conservative economist Joseph Schumpeter presented a surprisingly critical picture of Roman imperialism, in words that might sound familiar to present-day critics of U.S. "globalism":

... That policy which pretends to aspire to peace but unerringly generates war, the policy of continual preparation for war, the policy of meddlesome interventionism. There was no corner of the known world where some interest was not alleged to be in danger or under actual attack. If the interests were not Roman, they were those of Rome's allies; and if Rome had no allies, then allies would be invented. When it was utterly impossible to contrive such an interest—why, then it was the national honor that had been insulted. The fight was always invested with an aura of legality. Rome was always being attacked by evil-minded neighbors, always fighting for a breathing space. The whole world was pervaded by a host of enemies, and it was manifestly Rome's duty to guard against their indubitably aggressive designs.[14]

Still, the Roman empire has its twentieth-century apologists. British historian Cyril Robinson tenders the familiar image of an empire achieved stochastically, without deliberate design: "It was perhaps almost as true of Rome as of Great Britain that she acquired her world-dominion in a fit of absence of mind."[15] An imperialism without imperialists, a design of conquest devoid of human agency or forethought, such a notion applies neither to Rome nor to any other empire in history.

Despite their common class perspective, gentlemen historians do not achieve perfect accord on all issues. Gibbon himself was roundly condemned for his comments about early Christianity in the Roman empire. He was attacked as an atheist by clergy and others who believed that their religion had flourished exclusively through divine agency and in a morally flawless manner.[16] Gibbon credits Christianity's divine origin as being the primary impetus for its triumph, but he gives only a sentence or two to that notion, being more interested as a secular historian in the natural rather than supernatural causes of the church's triumph. Furthermore, he does not hesitate to point out instances of worldly opportunism and fanatical intolerance among Christian proselytes. Some readers may find his treatment of the rise of Christianity to be not only the most controversial part of his work but also the most interesting.[17]

Along with his class hauteur, the gentleman scholar is likely to be a male supremacist. So Gibbon describes Emperor Severus's second wife Julia Domna as "united to a lively imagination, a firmness of mind, and strength of judgment, seldom bestowed on her sex."[18] Historians do take note of the more notorious female perpetrators in the imperial family, such as Messalina, wife of Emperor Claudius, and Agrippina. They tell us that Agrippina grabbed the throne for her son Nero by poisoning her uncle and then her husband, the reigning Claudius. Upon becoming emperor, Nero showed his gratitude to his mother by killing her. Nero was not what we would call a family man; he also murdered his aunt, his ex-wife, and a half brother who had a claim to the throne.

Except for a few high-placed and notably lethal females, Roman women are virtually invisible in the works of most gentlemen historians. Even when noticed, they are not likely to be seen as of any consequence.[19] That there were no female historians to speak of in antiquity, nor for many centuries thereafter, only compounded the deficiency. In the last few decades, thanks mostly to the emergence of feminist scholarship, the research on Roman women has improved, despite the paucity of surviving data. Ordinary Roman women, we know, tended to die younger than their male counterparts because of malnourishment, mistreatment, exhaustion, and childbirth. Almost half of all Roman brides were under the age of fourteen, many as young as twelve, with consummation coming at the time of marriage even if before menarche. Women of all ages almost invariably lived under the rule of some male, be it husband, guardian, or *paterfamilias* (head of the extended family or clan).[20]

Through much of Roman history, females were denied individually given names as well as surnames. Prominent gens names such as Claudius, Julius, and Lucretius gave forth the obligatory feminine derivatives of Claudia, Julia, and Lucretia. Sisters therefore all had the same name and were distinguished from each other by adding "the elder" or "the younger" or "the first," "the second," and "the third." Thus Gaius Octavius's daughters were Octavia the elder and Octavia the younger. Denying them an individually named identity was one way of treating females as family property, mere fractional derivatives of the paterfamilias.[21]

Women of common caste performed much of the onerous work of society as laundresses, domestic servants, millers, weavers, spinners, and sometimes even construction workers, all in addition to their quotidian household chores. As far as we know, even when they labored in the same occupations as men, they were not permitted to belong to craft guilds.[22] Bereft of opportunities for decent livelihood, some of the more impecunious females were driven to selling their sexual favors. Prostitution was given standing as an employment and taxed as such. Owning a brothel was considered a respectable venture by some investors.[23] In general, the great mass of poor women had little hope of exercising an influence on political issues, though numbers of them must have participated in public protests.

The devoted, self-sacrificing wife was a prized character in Roman writing. Examples abound of matrons who faced exile or risked death to stand fast with their husbands.[24] But Roman matrons could also be rebellious on occasion. As early as 195 B.C., they successfully pressured the magistrates to repeal the *lex Oppia*, a law passed during the austerity of the Second Punic War restricting the use of personal ornaments and carriages by women.[25] That they would mobilize themselves in this willful manner sorely vexed many a patriarch.

By the Late Republic (approximately 80–40 B.C.) and during the first century of the empire, Roman matrons made a number of important gains relating to marriage, divorce, property rights, and personal independence. Some of them even owned substantial property, and administered commercial operations. During the civil strife following Caesar's death, the Second Triumvirate posted a list of 1,400 particularly wealthy women whose property was to be assessed. The women organized a protest in the Forum before the magistrates' tribunal, and demanded to know why they had to share in the punishment of the civil war when they had not collaborated in the crime. "Why should we be taxed when we have no share in magistracies, or honors, or military commands, or in public affairs at all, where your conflicts have brought us to this terrible state?"[26] Whatever influence women exercised in business affairs, they never gained full civil rights, nor could they sustain much visibility on the political landscape.[27]

Upper-class wives had the reputation of being overly generous with their sexual favors. Sallust clucks about the women who "publicly sold their chastity."[28] Horace fumes about the matron who becomes well practiced "in lewd loves, then seeks younger adulterers, while her husband's at wine."[29] Writing early in the second century A.D., Juvenal seems to anticipate the venomous misogyny that would soon pour from the pens of the Christian church fathers. Roman matrons, he tells us, are wanton hussies, engaged in their illicit pursuits at the expense of the hapless cuckolds who are their husbands. They have long discarded the virtuous devotions of their forebears, along with the "naturally feminine" traits of modesty, chastity, and domestic servitude.[30] In like fashion, a historian from our own era registers his disapproval of the growing sway exercised by high-placed improvident women in the Late Republic whose "unwholesome influence" engendered a "growing license" and "did much to debase the moral and social standards of the day."[31]

In truth, Roman matrons were doubtless no more promiscuous than their husbands, whose own commonplace dalliances were largely overlooked, given the double standard of that day. Under the patriarchal system, a man was free to kill an allegedly unfaithful wife, while himself patronizing prostitutes or keeping a concubine. The codes against adultery initiated by Emperor Augustus were aimed at wives, with no prohibitions imposed upon husbands.[32] One of the many Roman writers who see only virtue in Rome's earliest epoch and decadence in their own times is Valerius Maximus. He approvingly cites examples of husbands of yore who divorced their wives or otherwise treated them severely for acting in what we might consider mildly independent ways, such as walking abroad with head uncovered, talking to a common freedwoman, or attending public games without the husband's knowledge. "While women were thus checked in the old days, their minds stayed away from wrongdoing," Valerius assures us.[33]

Powerful men such as Julius Caesar often treated women from well-placed families as disposable strategic assets, to be bartered in arranged marriages designed to fortify one's fortune or help forge political coalitions—a practice that continued within European aristocratic circles down through the ages. Women were also a source of sensual divertissement for Caesar as for most other Roman men. A few—such as his first wife Cornelia, his longtime mistress Servilia, and, in his last years, Cleopatra—did win Caesar's love, though none could ever claim exclusive command of his sexual attentions.

Many Roman husbands were hopeless philanderers who fixed upon loveless marriages to advance their careers, pocket ample dowries, or simply enjoy a convenient concupiscence. Still there were instances of deep conjugal links being forged. Valerius gives several examples of husbands who were stricken at the loss of their wives. So does the younger Pliny, who himself expressed genuine love for his wife.[34]

Along with their gender bias, some gentlemen historians let slip a noticeable ethno-class bigotry. The progenitor of all historians of the Late Republic is Cicero. Hailed by Balsdon as "perhaps the most civilized man who has ever lived," Cicero has been revered by classics professors and Latin teachers throughout the ages.[35] This most civilized man was not above stoking the crassest ethno-class prejudices. Cicero sneered at the Greeks and Jews, both the slaves and freedmen among them, who rallied to the side of democratic leaders, declaring that "men of those nations often throw . . . our assemblies into confusion." The Greeks are given to "shameless lying," the Jews to "barbaric superstition."[36]

Some latter-day historians have taken their cue from Cicero. Theodore Mommsen describes the Roman Forum as a shouting fest for "everyone in the shape of a man" with Egyptians, Jews, and Greeks, both freedmen and slaves, being the loudest participants in the public assemblies.[37] Cyril Robinson notes that many proletarians were "of Greek or Oriental origin . . . [whose] loose and feeble character made them bad citizens." The "purity of Roman blood began to be contaminated by the admixture of this alien element." Those of "Oriental blood" were "incapable of assimilating the national habits of decency and restraint," although "not all Greeks, of course, were vicious or unwholesome characters."[38]

J.F.C. Fuller tells us that Rome's "Latin stock was increasingly mongrelized as Greeks, Asiatics, Spaniards, Gauls, and other [slaves] were absorbed through manumission and became citizens."[39] Another esteemed classicist, Jérôme Carcopino, flirts with a racist blood theory of history, writing that interbreeding between Roman aristocrats and their female slaves or freedwomen, followed by frequent emancipation or adoption of the offspring, left "many of the best families of the city infected with an actual hybridization, similar to that which has more recently contaminated other slave-owning peoples." This mixed breeding "strongly accentuated the national and social decomposition" of Rome.[40]

In ancient Rome, as in societies before and since, class oppression was supported by class bias. The lowly were considered low because of deficiencies within themselves. Class bias, in turn, was often buttressed by ethnic prejudice. Many of the poor, both slaves and free, were from "barbarian" stock, and this further fueled the tendency to loathe them as wastrels and brigands, troublesome contaminants of respectable society. So ethnic and class bias conveniently dovetailed for those who looked at their world *de haut en bas*, and this included not only the likes of Cicero but many of the writers who came after him.

2

Slaves, Proletarians, and Masters

Our hearts you see not; they are pitiful;
And pity to the general wrong of Rome—
—*JULIUS CAESAR* ACT III, SCENE 1

Rome's social pyramid rested upon the backs of slaves (*servi*) who composed approximately one-third the population of Italy, with probably a smaller proportion within Rome proper.[1] Their numbers were maintained by conquests, piratical kidnappings, and procreation by the slaves themselves. Slavery also was the final destination for individuals convicted of capital crimes, for destitute persons unable to repay debts, and for children sold off by destitute families. War captives were worked to death in the mines and quarries and on plantations (*latifundia*) at such a rate that their ranks were constantly on the wane.[2]

A step above the *servi* was the great mass of propertyless proletariat (*proletarii*), consisting of city-dwelling citizens (*plebs ur-*

bana), foreigners, and freedmen (ex-slaves). Rome had a downtown urban center of temples, ceremonial sites, emporia, public forums, and government offices. Downtown was encircled by a dense ring of slums. There being no public transportation, the proletarians had to be housed within walking distance of work sites and markets. The solution was to pile them into thousands of poorly lit inner-city tenements along narrow streets. Such dwellings were sometimes seven or eight floors high, all lacking toilets, running water, and decent ventilation. The rents for these fetid, disease-ridden warrens were usually more than the plebs could afford, forcing them to double and triple up, with entire families residing in one room. Some luckless renters could afford only dank cellars or cramped garrets not high enough to stand in.[3]

Charcoal braziers and oil lamps were a constant fire hazard. Building codes were not to appear in Rome for centuries to come. Tenants who escaped the typhoid, typhus, and fires that plagued the slums still lived in fear of having the structures collapse upon them, as happened all too frequently. The ingenuity for which Roman architecture is known was not lavished upon the domiciles of the poor. As Juvenal ironically describes it: "Rome is supported on pipe-stems, matchsticks; it's cheaper thus for the landlord to shore up his ruins, patch up the old cracked walls, and notify all the tenants. They are expected to sleep secure though the beams are about to crash above them."[4] Cicero himself owned tenement properties whose rental income he used to maintain his son as a student in Athens. In a letter to a friend, he sounds every bit the speculative slumlord: "[T]wo of my shops have collapsed and the others are showing cracks, so that even the mice have moved elsewhere, to say nothing of the tenants. Other people call this a disaster, I don't call it even a nuisance. . . . [T]here is a building scheme under way . . . which will turn this loss into a source of profit."[5]

The narrow rutted streets were crowded with tradesmen, artisans, jobbers, beggars, shoppers, and loiterers. Street vendors hawked salted fish, warm pans of smoking sausages, cups of pudding, and jars of wine. Musicians, acrobats, and jugglers, with their sad little trained animals, performed for the passing crowd. Large dirty pots placed at intervals along the streets served as pissoirs for passersby, a concession to fullers and laundry workers who—soap being unknown to the Romans—used the accumulated urine to treat or wash their cloth.[6] (Uric acid is still applied today in such cleansers as borax.) We can presume that the clothes were given a final rinse in fresh water.

For those who could afford it, wine was imbibed during and between meals. Romans of the Late Republic usually drank it more than half diluted with water. Wine was their coffee, tea, and spirits. "And olive oil was their butter, soap, and electricity: they cooked with it, anointed themselves with it at the baths, and burned it in their lamps."[7] The poor person's sustenance was grain, consumed in the form of bread and porridge.

With rampant poverty came a high crime rate. Rome had no street lighting and no police force to speak of. As night fell, the populace secured itself behind bolted doors. Only the opulent few, who could afford an ensemble of slaves and strongmen to light the way and serve as bodyguards, dared to venture abroad, and even they thought twice about it. Juvenal writes acerbically of the hazards posed by street toughs: "It makes no difference whether you try to say something or retreat without a word, they beat you up all the same. . . . You know what the poor man's freedom amounts to? The freedom, after being punched and pounded to pieces, to beg and implore that he be allowed to go home with a few teeth left."[8]

Most *plebs urbana* and their families lived from hand to mouth, toiling long hours for trifling sums. In the countryside, the *plebs rustica* fared no better than their city cousins. When possible, they would try to ease their straitened circumstances by taking on the more perilous chores offered by *latifundia* lords who, like American plantation owners of the antebellum South, sometimes preferred to use free laborers for risky tasks. By the owner's reckoning, the death of a day jobber merely increased the population of the netherworld, whereas the death of a slave represented the loss of a tidy investment.[9]

A rung above the propertyless *proletarii* were the small farmers, settled on their own parcels of land in the provinces around the city, with enough property to qualify for military service. And just above them was a small middle class of minor officials, merchants, and industrial employers, who lived in apartments situated away from the stench and noise of the inner city but still within manageable distance of the Forum and the baths.[10]

Looming over the toiling multitude of Rome in "almost incredible opulence" were "a few thousand multimillionaires."[11] One magistrate estimated that the number of solidly rich families was not more than 2,000.[12] This elite stratum, the "officer class," included the *equites* or equestrians, a class of knights, so designated because their property qualified them to serve in the cavalry—although by the Late Republic many of them probably had never been on a horse. The equestrians were state contractors, bankers, money-lenders, traders, tax collectors, and landowners.[13] They occupied a social rank just below aristocrats and well above commoners, serving as a reservoir for recruits into the aristocratic class, as families of old lineage died out from time to time. Being large property holders who generally had little sympathy for the poor, the knights shared many of the same interests as the nobility, although occasional conflicts did arise between the two elite groups.[14]

At the very apex of the social pyramid was the *nobilitas*, an aristocratic oligarchy representing families whose lineage could claim one or more members who had served as consul (the highest office of the Republic). Equestrians and nobles differed more in political lineage than family fortune. Both groups were members of the officer class; both held wealth in land, slaves, trade, and finance. Both lived in seemly mansions, enjoying gourmet meals served on plates of gold and silver, lavish gardens, game preserves, aviaries, stables of the finest horses, fish ponds, private libraries, private baths, and water closets. Their estates were situated on tracts the size of veritable townships, large enough to house swollen retinues of slaves and personal servants. Cicero was an equestrian who owned seven or eight estates and several smaller farms, along with his urban tenements and other business ventures.[15]

The old nobility too was not above pursuing speculative capitalist ventures. Thus Julius Caesar's friend and ally Crassus, a landed aristocrat, became one of the wealthiest men of the Late Republic by buying up urban sites upon which tenements had collapsed or been ruined by fire, then rebuilding new tenements whose rents provided ample recompense for his capital outlay.[16]

Class supremacism permeated republican Roman society right down to its domestic codes. There was a strict prohibition against marriage between a member of the aristocratic class and a citizen who had risen from the class of freedmen. Aristocrats also were forbidden to marry actresses and women of other such dubious professions.[17]

In Rome's Late Republic, as in any plutocracy, it was a disgrace to be poor and an honor to be rich. The rich, who lived parasitically off the labor of others, were hailed as men of quality and worth; while the impecunious, who struggled along on the paltry earnings of their own hard labor, were considered vulgar and deficient. Though he wrote later on, during the time of emperors, Juvenal might as well have been speaking of earlier republican society when he noted that a rich man's word was treated as good as gold because he was possessed of gold, but a poor man's oath "has no standing in court . . . Men do not easily rise whose poverty hinders their merit."[18]

Rome's oppressive class nature was nowhere more evident than in the widespread practice of slavery. Roman slavery was long treated none too harshly by gentlemen historians. Gibbon, for instance, tells us that a slave did not live without hope, given "the benevolence of the master." If he showed diligence and fidelity for "a few years" he might very naturally expect to be granted his freedom.[19] More recently, Jérôme Carcopino enthuses about Roman laws that "lightened [the slaves'] chains and favored their emancipation . . . The practical good sense of the Romans, no less than the fundamental humanity instinctive in their peasant hearts, had always kept them from showing cruelty toward the *servi*. They had always treated their slaves with consideration. . . . With few exceptions, slavery in Rome was neither eternal nor, while it lasted, intolerable."[20] No slaveholder could have said it better.

"It is not until recent times," notes K.R. Bradley, "that the realization has begun to set in among scholars that there is something distinctly unpalatable about slavery in antiquity. Indeed in some quarters apologetic influences are still at work."[21] One reputable historian who still celebrates the happy side of slavery is Lionel Casson. He accords a grudging nod to the ill-fated souls who labored under the whip in the fields or died in such numbers in the mines, saying only that they were burdened by "tasks that involved sweat and drudgery." Then he dwells upon the favorable conditions supposedly enjoyed by slaves who assisted in running luxurious households, or occupied government posts. Some even amassed substantial fortunes as investors. Sometimes "free men with bleak prospects would sell themselves into slavery in order to qualify" for these plum positions.[22] A great many manumitted *servi*, rhapsodizes Casson, "were able to escape from slavery and mount the steps of the social ladder, in some cases to the very top." One former *servus* gave his son an excellent education, and the boy grew to be the famous writer Horace. "In but two generations the family had risen from slavery to literary immortality."[23]

The impression one gets is that Roman slavery was a kind of affirmative action program, and Rome was a land of opportunity *ouvert aux talents*. In fact, such impressive instances of upward mobility were the rare exception. Manumission was usually granted only after many years of servitude. Even then, liberty was fettered with liabilities. Frequently the manumitted *servus* had to leave behind his spouse or children as slaves. Freedmen could neither serve in the military nor seek public office. They bore the names of their former masters to whom they continued to owe service and make payments.[24]

Slaves usually had to buy their freedom by meeting the original purchasing price. Obviously, the vast majority could not hope to accumulate such a sum. Some of the luckier ones had their freedom paid for by relatives who were already free and working. Only a select few had the opportunity to pocket tips as doorkeepers or performers, or glean windfall gratuities in specialized occupations such as skilled craftsmen, doctors, and prostitutes.

Manumission was largely motivated by the owner's desire to escape the onerous expense of having to feed and shelter chattel for their entire lives, especially ones no longer in the full productive vigor of their youth. Many of the manumitted were granted testimonial emancipation in the master's will, that is, only after his death deprived him of any further opportunity to exploit them would they be set free. As Bradley reckons, "most of the servile population probably never achieved freedom at all . . . [M]anumission was a real but fragile prospect for slaves, and it conceals the years of hardship that preceded its attainment."[25]

All slavocracies develop a racist ideology to justify their dehumanized social relationships. In Rome, male slaves of any age were habitually addressed as *puer* or "boy." A similar degrading appellation was applied to slaves in ancient Greece and in the slavocracy of the United States, persisting into the postbellum segregationist South of the twentieth century. The slave as a low-grade being or subhuman is a theme found in the writings of Plato and Aristotle. In the minds of Roman slaveholders, the *servi* including the foreigners who composed the larger portion of the slave population— were substandard in moral and mental capacity, a notch or two above animals. Cicero assures us that Jews, Syrians, and all other Asian barbarians are "born to slavery."[26] The Roman historian Florus sees the Spartacus slave rebellion not as a monumental struggle for liberty but a disgraceful undertaking perpetrated "by persons of the meanest class" led by "men of the worst character . . . eager to take vengeance on their masters."[27] Gibbon describes Rome's slave population as "a mean and promiscuous multitude."[28] More recently we have Sir Ronald Syme asserting that the Roman slave market was flooded with "captives of alien and often inferior stock."[29] Most present-day classical writers, however, do not embrace the slaveholder's supremacism, at least not overtly.

By definition the relationship between master and slave is a coercive one. Not surprisingly the master is preoccupied with questions of control, with instilling loyalty and obedience into these recalcitrant underlings, using a combination of lenient and harsh methods. In the first century A.D. the Roman agricultural writer Columella set forth advice on how best to manage servile farm labor. The slaveholder had to avoid excessive severity and gratuitous cruelty not out of humane consideration but because such things were counterproductive. Slaves could be better controlled if provided with decent living conditions, time off from work, and occasional opportunity to voice grievances.[30]

The uncertain promise of eventual emancipation sometimes made manumission an effective control mechanism. The slave was encouraged to observe long-term compliance in the hope of eventual freedom. Servile family attachments were another useful restraint. Married slaves with children were less likely to abscond and more ready to cooperate. And their offspring added to the owner's wealth. But the slave family existed only as long as it served the interests of the master. It was constantly in danger of disruption since the slave was a disposable form of property. Slave owners readily broke up servile families "when economic considerations made sale of their slaves attractive or necessary."[31]

Good treatment did not guarantee good slaves. One might recall Frederick Douglass's observation drawn from his own unhappy bondage in the American South: The slave who has a cruel master wishes for a kind one, and the slave who has a kind master wishes for freedom. Kindly treatment alone could eventually undermine control by nursing heightened expectations. It was necessary then to impose a coercive, fear-inspiring dominion. A Roman slave could be flogged, branded, mutilated, starved, raped, or crucified, without recourse to self-defense. "Against a slave everything is permitted," wrote Seneca, the Stoic, who inveighed against the cruel treatment of *servi* while availing himself of their services.[32]

In accordance with an ancient rule, if a master was murdered by one of his slaves, all the others in his household faced execution. In this way every *servus* might feel an interest in guarding the master's safety. A failure to report suspicious doings or secret plots could cost slaves their lives. One could only pray that one's master expired in an unambiguously natural fashion, for if there was any suspicion of foul play, the investigating authorities would put all the late owner's slaves to the torture.[33] Roman law did not admit the torture of a free man but required it to exact evidence from slaves, both male and female. But *servi* who betrayed their masters by volunteering damning information against them in court ended up being punished rather than rewarded.[34] For while prosecutors and plaintiffs wanted to win cases, they were disinclined to encourage disloyalty among slaves.

Those who think Roman slavery was such a benign institution have not explained why fugitive slaves were a constant problem. Owners did not lightly countenance the loss of valuable property. They regularly used chains, metal collars, and other restraining devices. Slaves who fled were hunted down and returned to irate masters who were keen to inflict a severe retribution.[35] Slaveholders consulted oracles and astrologers to divine the whereabouts of runaways; they posted bills offering rewards; they appealed to state authorities and engaged professional slave catchers (*fugitivarii*).[36]

Cicero enlisted two successive provincial governors in the search for a slave who had purloined some of his valuable books and fled abroad.[37]

Every slave society has known its uprisings. Rome was no exception. The three biggest rebellions, occurring in the last two centuries of the Republic, reached the level of open warfare, with many thousands of armed men on both sides, including the famous one waged by Spartacus and his brave hearts in 74–70 B.C. All were mercilessly crushed. There were numerous other slave uprisings but they were small-scale, short-lived, and unsuccessful, apart from the relatively few slaves who managed a permanent escape.[38]

Some domestic slaves who enjoyed the favored circumstances of a wealthy household doubtless were materially better off than many slum-dwelling plebs, though servile accommodations and food rations on even the richest estates were usually kept at meager levels. Some urban slaves could sneak away and participate in marketplace debates or even join guilds. But most endured long hours of service, daily humiliations, whimsical mistreatment, and the threat of heavy whippings. Ammianus Marcellinus tells of owners in his day who might have slaves flogged 300 times for a minor offense such as being slow to bring hot water.[39] The younger Seneca describes some of the indignities endured by household slaves:

> When we recline at a banquet, one slave mops up the disgorged food, another crouches beneath the table and gathers

up the leftovers of the tipsy guests. Another carves the price-
less game birds; with unerring strokes and skilled hand, he
cuts choice morsels along the breast or the rump. Luckless
fellow, to live only for the purpose of cutting fat capons
correctly . . . another, who serves the wine, must dress like a
woman and wrestle with his advancing years, he cannot get
away from his boyhood; he is dragged back to it; and though
he has already acquired a soldier's figure, he is kept beardless
by having his hair smoothed away or plucked out by the
roots, and he must remain awake throughout the night, di-
viding his time between his master's drunkenness and lust;
in the chamber he must be a man, at the feast a boy.[40]

Sexual exploitation of Rome's *servi* by their masters, though
pandemic, is ignored by virtually all present-day historians.
Among ancient writers it was openly acknowledged that slaves
should make their bodies available on demand. Horace parades his
preference for household slaves, both male and female: "I like my
sex easy and ready at hand."[41] And Petronius has an ex-slave in
his *Satyricon* reminisce about how he sexually serviced both his
master and mistress for fourteen years, an arrangement that Roman
readers doubtless found familiar and believable.[42]

The poet Martial—who was the closest thing ancient Rome
had to a gossip columnist—alludes repeatedly to sexual intimacies
that masters enjoyed with their household *servi*. He ironically hails
a certain Quirinalis for not needing a wife because he fornicates
with maid servants and fills his town house and country place

with the resultant offspring. "A genuine paterfamilias is Quirin-alis."[43] We hear nothing about how the maid servants felt about all this.

Affluent women sometimes took advantage of their class status to pursue carnal knowledge. So Martial chides one man whose seven sons all advertise the features of their mother's servile adul-terers, among whom are the cook, the baker, and even the hus-band's own sodomite underling. The poet refers to a woman of advanced years who uses her entire dowry to redeem her favorite lover from slavery, thereby ensuring regular satisfaction for herself; a master who beds his housekeeper; another who buys back his maid in order to keep her as his concubine; those who seek out slave boys for their pleasure; and a husband who lingers with maidservants while his wife accommodates litter-bearers: "You are quite a pair, Alauda."[44]

Martial himself longs for "a plump home-born slave." When he passes up the chance to buy "a lad" for 100,000 sesterces, a friend of his immediately meets the price. In his unsparingly coarse manner, Martial tells how his "cock grieves" over the lost opportunity.[45] Of course, the boy in question had no say in the matter. The owner unilaterally set the boundaries and chose the mode of gratification, using the child as he pleased. Slavers reg-ularly catered to pedophilic tastes, selling young boys and girls for sexual purposes. Depilatories were used to remove the hair on a boy's body, keeping him as young-looking as possible. Boys were made to ingest various potions thought to delay the onset of pu-berty. Even worse, slave dealers frequently resorted to castration, despite successive laws forbidding it.[46]

Such instances of child barter, rape, and sexual mutilation go unmentioned by those latter-day scholars who, like the slaveholders themselves, seem to have a keener sense of slavery's hidden benefits than of its manifest evils.

The image of a mutually loving master-slave relationship in ancient Rome, as Finley notes, seems "to draw modern commentators irresistibly into sentimentality and bathos."[47] But the relationship was anything but mutual. No matter how mawkishly costumed, Roman slavery cannot be passed off as a love relationship.

When a favorite of his named Sositheus, "a delightful fellow," died, Cicero observed "I am more upset than perhaps I ought to be over the death of a slave."[48] Here Cicero is monitoring his feelings, aware that the slaveholder must maintain proper class boundaries by not growing too attached to a mere *servus*. The love a master feels for his slave is patronizing and paternalistic. While the love a slave feels for his master is at least partially exacted by the steeply asymmetrical power relationship, generated as much by uneasy necessity as by genuine affection. No wonder it existed more firmly in the master's imagination than in the slave's heart. We will never know how Cicero's Sositheus, who lived and died in servitude, may have felt about their relationship had he been given an opportunity for freedom and decent employment.

During the American Civil War, many masters and mistresses in the Confederacy were astonished to find that their slaves— supposedly so well treated and so devoted and faithful—would manifest the most outrageous ingratitude at the first opportunity, insolently disregarding commands that could no longer be enforced, or fleeing to freedom, even enlisting in the ranks of the Union army to fight for the emancipation of their brethren. The journalist Whitelaw Reid, traveling through the South immediately after the war, noted the refrain repeated tirelessly by erstwhile slaveholders, "We have been the best friends the nigger ever had. Yet this is the way they treat us."[49] We can safely assume that this kind of hidden "ingratitude" existed among many Roman household slaves.

The "faithful slave" was a favorite theme among ancient writers, most of whom were themselves slaveholders. Both Valerius and Appian provide a number of stories of slaves who showed extraordinary devotion to their masters.[50] No doubt, touching friendships could blossom between master and slave. Vulnerable captives, torn from hearth and home, will sometimes seek survival and security by attaching themselves emotionally to those who hold life-and-death power over them. But we should not make too much of it. The Roman slaveholders, like the American slaveholders of the antebellum South, lived in persistent fear that their "faithfully devoted" slaves were quite capable of rising up and massacring their overlords. In the younger Pliny's words, slaveholders were permanently exposed to "dangers, outrages and insult . . . No master can feel safe because he is kind and considerate: for it is their brutality, not their reasoning capacity, which leads slaves to murder masters."[51] Hence the Roman proverb, "A hundred slaves, a hundred enemies."

The Panglossian view of benign bondage ignores the inhumanity that inheres in forced servitude. Slaves had to truckle to their

SLAVES, PROLETARIANS, AND MASTERS   43

masters and all other superiors. They were marginalized creatures often denied the most elementary social bonds. They suffered a nearly total lack of control over their labor, their persons, and in most regards their very personalities. Slaves themselves—not just their labor power—were commodities.[52] Presumably not thinking of his delightful Sositheus, Cicero made this perfectly clear when he remarked that it was preferable to lighten a ship in emergency by throwing an old slave overboard rather than a good horse. And the elder Cato advises his readers to sell old or sick slaves along with old or sick draught animals "and everything else that is superfluous."[53] So every slaveholder was locked into an intrinsically injurious construct that is the inescapable essence of slavery: The degrading exploitation of one human being so that another may pursue whatever comforts and advantages wealth might confer. Ultimately, the same can be said of all exploitative class relations perpetrated by those who accumulate wealth for themselves by reducing others to poverty.

3

A Republic for the Few

So often shall the knot of us be call'd
The men that gave their country liberty.
—*JULIUS CAESAR* ACT III, SCENE 1

As legend has it, Rome was founded in 753 B.C. and named after its first monarch Romulus. Early in the sixth century B.C., a succession of Etruscan kings reigned over the city. Detested by the common people because of its exploitative rule, the monarchy was overthrown around 510–509 B.C. and a republic was proclaimed. Executive rule passed to a pair of consuls, elected for one-year terms and subject to each other's veto. The consuls remained the highest magistrates throughout the history of the Republic. They levied and commanded Rome's armies, enforced the laws, gave audience to foreign delegations, and presided in the Senate and over the popular assemblies.[1]

Early Roman society was sharply divided between a landed aristocracy of patricians and a mass of commoners called plebeians.

Only patricians could enter the Senate or occupy leading governmental or religious posts. During the fourth century B.C., some of the more affluent plebeian families won access to top official positions, gaining seats in the Senate and entry into the nobility by winning the consulship. By the middle of the third century, plebeians and patricians had won the right to intermarry, and the richer elements of both groups melded into one aristocracy.[2]

The Republic was also an empire. During the fourth and third centuries B.C., Rome embarked upon a series of conquests and alliances that extended its dominion over most of the Italian peninsula. With the defeat of its arch commercial rival, Carthage, in what is known as the First Punic War (264–261 B.C.), Rome took control of Sicily, Sardinia, and Corsica. In the Second Punic War (218–202 B.C.), the Carthaginian general Hannibal launched his famed invasion of Italy, crossing the snow-covered Alps with an army and a troop of elephants. Hannibal fought his way down the peninsula, destroying two Roman armies in the doing, only to be worn down and eventually defeated.[3] Rome expelled Carthage from Spain, turning the greater part of the Iberian peninsula into Roman provinces.

In 146 B.C., after a half-century of peace, Rome attacked and destroyed Carthage itself, transforming its territory into a colonial province called Africa (roughly coextensive with present-day Tunisia). Contrary to popular myth, the invaders did not pour salt or lime into Carthage's topsoil in order to leave it forever barren. Carthage eventually flourished once again but as a Roman provincial city.

The Roman imperialists then moved eastward to fish in troubled waters, intervening to assist Greek cities threatened by Macedonian and Syrian armies. But after beating off these threats, Rome subjugated the Greeks themselves, welding their numerous polities into one province. By the end of the second century B.C., Rome reigned as supreme mistress of the Mediterranean.

As with other imperial powers before and since, the Roman empire brought immense wealth to its ruling class and imposed heavy burdens on its common citizenry. The aristocracy pursued a policy of almost continuous warfare. War offered opportunities to plunder the treasure of other countries and take advantage of depressed land markets in Italy itself. Many small landholders, the mainstay of the Roman infantry, fell in battle. Many more had to serve long enlistments that left them unable to tend their farms. Wealthy investors bought up these holdings for a pittance. War also brought a replenished supply of captive slaves to till the newly acquired tracts.

The *ager publicus*, the publicly owned fertile lands in regions south and east of Rome, had been farmed for generations by collectives of smallholders who paid a modest rent to the state treasury. These collectives, run by free labor, had produced enough to victual the entire city. That Rome could be fed by common farmers, with not a penny of profit extracted by the rich, was more than the rich were willing to tolerate. To protect the smallholders a law was passed that forbade any individual to hold more than 500 *iugera* (about 310 acres). "For a while," writes Plutarch, "this law restrained the greed of the rich and helped the poor. . . . But after a time the wealthy men, by using the names of fictitious tenants, contrived to transfer many of these holdings to themselves, and finally they openly took possession of the greater part of the land under their own names."[4]

By the second century B.C., through a combination of opportunistic buyouts and sheer violence, the wealthy few carved out from the *ager publicus* vast estates for themselves, to which they had no right except that imposed by their money and their hired thugs. In time, the laws were changed to allow unlimited concentration of public and private lands in their hands.[5] As Appian reports, "the powerful [landholders] were becoming extremely rich, and the number of slaves in the country was reaching large proportions. Meanwhile the Italian people were suffering from depopulation and a shortage of men, worn down by poverty, taxes and military service."[6]

The dispossessed farmers emigrated to towns and provinces where they joined the ranks of the proletariat, serving as a cheap labor supply and contributing to the growth of new urban markets and city slum congestion. Some remained in the countryside, living from hand to mouth as landless jobbers.[7]

Large-scale mining and agriculture were carried out, then as now, by rich owners whose prime concern was the maximization of profits, with little thought given to the attrition visited upon the workforce or the land. As the elder Pliny observed, men relentlessly accumulated landed property and probed the earth, "digging into her veins of gold and silver and mines of copper and lead; we actually drive shafts down into the depth to search for gems and certain tiny stones; we drag out her entrails in search of a jewel merely to be worn upon a finger! How many hands are worn away with toil that a single knuckle may shine resplendent! . . . All these avenues from which wealth issues lead but to crime and slaughter and warfare. . . ."[8]

With a further touch of wisdom Pliny continued: When compared to all the universe, the earth is "but a pinprick," yet "here it is that we fill positions of power and covet wealth, and throw mankind into an uproar." Here we launch "civil wars and slaughter one another to make the land more spacious!" And here "we expel the tenants next to us and add a patch of turf to our own estate by stealing from our neighbor's—to the end that he who has marked out his acres most widely and banished his neighbors beyond all record may rejoice in owning—how small a fraction of the earth's surface? or when he has stretched his boundaries to the full measure of his avarice, may still retain—what portion, pray, of his estate when he is dead?"[9]

The Republic's political structure was not fashioned whole in accordance with some rational design. It emerged from prolonged conflict between the citizenry and the aristocracy, a jerry-built mixture of popular protections and elite entrenchments. Less than two decades after the kings were expelled, the people began a struggle, lasting over 200 years, to win the right to popular elections and legislative assemblage. The commoners demonstrated and rioted, embarking on highly organized strike actions or "secessions" when called upon to serve as soldiers. Democracy, a wonderful invention by the people of history to defend themselves from the power of the wealthy, took tenuous root in ancient Rome.

Still, as a democracy Rome left much to be desired. In the Forum, the central marketplace and open plaza of the city, candidates and commoners could mill about in informal groups, dilating on sundry issues. But full-dress debates before the entire assemblage were limited to those invited to speak by the summoning magistrate. Ordinary citizens could not directly participate, except occasionally to applaud, cheer, shout, or groan. And citizens could vote only "yea" or "nay" on proposals submitted by one of the magistrates, without the right to amend any clause.

Lacking a representative system, the assemblies were open to all citizens. In actual practice, only a relatively small portion of the eligible population could be accommodated in the open-air venues, usually the more prosperous and mobile who had the time and wherewithal to attend. Yet common plebs and to a much lesser degree even foreigners and slaves sometimes made their presence felt. In the Centurial Assembly (*comitia centuriata*), which elected consuls and praetors, voting took place in block units organized around traditional military groupings that were heavily rigged to favor the propertied classes. More democratic was the Tribal Assembly of the People (*comitia tributa*), in which each family tribal group voted as a unit. It however was weighted to favor rural over proletarian voters. Reformers like the Gracchi brothers and Julius Caesar regularly preferred the Tribal Assembly to the Centurial Assembly when trying to pass reform legislation.[10] With enough unity and mass mobilization, poor city dwellers in alliance with voters from outlying districts might pass measures that were opposed by the dominant aristocratic faction in the Senate.

The various magistrates (consuls, praetors, aediles, and quaestors) were elected by the assemblies.[11] To be elected to any of these top four ranks of magistracy carried life membership in the Senate. The closest thing to a popular democratic office was the Tribunate of the People, created after decades of popular agitation and threats of armed secession. Ten tribunes elected each year by the assemblies were to act as the protectors of popular rights. They could veto bills and even senatorial decrees. They eventually gained the right to submit legislation themselves and prosecute errant officials. One had to be of plebeian lineage to qualify as a tribune, one of the few instances in the Late Republic when the patrician-plebeian distinction still obtained.

A tribune who won favorable attention from the senatorial elites might eventually be supported by them in running for the quaestorship. If victorious, he gained admission into the Senate. The promise of such a prestigious advancement blunted the democratic verve of many a tribune. Furthermore, one tribune's proposals could be vetoed by any of the other nine, thus dampening the efforts of a dedicated innovator. By the second century B.C. despite exceptional moments of independence—tribunes were as likely to be instruments of the Senate as champions of the people.[12] Members of the Senate (if they were of plebeian ancestry) could hamstring the tribunate by getting themselves elected tribunes, as did the conservative Cato. Still the tribunate was greatly valued by the common people as the key protection of their republican liberties.

Ordinarily, elections were contested by candidates who were either wealthy themselves or bankrolled by wealthy backers. Those with modest purses had but a dim chance at the polls. Bribery and the buying of votes were widespread. Rarely did candidates proffer discernible programs. To distinguish himself from his opponents, a candidate emphasized his personal integrity and leadership, the prestige of his family name, his association with important personalities of the day, his public service, and his heroic war record—a favoring of style over substance that present-day voters might find familiar.[13]

In sum, the Roman political system permitted the wealthy few to prevail on most issues.[14] One historian finds nothing wrong with this: "There was, indeed, some justice in a system whereby those who bore the chief burden of fighting and financing the city's wars, should also possess the chief voice in directing the city's course."[15] In fact, the very rich did not bear the chief burden of fighting. That dangerous task fell mostly on the shoulders of yeomen and townsmen, and later even the proletariat. The rich did bear much of the financial burdens of war, often using their own funds to raise armies. But they usually were more than recompensed by pocketing the lion's share of the booty.

Rather than contributing to the commonweal, the wealthy fed off it. They avoided paying rents for the public lands they or their forebears had expropriated. Cicero's aristocratic wife, for instance, paid no taxes or fees for public forest lands whose timber she marketed for personal profit.[16] Senators paid no taxes and little of the other costs of governance. The money they lent to the state was paid back to them with interest from funds the state raised by taxing less privileged populations at home and abroad. This system of deficit spending—of borrowing from the rich and paying them back by taxing poor commoners—amounted to an upward redistribution of income much like the kind practiced by indebted governments today, including our own.

The most powerful governing body was the Roman Senate. Numbering several hundred men of wealthy background who had served, or continued to serve, as magistrates, the Senate deter mined foreign policy, appointed provincial governors, and held the purse strings of the Republic. The Senate's approval was sought for most measures before they were submitted to the assemblies. The Senate controlled recruitment and deployment of army units and top military appointments. And it made decisions on war and peace, after formal consultation with the popular assembly.

Within the Senate itself was the inner circle of nobles (*nobiles*) who exercised a controlling influence over the election of major magistrates, especially the consuls and praetors who wielded executive and military power, and the censors who supervised public morals and voting lists. Candidates from families of senatorial renown generally won the higher magisterial offices. During most times, "twenty or thirty men from a dozen families" held what was almost "a monopoly of power."[17] Thus, seven Metelli gained the consulship within fifteen years.

Inequalities prevailed within the Senate itself. No senator could speak unless called upon by the presiding consul, and those of consular rank (the nobility) were always invited to speak first, often leaving little time for senators of lesser eminence. Sallust, himself a low-ranking senatorial newcomer, complained that a small faction of senators governed, "giving and taking away as they please; oppressing the innocent, and raising their partisans to honor; while no wickedness, no dishonesty or disgrace, is a bar to the attainment of office. Whatever appears desirable, they seize and render their own, and transform their will and pleasure into their law, as arbitrarily as victors in a conquered city."[18]

The nobles maintained their influence mostly with their wealth, social prestige, and the protection and patronage they extended to their paid followers or clientele (*clientela*), along with the threats and actual applications of force they might employ. As necessity dictated, they used their clientele as voting blocs, agitators, and armed cadres. This system wedded portions of the lower class to the rich. Influential patrons spent many a morning at home in audience to a throng of followers who came to press for a favor, pass on useful information, receive an assignment, pay their respects, and secure a modest handout of money or food. As Max Weber notes, patronage created relationships of personal dependence that gave Roman political life its private armies and lasting semi-feudal character.[19]

In the second century B.C., the senatorial nobles began to divide into two groups, the larger being self-designated as the *optimates* ("best men"), who were devoted to upholding the politico-economic prerogatives of the well-born. Cicero describes the optimates as "the foremost men and saviors of the state."[20] The smaller faction within the nobility, styled the *populares* or "demagogues" by their opponents, were reformers who sided with the common people on various issues. Julius Caesar is considered the leading *popularis* and the last in a line extending from 133 to 44 B.C.

The optimates sometimes encountered opposition within the Senate itself, and not just from the smaller group of *populares*. Asconius notes that the optimates opposed a quorum requirement because low attendance in the Senate allowed them more readily to carry the vote.[21] Brunt believes that many senators, even a majority, were open to compromise with Caesar, but they were overawed or in other ways beholden to the Senate's leading figures.[22]

Sympathy for the optimates is part of a long-standing tradition. Tacitus, himself a senator, describes the Senate oligarchs who assassinated Caesar and fought against Octavian and Mark Antony as "the most ardent patriots" and "the last army of the Republic."[23] Four centuries later, St. Augustine would write that the assassins were "a party of noble senators, who had conspired to defend the liberty of the Republic."[24] And in the late eighteenth century, Gibbon saw the oligarchs as "the republicans of spirit and ability [who] perished in the field of battle."[25]

Many present-day historians also look with undampened enthusiasm upon this Republic for the Few. Dickinson waxes rhapsodic about Rome's constitutionalism while saying next to nothing about its severe economic inequality and undemocratic political features. Grant would have us believe that senatorial consulship candidates "possessed the inherited training of their class, which very often produced . . . an attitude of selfless sacrifice to the needs of the community as a whole." Robinson heaps praise on senatorial elites bred to a strong tradition of subordinating their individual ambitions to the commonweal. And Scullard reassures us that the Roman constitution—a "balanced" mix of regal, aristocratic, and democratic powers, as represented respectively by the consuls, the Senate, and the assembly—was never seriously threatened by the enormous influence of the Senate. That august body "contained the men who possessed the greatest administrative experience and political wisdom."[26]

The practice of hailing a "balanced" or "mixed" constitution as the finest and most stable of all governing arrangements goes back to ancient times. Referring to the three forms of governance: "kingship, aristocracy, and democracy," Polybius argues, "It is clear that we should regard as the *best* constitution one which includes elements of all three species. . . ."[27] Cicero concurs, favoring a system with all three, though seemingly not in equal measure.[28] Indeed, it is not clear what an "equal" blend of the three could be, given their inherently contradictory and antagonistic essences. It has long been presumed that the diversity of constitutional forms makes for an optimal result. In reality, it creates a system of impediments that makes popular reform nearly impossible.

As with Polybius and Cicero, so with Aristotle, and so with the framers of the United States Constitution in 1787 (who were heavily influenced by their reading of the classics and their own propertied-class concerns)—all have been mindful of the leveling threats of democratic forces and the need for a constitutional "mix" that allows only limited participation by the *demos*, with a dominant role allotted to an elite executive power.[29] That same concern predominated among those who contrived the constitution of today's capitalist Russia. Such has been the real nature of the mixed constitution. Diluting democratic power with a preponderantly undemocratic mix does not create an admirable "balance" and "stability." In actual practice, the diversity of form more often has been a subterfuge, allowing an appearance of popular participation in order to lend legitimacy to oligarchic dominance.

Unfortunately, many classical historians are less discomforted by senatorial plutocracy than by proletarian egalitarianism. Their fear is that the people and their demagogic leaders are given to committing "democratic excesses," a concern that goes back at least to Plato. Theodore Mommsen, for one, could not contain his distaste for radical reformers of the Late Republic such as the praetor Marcus Caelius Rufus, an aristocrat who in 48 B.C. launched a campaign to cancel all debts and free the slaves. Rufus was accused of planning to seize the town of Capua with armed slaves. The following year, the tribune Publius Dolabella and others incited street frays against house rents and creditor claims. To Mommsen, both Rufus and Dolabella were "fools" and "the communists of that day," instigators of "a rabble engaged not in political activity but solely in a bandit war against property."[30]

The impetuous multitude, we are told, needs to be restrained by aristocratic moderation and probity, the latter ingredients existing more persistently in the imaginations of some commentators than in actual history. There is no denying that the Senate oligarchs were concerned about preserving the rule of law—as

long as it served the interests of wealth, and thwarted the reformers who sought some modest redistribution of income and privilege. In Roman constitutional practice, there was nothing to
prevent the Senate from passing any decree it so desired. The
nobles protected the constitution—an unwritten one based on custom and practice—to the extent that it fortified their oligarchy.
It was *their* constitution, *their* law, and indeed *their* Republic, made
to accommodate "sacred traditions" including, above all, their
long-standing class interests. This point is regularly eschewed by
those who hail the senatorial aristocrats as defenders of republican
virtue.

4

"Demagogues" and Death Squads

Set honor in one eye and death i' the other.
—*Julius Caesar* Act I, scene 2

*T*hroughout the ages, in keeping with their ideological proclivities, gentlemen historians have tended to dismiss the *populares* of the Roman Republic as self-aggrandizing demagogues who affronted constitutional principles by encroaching upon the Senate's domain. Among the first to impress this image upon history is Cicero, who charged that popular agitators were psychologically unbalanced "owing to a sort of inborn revolutionary madness, [they] batten on civil discord and sedition." They are "reckless and abandoned men" possessed of "vicious aims," whose "own natural disposition incites them against the state."[1] In our own era, historians such as P. A. Brunt tell us, "[Rome's] established structure was under attack only by agitators, often or always self-interested adventurers. . . ."[2]

One of the more prominent of these "agitators" was Tiberius Gracchus, a man of aristocratic birth and strong democratic leanings. More than three decades before Julius Caesar was born, Tiberius addressed some of the afflictions that beset Rome and Italy, most notably the crying need for a more equitable land distribution. Elected to serve as a tribune in 133 B.C., Tiberius Gracchus mobilized people from within and without the city in order to pass his *lex agraria*, which sought to revive the dead-letter law of 367 B.C., limiting the amount of public land that could be leased to any individual. The surplus acreage expropriated by large holders was to be redistributed to the poor by three elected commissioners.[3]

In drafting his law, Tiberius consulted a number of eminent citizens including magistrates and former magistrates. Wealthy individuals who deserved to be penalized for the crimes associated with their land grabs were only obliged to surrender their illegal holdings to those most in need of land. "And for this they were compensated. Surely many would agree that no law directed against injustice and avarice was ever framed in milder or more conciliatory terms," argues Plutarch in a surprisingly sympathetic cast. The land was being bought back at a fair market price from those who had stolen it. "Even though this act of restitution manifested such tender regard for the wrongdoers, the common people were content to forget the past so long as they could be assured of protection against future injustice." The wealthy landowners, however, detested the *lex agraria* "out of sheer greed," and they hated Tiberius for proposing it, continues Plutarch. They did their utmost to turn the people against the law, alleging that Tiberius's real intent was to foment revolution, impose his autocratic will, and undermine the foundations of the Republic.[4] These same charges were to be leveled against Caesar almost a century later.

Fragments of Tiberius's speech, by which he introduced his *lex agraria*, have come down to us. With bitter eloquence he describes the plight of landless commoners, many of whom were army veterans: "Hearthless and homeless, they must take their wives and families and tramp the roads like beggars. . . . They fight and fall to serve no other end but to multiply the possessions and comforts of the rich. They are called masters of the world but they possess not a clod of earth that is truly their own."[5] Such class-conscious sentiments voiced before an assemblage of plebs stoked the rancor of the oligarchs. "[T]he conspiracy that formed against [Tiberius] seems to have had its origins in the hatred and malevolence of the rich rather than in the excuses that they put forward for their actions," writes Plutarch, who describes Tiberius Gracchus as one who chose his words with care while appealing to men's sense of compassion.[6]

Most other historians have a different view. Dio Cassius sees Tiberius as "turning aside from what was best" (his prominent family connections and fine education) in order to drift "into what was worst" by "bedeviling and disturbing all established customs," and making "any statement or promise whatever to anybody."[7] A chorus of latter-day scholars agree, claiming that Gracchus "did untold harm to the Republic," was "high-handed," "rash," "self-righteous," "plunged into illegal courses," and "unnecessarily provocative and ill-judged."[8]

What exactly were the rash and illegal methods that Tiberius

Gracchus pursued? Instead of putting his land-reform bill before the Senate, which was loath to consider it, he chose a more democratic course established a hundred years earlier, though seldom invoked since. He took the measure straight to the Tribal Assembly of the People, which was well attended by commoners far and wide in anticipation of such a move. The bill passed but was unexpectedly vetoed by another tribune, Marcus Octavius, an ally of the optimate coterie. This move arguably was itself unconstitutional since a tribune's veto was intended to protect the citizenry against official tyranny and not stifle the vox populi on substantive issues.[9]

On the advice of some leading citizens, Tiberius took the dispute about Octavius's veto to the Senate, where "he was treated so contemptuously by the rich," according to Appian, that he returned posthaste to the Forum. There he proposed that Octavius be deposed. True, a tribune was inviolate because he stood as the people's protector. "But if a tribune should depart from his duty, oppress the people, cripple their powers, and take away their right to vote," argued Gracchus, "he has by his own actions deprived himself of his honorable office by not fulfilling the conditions upon which he accepted it." Tiberius overwhelmingly won the votes of the tribes, and Octavius was removed from office, thus allowing passage of the *lex agraria*.[10]

Tiberius proposed other reforms. He wanted to reduce the period of military service (at the time it went from age seventeen to forty-six), give people the right to appeal jury verdicts, and allow equestrians to sit on juries hitherto composed exclusively of senators. After noting these efforts, Plutarch departs from his otherwise sympathetic view of Gracchus and concludes: "In short, Tiberius's program was designed to cripple the power of the Senate in every possible way, and it was inspired by motives of anger and party politics rather than by considerations of justice and the common good."[11]

Shortly after the *lex agraria* was passed, an Asian king bequeathed his kingdom and its revenues to the Roman state. Tiberius proposed that some of this windfall be used as start-up capital for the needy farmers who were allotted land parcels under the new law. This incurs the disapproval of some latter-day historians. For Mommsen, his move was tantamount to "tampering with the public finances." For Handford, it was a "serious encroachment on the Senate's hitherto undisputed control of financial and foreign affairs."[12]

Tiberius then sought reelection to a second term. As officers of the state, senior magistrates were prohibited from seeking immediate reelection to the same office, but the tribunate was an office of the plebs. Tiberius's bid was neither illegal nor unprecedented. Yet this move too has been roundly condemned by various modern-day historians as "tactless and provocative," symptomatic of "mob leadership," "transgressing traditional observances," and showing "undue hastiness and folly."[13]

Tiberius Gracchus's *lex agraria* would have given thousands of uprooted families a chance to work the land, thereby easing the congestion within Rome. It would have reversed the depopulation of the Italian countryside, and replenished the yeomen stock. Fac-

ing a popular upsurge against their illegal land holdings, the oligarchs could not easily attack Tiberius's law. So they attacked
Tiberius himself. They took every opportunity to denounce him
as a demagogue and tyrant who was intent upon crowning himself
king. They deprived him of a sufficient expense allowance to ad-
minister the land-reform program. The chief promoter of these
affronts was Publius Nasica, one of the largest owners of public
lands, who bitterly resented being obliged to surrender any of the
ager publicus, and who, as Plutarch writes, "abandoned himself
completely to his hatred of Tiberius."[14] Having stolen the *ager
publicus* for themselves, the big owners now were convinced it
rightfully belonged to them.

Tiberius feared he would be assassinated for his reformist efforts. His apprehension proved well grounded. When the Tribal
Assembly gathered to vote on Tiberius's reelection, Nasica, with
other senators and a large gang of hired thugs, descended upon
the meeting and slaughtered him and some 300 of his supporters,
none of whom had taken up arms. When Mommsen writes that
Gracchus had a "bodyguard from the gutter," he is referring to
this complement of unarmed Romans of humble station who stood
by Tiberius and gave their lives on behalf of equitable reforms.[15]

The common people felt bitterly about the killings and spoke
openly of revenge. When they encountered Nasica, writes Plutarch, "they did not try to hide their hatred of him, but grew
savage and cried out upon him wherever he chanced to be, calling
him an accursed man and a tyrant" who had murdered "an invi-
olable and sacred person." Fearing for Nasica's safety, the Senate
voted to send him to Asia though it had no need of him there.

Nasica departed Italy undercover even though he was Rome's high priest (*pontifex maximus*). He wandered about ignominiously in foreign lands for a brief period, then took his own life at Pergamum (close to the Aegean coast of present-day Turkey).[16]

By recourse to an improbable anecdote, Lucius Annaeus Florus condones Tiberius's murder. He tells us that the tribune fled to the Capitol with his attackers in hot pursuit. There he exhorted the people to save his life, but he touched his head with his hand suggesting that "he was asking for royalty and a diadem." This gesture so incensed the crowd that they were easily roused to take up arms and join in putting Tiberius to death "with apparent justice."[17] That Tiberius would start negotiating for a crown while being pursued by a gang of assassins, and that an otherwise sympathetic audience would suddenly turn upon him with weapons because he touched his head, all seems perfectly plausible to Florus.

It is a time-honored practice to blame "rash" and "provocative" reformers for the violence delivered upon them by reactionary forces. Speaking for any number of modern-day historians, Andrew Lintott says the hostility of those who attacked Tiberius Gracchus "was not simply inspired by the land bill itself but by the tactics which Gracchus employed."[18] Cyril Robinson blames the hecatomb of 133 B.C. on its victims, referring to "the reckless and irregular tactics of the Gracchian democrats." The civil violence that brought death to Tiberius is something "for which partially at least he shared the blame."[19] Scullard goes further: the oligarchs, the murderers themselves, are not to be blamed at all. The "pru-

dent" senators were forced to confront "the over-zealous reformer."
"The urban mob that thronged the assembly in Rome . . . was
becoming increasingly irresponsible and unrepresentative of the
needs of the people as a whole," leading to "mob-rule or dictatorship."[20]

These critics do not tell us what reform program Tiberius could
possibly have legislated that would not have incurred the ire of
the wealthy landholders. Even if he had followed the traditional
course, leaving the *lex agraria* to the tender mercies of the Senate,
and had employed the utmost finesse and moderation, the large
holders still would have buried the measure. As it was, Tiberius's
law was more than generous in offering an undeserved compensation to the rich, undeserved because they themselves had never
paid restitution for the land they had swiped years before, nor for
the injuries they had inflicted on the smallholders of that day.

The truth is, Tiberius's sin was more substantive than stylistic.
It was not that he failed to hew closely to established practice.
The Senate itself often departed from its own constitutional procedures when expediency dictated—as when they launched their
armed assault to massacre Tiberius and hundreds of his supporters.
It was that he attempted to reverse the upward redistribution of
wealth. He had the audacity to advocate reforms that gave something to the poor and infringed upon the rapacity of the rich.

After Tiberius Gracchus's assassination, the Senate hesitated to
abolish the three-person commission that was in charge of land
reform. "From fear of the multitude," as Plutarch puts it, the
nobles allowed the distribution of public land to proceed.[21] But
they contrived to undermine the commission's workings. By 129,

they had taken many disputed cases out of its hands and entrusted them to the consuls, whose frequent and deliberate absences greatly impeded the program. In time, land reform was entirely undone.

Considered among the greatest of *populares*, second perhaps only to Julius Caesar, was Tiberius's younger brother, Gaius Gracchus. Being keenly aware of his brother's fate, Gaius was reluctant to pursue office. His mother Cornelia, a woman of some note, demanded that he refrain from the perils of public life so that she might have some peace from pain: "You . . . the only survivor of all the children I have had . . . Stand for the tribunate after I am dead . . . when I shall no longer be aware of it."[22] But Gaius found it impossible to withstand the entreaties of those who desired reform. He eventually emerged as an eloquent and fiery speaker, one of the greatest orators Rome ever produced. Against the combined opposition of all the distinguished nobles, he was elected tribune in 123 B.C.

Upon assuming office, he embarked on a comprehensive reform program that included the redistribution of public lands on behalf of the indigent, the construction of roads into more fertile districts in order to advance Italian agriculture, the sale of grain to impoverished plebs at a reduced price, and shorter enlistment terms and free clothing for soldiers. Gaius also advocated granting Italian allies the same voting rights as Romans so that they might live as citizens rather than subjects. He put equestrians on juries, thus breaking the Senate's monopolistic privilege of serving as jurors in criminal cases. And he proposed adding 200 new seats to the Senate, to be occupied by the knightly order.

Gaius Gracchus recommended that the various classes should vote not in hierarchical sequence that favored the nobility but by lot, "thus all being made equal in political influence whatever their wealth."[23] He introduced a bill that prohibited any magistrate who had been deposed by the people from holding office again. Another bill of his reaffirmed the ancient principle that protected a citizen's life against summary judgments by magistrates—as when the Senate put his brother Tiberius to death without trial, and murdered many of his supporters.

Plutarch notes that Gaius Gracchus supervised every project with extraordinary speed and application, impressing even those who disliked him. Gaius was "attended by a host of contractors, craftsmen, ambassadors, magistrates, soldiers, and men of letters, all of whom he handled with a courteous ease that enabled him to show kindness to all his associates. . . . In this way he gave the clearest possible proof that those who had represented him as a tyrannical, overbearing, or violent man were uttering nothing but malicious slanders."[24]

In 121, in response to Gaius's initiatives, the Senate passed what was later called the *senatus consultum ultimum*, a decree that allowed for a suspension of republican rights "in defense of the Republic." It gave magistrates license to discharge absolutist power, including political repression and mass murder. After repeated threats against his life, Gaius and 250 supporters, including another *popularis,* Fulvius Flaccus, were massacred by the optimates' death squads in 121 B.C. These assassins then rounded up and summarily executed an additional 3,000 democrats. The victims' relatives were forbidden to mourn publicly for the dead.[25]

Given the magnitude of these crimes, it is disheartening to find that through the ages, many historians have been more critical of the victims than of their victimizers. Cicero is among the earliest commentators to denounce the Gracchi and voice approval of their murders. He saw them as demagogues who pandered to the worst elements.[26] Likewise Dio writes that Gaius "was naturally intractable" and easily "played the rogue," becoming a mortal threat to "the nobility and the senatorial party."[27] Florus dismisses the reform struggles waged by the Gracchi as "seditions."[28] Valerius Maximus repeatedly denounces the Gracchi for engaging in "villainous attempts." He treats Gaius's death as "a good example," and applauds the Senate's "wisdom" in killing Tiberius Gracchus "who dared to promulgate an agrarian law." The Gracchi and their "criminal supporters . . . paid the penalty they deserved."[29] For Velleius Paterculus, the Gracchi were animated by "pernicious views." Gaius was prompted by a desire "to prepare a way for himself to a kingship." And the murder of Fulvius Flaccus, his ally, was justified because he shared Gaius's "king-like power" and "was equally inclined to noxious measures."[30]

In the early Christian era we have St. Augustine telling us that the Gracchi transgressed against society "when they threw everything into confusion"; they and other *populares* that came after them pursued "civil wars, most iniquitous and unjustifiable in their causes."[31] Modern writers like H.H. Scullard say that Gaius "unwisely formed a bodyguard of friends" that "provoked" the optimates into killing him.[32] Christian Meier justifies the optimates' homicidal fury, arguing that Gaius defied the "unwritten law" as defined by the Senate, and "it seems" his supporters were the first to resort to violence.[33] Otto Kiefer sidesteps the whole issue of aristocratic culpability by using a neutral construction: the Gracchi "perish[ed] in furious street fighting."[34]

That the *senatus consultum ultimum* was used to cut down Gaius Gracchus and thousands of his followers seems not to trouble P. A. Brunt, who argues legalistically that the decree did not confer any new authority but simply allowed the magistrates to disregard existing statutes by "acting on the principle that the highest law was the public safety."[35] But the "highest law" is often a cloak for the lowest deeds. Were the Gracchian reformers endangering society? Or were they infringing upon the prerogatives of the few? To be sure, like most ruling elites, the optimates saw no difference; to them, any trespass against their privileged interests was tantamount to endangering the social order as they knew it.

After the massacres of 121, violent expropriation of land by the rich and powerful owners accelerated.[36] The land commission was dissolved outright in 118 at the instigation of the Senate, and allotments to smallholders became a thing of the past. By 111, the rents that the big landholders had paid to the state for use of public lands were abolished, thereby effecting a complete privatization of the *ager publicus*. The fertile public lands now belonged completely to wealthy absentee slaveholders.[37]

About twenty years after Gaius Gracchus was murdered, another *popularis*, Lucius Appuleius Saturninus, while serving as a tribune, proposed a law to distribute affordable grain to the proletariat. He also sought to establish a court to hear cases of "debasing the majesty of the state," a measure directed against the optimate faction. He was joined by another reform-minded senator, Gaius Servilius Glaucia. In 100 B.C., the Senate declared another *senatus consultum ultimum*, under which both men were placed under custody in the Senate House. An optimate death squad broke into the Senate House from the roof and murdered them. The killers were never prosecuted.[38]

Marcus Livius Drusus, a tribune, wanted to extend the voting franchise to larger portions of Italy, distribute corn at subsidized prices, provide land allotments in the manner of the Gracchi, and set up a compromise plan for reforming the law courts. For his efforts he was stabbed to death in 91. His assassin was never sought out.[39]

Another tribune, Sulpicius Rufus, a friend of Drusus, attempted to carry on with these reforms. After a number of open clashes with reactionary forces, he was hunted down by the optimates' death squads and killed, probably in 88 B.C. Even a conservative like Velleius allowed that the limited concessions advocated by Drusus were intended to placate the multitude so that, being grateful for small favors, they might consent to the far larger rewards dispensed to the wealthy.[40] Most ancient and modern historians dismiss these post-Gracchian reformers as "demagogues."[41]

A leading *popularis* was Gaius Marius (Caesar's uncle by marriage), who came from a minor provincial family and lived the life of a peasant and soldier in his earlier years, eventually winning fame as a general. In 119 B.C. he was elected a tribune of the people, then consul in 107 and five more times thereafter, an unusual honor. Marius was the first to waive property qualifications for military service and enlist even the penniless proletarians, a reform largely impelled by the increasing shortage of property-owning yeomen. In alliance with Saturninus and Glaucia, he pushed for the provision of land for his army veterans and for subsidized grain sales. Eventually he broke with Saturninus and failed to stop his death. In 87, locked in struggle against Sulla, Marius joined with Lucius Cornelius Cinna to storm Rome and kill hundreds of aristocrats and their collaborators. He died of pleurisy the following year at the age of seventy-one. Despite his spectacular career, Marius had no clear policy for political reform. Much of his popularity and subsequent legendary reputation among the common people came from his relatively modest provincial origins, his early military exploits, his willingness to promote commoners to responsible positions, and his occasional ability to scourge the nobility.[42]

Foremost among reactionary leaders who regularly transgressed republican rights in service to aristocratic interests was Lucius Cornelius Sulla, who in 88 B.C. marched his forces right into Rome in violation of an ancient constitutional prohibition against bringing armies within city limits. In 87, thousands of unarmed citizens, including a number of wealthy equestrians who were followers of Cinna,[43] were slaughtered by Sulla's death squads, their primary crime being their desire to revive the egalitarian reforms of Sulpicius Rufus, including a more democratic voting system for the Tribal Assembly. "[T]he Forum was heaped with bodies and the sewers ran with blood" is the way one writer describes the slaughter of Cinna's democrats.[44] Cinna himself was murdered by traitorous lieutenants soon afterward.

After several years of foreign wars, Sulla reentered Rome in 82. He defeated a rebellious Samnite army and butchered all its troops including those who had surrendered. He then issued a proscription (*proscriptio*) against hundreds of Romans, to which hundreds more were added in the passing months. A proscription consisted of a list of persons who were declared outlaws by the state authority. Their property and possessions were confiscated, and in effect a bounty was put on their heads. Their killers were rewarded and their protectors punished. As a method of political purge, proscription was brought to brutal perfection by Sulla. He slaughtered some fifty senatorial opponents suspected of not being cooperative enough, along with 1,600 knights and 2,000 commoners (some estimate as many as 10,000 victims), so determined was he to eradicate the democratic faction that opposed him.[45] Many fell victim on the flimsiest suspicions, some because their possessions were coveted by the executioners. As in any inquisitional terror, many came forward as accusers, pointing their finger at others in order to demonstrate their own loyalty and keep themselves above suspicion.[46]

Like other dedicated reactionaries before and since, Sulla also employed his dictatorial power to accumulate a huge personal fortune.[47] Declaring himself *dictator* not for the usual six months but indefinitely, he removed control of the criminal courts from the Assembly and gave it to the Senate. He appointed 300 new members to the Senate selected primarily for their conservative proclivities, and increased the number of state priests. He ruled that tribunes could never aspire to higher office, so to block the ascent of democratic leaders like the Gracchi. Nor could they any longer convene meetings of the people or initiate legislation in the Assembly. All legislative proposals had to receive the Senate's preliminary assent. And although the tribunate's veto power was not abolished—probably because the Senate could use it to block a troublesome consul—it was seriously circumscribed.

Sulla undid Gaius Gracchus's court reform, restoring a senatorial monopoly over the judiciary. In sum, he rolled back hard-won democratic gains and installed a strikingly reactionary constitution. The Senate emerged with nearly complete control over legislation, courts, and executive magistrates, with more powers than it had enjoyed centuries past.[48]

Sulla abolished the right of the plebs to buy cheap grain, thereby imposing serious hardship on them. During his dictatorship, and into the following decades, usurers or larger landholders drove half the rural residents of Italy from the countryside. Their farms were transformed into plantations, vineyards, olive groves, orchards, and pastures for cattle and sheep, worked by slave labor and tenant farmers—a momentous social upheaval involving immeasurable suffering, yet scarcely mentioned by public figures or historians of that day.[49]

The struggle around Sulla's new order continued long after his retirement in 81 and his death in 78. An immediate demand made by the democrats was for the restoration of the rights and prerogatives of the people's tribunate. In 76, the tribune Cnaeus Sicinius dared to speak of restoration, for which he died a victim of "patrician perfidy," reports Sallust.[50] A *popularis* proscribed by Sulla was Quintus Sertorius, who advocated citizenship for the peoples of the Iberian peninsula, and who for a number of years waged a resourceful guerrilla war against Sulla's forces in Spain. One of Sulla's colleagues offered any Roman who killed Sertorius a huge cash award and 20,000 acres of land.[51] Sertorius was eventually hunted down and assassinated in 73. Looking back on Sulla's reign, Cicero wrote, "All was basically admirable, though temper and moderation were somewhat lacking."[52]

Some historians have not a critical word about Sulla's "reforms." Scullard manifests none of the concern about the loss of constitutional balance and freedom that he unfailingly evinces when discussing the Gracchi: "As army commander and dictator [Sulla] could act with greater independence." Sulla understood that the Senate had to "resume firm control and become an effective governing body once again." In a similar vein, Mommsen refers to Sulla's "patriotic and judicious moderation" and his steadfastness in establishing the oligarchy on a more independent footing. Meier tells us that Sulla "was simply a realist" who "simply performed the tasks that he felt incumbent upon him, though admittedly in a somewhat unconventional fashion." And Keaveney devotes an entire book to promoting a mostly positive view of the dictator, with appreciation for his restorative efforts and republican virtues.[53]

* * *

In 66 B.C., the reform-minded tribune Gaius Manilius introduced a law to democratize the voting system in the tribal assembly. Domitius Ahenobarbus, a leading protagonist in Sulla's reign of terror and a violent opponent of popular reform, had members of his *clientela* attack the assembly and kill a number of Manilius's partisans. The Senate congratulated Ahenobarbus for his civic spirit and annulled Manilius's law.[54]

Of special note is Publius Clodius Pulcher, a tribune allied with Julius Caesar. Clodius affected an older spelling of his patrician family name, Claudius, as being more in keeping with common-style pronunciation. He even renounced his patrician rank and had himself adopted into a noted plebeian family so that he might serve as a tribune in 58. From that office he sponsored a law to curb the partisan use of censors. He outlawed executions of citizens without trial, a measure aimed at the death-squad killings. And he got a law passed that reestablished the right to organize the *collegia*, the popular craft guilds and unions. Many guilds had been abolished by senatorial decree six years earlier. Clodius's law put these people's organizations on a legal footing and on a paramilitary basis, readying them for armed defensive action against the optimates' private armies. Their ranks consisted of freedmen, the poorer citizenry, and even slaves. He proposed a law to give full political rights to all freedmen and many slaves.[55] The Senate oligarchs constantly tried to drive a wedge between Clodius and the citizenry by alleging that his followers were made up exclusively of slaves and criminals.

Clodius fought to have free grain allotted to the proletariat, and he prohibited the magistrates from using "bad omens" and other priestly pap to obstruct popular assemblies.[56] The free grain distribution modestly improved the material welfare of the plebs, the liberalizing of assembly procedures enhanced their sovereignty, and the organizing of *collegia* augmented their political power.

Most of our gentlemen historians, both ancient and modern, disapprove of Clodius's efforts at grassroots mobilization on behalf of a popular agenda. In 57, a scandalized Cicero denounced Clodius as a rapscallion of the worst sort for going "from street to street openly offering the slaves their freedom . . . and he takes slaves for his advisers."[57] Others uncritically embrace Cicero's opinion. Plutarch calls Clodius "the boldest and vilest" and "the most notorious and low-lived demagogue of his time." Asconius dislikes Clodius for inciting "the sediment of the city's slave population." Velleius looks not too harshly upon his murder (discussed below), calling it "an act of bad precedent, but beneficial to the public."[58]

Latter-day historians are almost unanimous in denouncing Clodius as "loose and dissolute," a "rogue," "scoundrel," "unscrupulous adventurer," "reckless demagogue," and "gang leader" who "organized street-rowdyism" and "recruit[ed] men for violence," "an anarchic tribune of the people."[59] Gelzer labels Clodius "a demagogue of the wildest kind" for advocating free grain distribution and organizing political clubs among the proletariat. Lintott, sounding much like Cicero, assures us that Clodius pursued "urban political power as an end in itself," and needed to be resisted "by bands of professional fighters, whether mercenary thugs, gladiators, or soldiers."[60]

To be sure, Clodius was capable of raffish ventures. In 61 he was accused of dressing as a woman and stealing into the inner sanctum of the Vestal Virgins in order to tryst with Caesar's second wife, Pompeia. The authorities pronounced the incident a sacrilege. Caesar did not react too harshly against his political ally Clodius, but he did divorce Pompeia. He insisted that she had not slept with Clodius, nevertheless "Caesar's wife must be above suspicion." Clodius was brought to trial but acquitted by a 31–25 vote because, Cicero charged, the jury was populated by a needy disreputable lot whose sympathy for the accused was won with bribery. Afterward in the Senate, Cicero pronounced sentence on him: "Clodius . . . the jury has not preserved you for the streets of Rome, but for the death chamber,"[61] a menacing prognostication that was to prove all too true.

On 18 January 52, Clodius was traveling along the Appian Way with about thirty slaves. He encountered a band of 300 mercenaries, mostly gladiators, led by the optimate Titus Annius Milo, a friend of Cicero and husband to Sulla's daughter. Wounded in the ensuing fray, Clodius was carried to a nearby inn. At Milo's command, the gladiators pursued their prey, killed the innkeeper, then dragged Clodius out to the highway, stabbing him repeatedly until they finished him off.[62]

As word spread around the city, the stunned population lingered all night in the Forum. The next day, an outraged crowd carried the corpse, naked so as to expose its many lacerations, into the Senate House. There they made a pyre of seats and tables and burned the body and the building. They then proceeded to the murderer's house, holding it under siege until driven off by Milo's archers. The proletariats rampaged through the city, beating and killing those they suspected of sympathy with Milo, attacking especially persons who were richly attired.[63]

Milo was brought to trial, with Cicero serving as his attorney. In that time-honored fashion of defense lawyers who have no case, Cicero defended his client by attacking the victim, accusing "the audacious and despicable monster" Clodius of being "a robber and a traitor," who incited "the frenzied attacks of scum." In contrast, Milo was "a fine and gallant gentleman" who acted only to defend himself. Clodius had sought to thwart Milo's bid for the consulship; he was a revolutionary menace to the Republic while Milo was Rome's stalwart defender. Clodius repeatedly threatened Milo's life, but "[n]othing in the world could have induced Milo either to [kill Clodius] or even want it done." Clodius had been lying in wait to ambush Milo because he was driven by rage and hatred. But in Milo "there was no trace of such sentiments."[64]

Here Cicero was dissembling, as was his wont. In an earlier private letter he himself had acknowledged that Milo was openly threatening to murder Clodius: "I think Publius [Clodius] will be brought to trial by Milo, unless he is killed first. If he now puts himself in Milo's way in a rough-and-tumble I don't doubt that Milo will dispatch him with his own hands. He has no qualms or hesitations about doing so."[65]

During the trial, popular feelings were running so high against Milo as to unnerve Cicero, preventing him from finishing his defense oration. Milo was found guilty and forced into exile, the severest penalty that could be imposed upon an aristocrat. To their credit, many historians do not accept Cicero's charge that Clodius attacked Milo. An armed body of thirty is not likely to ambush an armed contingent of 300, especially if the latter includes a substantial number of highly trained gladiators. Most describe the murder on the Appian Way as a chance encounter: the two parties just happened to be passing each other, and sparks flew causing an unpremeditated clash. Appian tells us that Clodius and Milo eyed each other suspiciously as they passed by, but then one of Milo's slaves, "either by order or because he wanted to kill his master's enemy," drove a dagger into Clodius's back.[66] It is difficult to imagine that a slave could gain such easy access to the well-guarded Clodius, or that he would take such a risky and consequential initiative on his own.

A month after Clodius's death, Q. Metellus Scipio charged that Milo's defense had been a lie. Metellus maintained that Clodius, accompanied by twenty-six slaves, had set out from Rome to address officials in Aricia, and that Milo, with a complement of over 300 armed men, had rushed to overtake him. Eleven of Clodius's men lost their lives in the attack and others were wounded, while only three of Milo's men sustained injuries. According to Metellus, the next day Milo rewarded twelve of his men, probably gladiators, with payments for their service against Clodius. He also freed a number of them, so they could testify in court as freedmen if need be.[67]

Some time after Metellus went public, a well-known freedman named Aemilius Philemon announced that he and four other persons had witnessed the murder of Clodius. When they protested, they were abducted and held captive for two months in a house belonging to Milo. This report stirred much feeling against Milo. In his trial statement, Cicero never once refers to the particulars raised by Metellus or Philemon, not even for purpose of refutation.[68] Nor does he explain why Milo was coursing the Appian Way with such a large heavily armed force of professional killers. Instead Cicero claims with a straight face that Milo's retinue consisted largely of a boy's choir and a collection of female servants, "whereas Clodius who was habitually escorted by whores, prostitutes, and homosexuals" now had a group of toughs who looked like they could have been handpicked.

Why then did Clodius get the worst of it? Because Milo always made it a practice of being ready for him, argued Cicero. And, as the gods of war would have it, the outcome of armed clashes are never predictable. Furthermore, Clodius, "drowsy from too much lunch and drink," mistakenly thought he had cut off his prey from the rear, only to find himself in the midst of Milo's followers.[69] We are left to conclude that, having thus blundered, he and a number of his accomplices were then cut to pieces by Milo's implacable choirboys and maids.

Four years after killing Clodius, Milo returned from exile to join forces with others in Italy in an attempt to stir a rebellion against Julius Caesar. He was swiftly captured and executed by the praetor Pedius, Caesar's nephew.

With Clodius out of the way, the optimates launched death-squad attacks upon his partisans, similar to the kind they had employed in the past against the followers of the Gracchi and other *populares*.[70] In sum, just about every leader of the Middle and Late Republics who took up the popular cause met a violent end, beginning with Tiberius Gracchus in 133 and continuing on to Gaius Gracchus, Fulvius Flaccus, Livius Drusus, Sulpicius Rufus, Cornelius Cinna, Marius Gratidianus, Appuleius Saturninus, Cnaeus Sicinius, Quintus Sertorius, Servilius Glaucia, Sergius Catiline (discussed in the next chapter), Clodius Pulcher, and Julius Caesar. Even more reprehensible, the optimates and their hired goons killed thousands of the *populares'* supporters.

Could it really be that the reformers' *tactics* were so disquieting as to justify mass murder by the "bludgeon-men" (as Mommsen calls the optimates' death squads)?[71] Something other than procedural niceties and personal rivalry was at the root of all this ruling-class butchery. The *populares'* real sin lay not in their supposedly unconstitutional methods but in the economic democracy of their programs. Were the Gracchi violating custom and constitution when they essayed under the law to reclaim the *ager publicus* for the smallholders whose forebears had tilled it for centuries? In any case, what constitutional right justified the repeated use of death-squad violence against them and other *populares* and thousands of their followers for the better part of a century?

As with just about every ruling class in history, the Roman nobility reacted fiercely when their interests were infringed upon, especially their untrammeled "right" to accumulate as much wealth as possible at the public's expense. If not their only concern, accumulation was a major preoccupation. In a word, the nobles were less devoted to traditional procedures and laws than to the class privileges those procedures and laws were designed to protect. They never hesitated to depart from their own "hereditary constitution," resorting to extraordinary acts of bloody repression when expediency dictated. They treated egalitarian reforms and attempts to democratize the Republic's decision-making process as subversive of republican rule. What should not go unnoted is how readily some past and present historians embrace this same position.

5

Cicero's Witch-hunt

But men may construe things after their fashion,
Clean from the purpose of the things themselves.
—*JULIUS CAESAR* ACT I, SCENE 3

*T*he great orator Marcus Tullius Cicero looms large in any
consideration of the Late Republic. He was a key participant in its affairs, and his writings constitute by far
the largest surviving primary source we have of that era. Moreover,
his ideological proclivities dovetail with those of regiments of historians down through the ages, making him a great favorite
among them. Sir Ronald Syme hails Cicero as "a humane and
cultivated man, an enduring influence upon the course of all European civilization."[1] Other admirers trumpet him as a "consti-
tutionalist" of "honorable and unselfish ideals," a leader devoted
to "standards of duty, kindliness and public spirit," "singularly
genuine, refined and lovable," "one of Rome's leading sons" and
"most precious gems," who refused "to live under a tyranny."[2]

Almost everyone shares that opinion of Cicero. "Contemporary American and British ancient historians are divided between Ciceronians (95 percent) and Caesarians (a mere handful), and the division reflects their current political attitudes," observes Arthur Kahn, one of the handful.[3] Another of the handful is Friedrich Engels, who called Cicero "the most contemptible scoundrel in history."[4]

Born in Arpinum (a municipality southeast of Rome) of a wealthy equestrian family, Cicero went to Rome for his education and eventually established himself as the city's leading barrister. Early in his career he proved himself an able mouthpiece for the aristocracy by successfully pleading the cases of "large numbers of young men of illustrious and noble families" accused of ill-discipline and cowardice in war.[5] Quaestor in 75, aedile in 69, and praetor in 66, he forged links with leading citizens whenever possible, learning the locations of their town and country dwellings, and what friends and neighbors they had.[6]

For all his prodigious kowtowing to the nobles, they never considered him much more than a useful upstart. Cicero himself fretted about their ingratitude: they "have never made me the slightest return or recompense, material or even verbal."[7] In 56, he complained of "certain gentlemen" who objected to his owning a villa that once belonged to a leading optimate. When the aristocratic Metellus sneeringly asked Cicero, "Who was your father?" it must have cut the orator's heart. We can forgive his retort and even favor it with a smile: "I can scarcely ask you the same question since your mother has made it rather difficult to answer."[8]

Cicero fumed in particular about Brutus's gaucherie in declining his hospitality, and for taking "a brusque, arrogant, ungracious tone toward me even when he is asking for a favor." Yet he managed to convince himself that Brutus was very fond of him.[9] At one point, he concluded rather plaintively, "Now it's time for me to love myself since *they* won't love me whatever I do."[10] And love himself he did. Dio Cassius notes that Cicero "was the greatest boaster alive and thought no one equal to himself."[11]

A self-enriching slaveholder, slumlord, and senator, Cicero deplored even the palest moves toward democracy. Rulers, he insisted, should always be persons of the affluent class: "When you appoint a judge it is perfectly proper to be guided by considerations of property and rank."[12] In 66, when Gaius Manilius, a people's tribune, introduced a law that granted freedmen the right to vote along with their former masters, Cicero was part of the senatorial majority that immediately rejected it.[13] He also denounced the secret ballot, introduced several generations earlier in 139 B.C. by Aulus Gabinius, a tribune and grandson of a slave, whom Cicero dismissed as "a vulgar and insignificant fellow." The secret ballot made it easier for the plebs to do mischief, he believed. It was "a subterfuge" that "ensured the secrecy of a wrong-headed vote thus keeping the aristocracy in the dark about what each man thought."[14]

He regarded the people as worthless groundlings, akin to criminals and degenerates, "the common herd," the "masses and worst elements . . . many of them simply out for revolution." He denounced those of pedestrian occupation, "the artisans and shopkeepers and all that kind of scum" who align themselves with dangerous demagogues, "the wretched half-starved commoners who attend mass meetings and suck the blood of the treasury."[15] To him, their restiveness was an outgrowth of their own personal malevolence rather than a response to unforgiving material circumstances. Privately he referred to "my army of the rich" and noted that "the safety of the state is to the advantage of all good men, but most clearly benefits men of fortune"—which was the way he thought it should be.[16] In 59, he wrote to his wealthy confidant Atticus, "My only policy now is hatred of the radicals."[17]

While unsparingly praised by generations of classicists for his principled ways, Cicero was often an unprincipled opportunist and dissembler. In 50 B.C., for example, with Caesar's fame and power ascendant, he persuaded the Senate to decree a thanksgiving service in Caesar's honor, and himself delivered a hypocritical panegyric—which he privately recanted shortly thereafter in a letter to Atticus: "I was not exactly proud of my palinode. But goodnight to principle, sincerity, and honor!"[18]

Celebrated throughout the ages as a champion of constitutionalism, Cicero actually was quite capable of playing fast with constitutional rights. His role in what became known as "the Catiline conspiracy" affords sorry evidence of this.

Born of an old patrician family in decline, Lucius Sergius Catiline had served with Sulla in his occupation of Rome and participated in the dictator's ruthless proscriptions in 81–80 B.C. After holding several magistracies over the years, he was indicted for extortion while serving as governor of Africa in 66, but won acquittal. About this time Catiline emerged as a late-blooming *po-*

pularis. Most writers see Catiline as propelled purely by ambition, lacking any dedicated attachment to the popular cause. But he did take up the cudgel on behalf of the poor with pronouncements like the following: "Ever since the state fell under the jurisdiction and sway of a few powerful men, it is always they who receive tribute from foreign kings and princes and rake in taxes from every people and tribe. . . . Thus all influence, power, office, and wealth are in their hands or where they choose to bestow them; all they leave for us is danger, defeat, prosecutions, and poverty."[19]

Catiline's diatribes registered in Cicero's mind as nothing less than subversion, a revolutionary assault upon the constitution and all of Roman society. He charged Catiline with plotting murderous deeds to grab state power. Writing twenty years after the events Sallust (though no friend of Cicero's) uncritically accepts all of Cicero's worst criminations. He maintains that Catiline and a confederate made ready to assassinate the consuls-elect on 1 January 65 and grab the offices for themselves. "Because their murderous intent was discovered, they postponed its execution until 5 February, when they planned to destroy most of the senators as well as the consuls." But Catiline was in too great a hurry to give the signal to his accomplices in front of the Senate House, asserts Sallust, and the attack never came off. Hence they failed in what would have been the "most heinous crime in the annals of Rome."[20]

As is often the case, Sallust leaves us with more questions than answers. He does not explain how the conspirators could hope to make themselves consuls by murdering the two consuls-elect. And once uncovered, why were they not prosecuted by the authorities?

Instead they felt perfectly free to reschedule their skulduggery for the following month, even escalating it to include the massacre of hundreds of senators. Then why was this grandiose scheme permanently called off merely because of a premature signal?

In 64, acting not at all like an aspiring mass murderer, Catiline waged an electoral campaign for consul, perhaps with the backing of Crassus and Caesar, gathering much popular support in the doing.[21] In an attempt to stop him, the nobles reluctantly threw their weight behind Cicero's candidacy. Their problem with Cicero was that he was a *novus homo*, a "new man," the first in his family ever to serve in the Senate. The Roman nobility was composed of individuals, both patrician and plebeian, who could claim a consul in their lineage. Occasionally the nobles recruited a candidate for consulship—and thereby for the aristocracy—whose senatorial ancestry had stopped at a lower office, but rarely would they deign to support a *novus homo*, someone like Cicero who had no senatorial ancestors whatsoever.[22] Sallust, himself a *novus homo*, explains it, "A self-made man, however distinguished he might be or however admirable his achievements, was invariably considered unworthy of [the consulship], almost as if he were unclean."[23]

But by 64, Cicero was proving himself a capable paladin to the plutocracy, while Catiline was emerging as a patrician turncoat, who roiled the optimates with bruising broadsides calling for debt cancellation and land redistribution. Forced to choose between their class snobbery and their class interests, the oligarchs decided on their interests. When necessity dictates, every ruling class has recruited serviceable talent from the ranks below. So the optimates held their noses and threw their weight behind the pushy orator from Arpinum. By being the first man in his family to hold a consulship, a new man thereby won aristocratic status for himself and his descendants. It was a relatively rare achievement and it was Cicero's, as he never tired of reminding others.

In the 64 campaign, Cicero drew upon the advice set down by his brother Quintus in a manual summarizing their discussions about campaign tactics. He was to avoid specific issues, and generally present himself as an unflinching upholder of the Senate's authority, devoted to orderly rule and the reactionary Sullan constitution. At the same time, he was to heap slander upon his opponents, Antonius and Catiline (several other candidates posed no serious challenge), defaming them as "two assassins from boyhood, both libertines, both paupers," charging Catiline with being so cunningly efficient "in his lust that he has raped children in smocks practically at their parents' knees."[24]

At one point in the campaign, when a radical tribune denounced Cicero as unworthy of a consular post, he responded by charging the tribune with being part of a fell design that threatened the commonwealth. From then on, conspiracy and subversion would remain Cicero's theme in the electoral campaign, throughout his consulship, and for much of his life.[25] He would stigmatize any attempt at reform, as part of a larger stratagem to subvert the Republic.

In the summer of 64, Cicero and Antonius won election as consuls to serve in 63. Catiline was defeated by a narrow margin. Through a combination of bribery and threat, the financially strapped Antonius was dissuaded from exercising a restraining veto on his co-consul, leaving Cicero with a free hand to act as he wished. In 63 Catiline waged another campaign for the consulship (to serve in 62). Cicero had the election delayed until late in the summer after many of Catiline's supporters were obliged to return to their provincial homes, thereby contributing to his second defeat. At the time Cicero informed the Senate that Catiline had planned to assassinate him. The charge was never clearly explained, and failed to convince the senators.[26]

During his tenure in office, Cicero lifted not a finger on behalf of the people, and vigorously opposed all reform proposals. He and his Senate collaborators quashed motions designed to cancel debts, effect land distribution, and allow the offspring of those exiled by Sulla to occupy public office.[27] As his undistinguished consulship was winding down to its final months, he escalated his vendetta against Catiline, charging him with orchestrating a revolutionary conspiracy of immense proportions. Catiline supposedly was pursuing this diabolic design throughout 63, at the very time he was energetically campaigning for the consulship. Here was a "crisis" that might serve Cicero famously. With little time left in office to mark his own greatness, the vigilant consul would leap into the fray, close the breach, and stay the perpetrator's hand. This feat, he insisted, would cause future generations to sing hosannas to his name, as indeed they have. All he needed was a prominent but not overly powerful enemy who could be identified with the lower classes. The defeated Catiline fit the bill perfectly.

The unrest in certain provinces only added to the alarmist atmosphere that Cicero was confecting. In Etruria (Tuscany) im-

poverished army veterans, aggrieved smallholders, and dispossessed farmers were arming themselves and rallying around their
leader Manlius. As Manlius explained in his declaration to the
Roman proconsul: "[O]ur object in taking up arms is not to attack
our country or to endanger others, but to protect ourselves from
wrong. We are poor needy wretches. The cruel harshness of moneylenders has robbed most of us of our homes. . . . We are not
seeking dominion or riches. . . . We beseech you and the Senate
to rescue your unhappy fellow citizens, to restore to us the legal
protection snatched from us."[28]

Manlius sounded more like someone petitioning for a redress
of grievances than a rebel breathing insurrectionary hellfire. Still
Cicero damned him for being in league with Catiline in a campaign to destroy Rome. Manlius and his supporters had backed
Catiline in the previous election. But there is nothing to indicate
that they were collaborating in an impending revolution.

In Rome, anonymous letters were sent to leading senators warn-
ing of a massacre. One nervous senator read a letter on the Senate
floor reporting that disgruntled veterans were massing in Etruria
to descend upon Rome on 27 October, at which time the city
would be set aflame by revolutionary incendiaries lurking within
its gates. On 1 November, other rebels would seize Palestrina (a
town just east of Rome), and from there launch an attack upon
the city. No one called for an investigation of the wild claims
proffered in these letters—nor of the letters themselves so mysteriously distributed.[29]

Cicero's jeremiads were having their intended effect. The Senate
passed a *senatus consultum ultimum* suspending the constitution and

giving the consul extraordinary emergency powers. Panic and gloom seized certain sectors of the city. As often happens, people saw evidence of the menace in the very precautions taken against it. Senators and other notables packed and fled. Private residences and government buildings were left unattended. Investment values plunged. But 27 October came and went, so too the first of November, and nothing happened. No army took the field in Etruria, no insurgents seized Palestrina, Rome went unmolested.[30]

At about this time, Catiline offered to place himself under Cicero's custody in order that he be as free as possible from suspicion of promoting insurrection. Cicero refused to accommodate him. It better served his purpose to have his prey skulking about as an untrammeled menace. Catiline voluntarily took up residence at the house of Metellus Nepos, the praetor, in a display of good faith. In contrast, Cicero took to accompanying himself with a large contingent of bodyguards. He began wearing a breastplate beneath his clothes that he would purposely uncover,[31] treating these well-advertised precautions as further evidence of Catiline's diabolic intent.

On 7 November 63, Cicero convened an extraordinary meeting of the Senate. While many senators doubted his charges, they dared not risk putting themselves under suspicion by challenging him. When Catiline entered the House, his colleagues shrank from greeting him or sitting near him, as Cicero gleefully pointed out. Their timorous reaction to the climate of fear only reinforced it. The consul launched into his speech, accusing Catiline of "actually plotting the destruction of every single one of us, and of all Rome, and of everything upon the face of the earth." Catiline was "determined to plunge the entire world into fire and slaughter." His conspiracy constituted "the most ferocious and appalling and deadly menace to our country." He and his confederates were ready to "besiege the Senate House with their swords, and mobilize their firebombs and brands to plunge the city into flames." In subsequent invectives Cicero was to repeat this charge again and again: Catiline intended "to burn down the entire city and kill you all"; his goal was "nothing less than the extermination of the Roman people."[32]

Cicero addressed Catiline directly as a man of "evil spirit," who had launched repeated attempts upon Cicero's own life: "Although I was well aware that my death would be a disaster to our state, I employed only my unaided endeavors to frustrate your plots. . . . There are all your attempts, for example, to kill myself. . . . Many of your [dagger] thrusts were so lethal that it seemed they could not fail to hit their mark. All the same, by some sort of sideways movement or dodge, I managed to elude them."[33] Ten years later, Cicero would again portray himself as the moving target of a *popularis*: "Many is the time that I . . . have narrowly managed to escape from Publius Clodius' weapons and gory hands."[34] One can only marvel at how the fleshy orator nimbly evaded his presumably determined assailants.

During his speech in the Senate, Cicero repeatedly indulged in threats against Catiline's life, noting that he was timing Catiline's execution to coincide with the roundup of other like-minded blackguards. To convince the Senate that summary executions were not without precedent, he repeatedly and approvingly mentioned the murder of Tiberius and Gaius Gracchus and other leaders of high social rank on mere "suspicion of treason."[35] But many senators found the charges hard to believe, which probably explains why they made no attempt to detain Catiline. Sensing that he was not carrying his audience, Cicero criticized those colleagues who refused to see "the disasters" that menaced them. And again the next day before the Assembly, he complained that "there were quite a number of people who did not believe what I was telling them."[36]

Nevertheless, the orator's repeated accusations managed to create a witch-hunt atmosphere that Catiline's calm denials could not sufficiently dispel. The dispirited Catiline quitted Rome the night after Cicero's first invective. If we are to believe him, he departed not to organize a revolutionary opposition in Italy, but reluctantly when the consul's denunciations and threats in the Senate made his position untenable, causing him to fear for his life. Catiline dispatched letters to men of consular rank and other members of the aristocracy, describing himself as "beset by false accusations" and unable to cope with the intrigues of his enemies. He informed them that he would go into exile at Massilia (Marseilles).[37]

Within days after his departure, Catiline must have had second thoughts about exile. Instead of going to Massilia, he joined the restive denizens led by Manlius in Etruria. That he had intended to do so all along has been the accepted opinion among most historians, beginning with Cicero. Indeed, it is possible that he lied in order to throw any pursuers off his track. It is just as likely that he changed his mind as he issued forth.[38] He realized he could never expect to return to Rome and live unmolested, and he feared being hunted down by the consul's armed guards while abroad. In any case, a fearful barren life in exile did not fit his temperament. So he embarked upon one last desperate gambit, joining the dispossessed in northern Italy who were now taking up arms to defend themselves from foreclosures and usurious debt collectors.

This is suggested in the letter produced by the arch-conservative Quintus Catulus, which he said came from Catiline. It read in part:

> I was provoked by wrongs and insults and . . . found myself unable to maintain a position of dignity. So I openly undertook the championship of the oppressed, as I had often done before. . . . It was because I saw unworthy men promoted to honorable positions, and felt myself treated as an outcast on account of unjust suspicions. That is why I have adopted a course of action, amply justified in my present circumstances, which offers a hope of saving what is left of my honor. I intended to write at greater length, but news has come that they are preparing to use force against me.[39]

When word of Catiline's arrival in Etruria reached Rome, the Senate declared him and Manlius public enemies. On 9 November, before the Assembly, Cicero delivered a set piece in the art of demonization: "Imagine every type of criminality and wickedness that you can think of; [Catiline] has been behind them all. In the whole of Italy there is not a single poisoner, gladiator, robber,

assassin, parricide, will-forger, cheat, glutton, adulterer, prosti-
tute, corrupter of youth, or youth who has been corrupted, indeed
any nasty individual of any kind whatever, who would not be
obliged to admit he has been Catiline's intimate. Whenever, all
through these years, there has been a murder, the murderer has
been he." Catiline even encouraged his young male lovers to murder their parents and "personally lent a hand" in such misdeeds,
Cicero assured the Assembly. The orator did not explain why the
depraved patrician had never been prosecuted for any of these
horrific exploits.[40]

Cicero's strategy was enjoying some success: Demonize and isolate
Catiline, push him to the wall, and goad him into an act of unlawful resistance, all the while creating a climate of alarm within
the city. The orator-cum-savior would then use the "perilous emergency" as an opportunity to restore, in the manner of Sulla, the
unchallenged authority of the inner circle of aristocratic senators,
thereby earning their eternal gratitude, and winning supreme
glory for himself.

Still, the lurid scenario he conjured was wanting in one essen-
tial component: evidence. Not one person had been harmed, not
a house torched, not an arms cache uncovered, not a hilltop or
vantage point seized by the insurrectionists, not a trace of anything nefarious afoot, not a perpetrator rooted out and apprehended. The squadrons of incendiaries and armed cadres never
materialized. Subversion and mass murder were nowhere to be

found except in the hyperbolic screeds emanating from the over-heated consul.[41]

With Catiline now ensconced in Etruria, another month passed and still nothing materialized. Cicero easily explained why; the insurrection had been stymied by his unmatchable vigilance: "I myself am on guard. The interests of our country are in my watchful care." And "My courage, wisdom, and foresight [have] preserved the state from the gravest of perils."[42]

A dramatic turn came on 3 December, when an excited Cicero summoned the Senate into another emergency session. He announced that he had planted informers in a secret clique of aristocrats who were confederates of Catiline. Acting on tips from his undercover agents he had arrested a delegation of Allobroges (from Gaul) who were in Rome seeking redress from the extortions of Roman officials and usurers. A certain Umbrenus, a moneylender active in Gaul, and probably an agent of Cicero, approached the unsuspecting Gauls and informed them of Catiline's conspiracy to overthrow the Roman Republic. He even named the conspirators. Fearing that they were being set up by a provocateur, the Allobroges informed a senator, who regularly acted as their patron in Rome. He in turn informed Cicero, probably not realizing that he was thereby drawing the Gauls into the consul's net.[43]

The next morning Cicero had the Allobrogian envoys arrested as they were wending their way out of the city, along with someone named Titus Volturcius, a provincial Italian who supposedly had entered in league with Catiline's conspirators. The envoys were now implicated. Either they cooperated (with the promise of ample monetary reward) or risked dire retribution. The Gauls chose to cooperate fully with Cicero. Following his instructions, they managed to get introduced to the aristocratic conspirators, and asked from them "a written undertaking" under their personal seals that the Allobroges could carry to their countrymen.[44]

Cicero then summoned the aristocrats who, acting not at all like guilty conspirators, obligingly answered his call only to find themselves under arrest.[45] "It was to be suspected," Kahn writes, "that Umbrenus himself was in Cicero's hire, and Volturcius, the conspirator caught along with the Gauls, was almost certainly a paid informant. He had only recently joined the conspiracy and, upon capture, with inordinate alacrity offered to turn state's evidence." Volturcius corroborated the whole litany of horrors Cicero had been highlighting. He claimed that at a signal for an uprising, youths of noble families were to murder their fathers. But Cicero "did not press Volturcius to name any of the prospective patricides."[46]

The letters of the apprehended aristocrats revealed no precise evidence of criminal intent, and probably were primarily statements of support for the Allobroges' redress of grievances. If they had contained mention of arson, massacre, or seizing state power, we certainly would have heard about it from Cicero.

Still the orator held forth about the impending apocalypse. He noted that when Catiline had "broken out of the city a few days ago" (actually Catiline had departed unimpeded nearly a month before), "he left behind him at Rome the associates of his odious designs, the ferocious leaders . . . whose madness and malignancy knew no limits." One of these maddened malignant conspirators was none other than Publius Lentulus Sura, an eminent praetor and former consul, a friend of Catiline's, and Mark Antony's stepfather. Lentulus had written a supportive letter to Catiline, which Volturcius supposedly was asked to deliver. It urged Catiline to "stand firm" and enlist the aid of all "even of the lowest classes."[47] That being the only portion of Lentulus's letter that Cicero quotes and therefore the only portion known to us, we might expect it is the most damaging. Yet it hardly bespeaks a sinister conspiracy to destroy Rome. "Stand firm" in the face of unrelenting calumny is not exactly a call to overthrow the state and butcher all its inhabitants. Rather Lentulus seems to be calmly advising his friend to rally enough support to withstand Cicero's onslaught. And if Catiline and Lentulus had long been conspiring with armed slaves and plebs, then Lentulus's suggestion that he enlist even "the lowest classes" seems oddly redundant and out of date with what supposedly already had been brewing among the conspirators.

Appearing in the Forum later that day, Cicero announced that it was now conclusively proven that Catiline planned to invade Rome and massacre the entire citizenry; the five confederates had been plotting an insurrection from within; and Lentulus intended to make himself king of Rome. Another conspirator, Cethegus, a man of some wealth, possessed a private collection of fancy high-priced daggers and swords that Cicero eagerly confiscated and treated as the arsenal intended for Catiline's rogue army.[48] The five were guilty, Cicero assured the assembled crowd. More conclusive than any evidence was "their pallor, the look in their eyes, the set of their features, their silence. As they stood there stupefied, gazing fixedly upon the ground or occasionally glancing furtively at one another, their guilt was quite as manifest from their own appearance as from any one else's testimony."[49]

A different conclusion is reached by the few dissenting historians who note that the "evidence" against the five had been proffered by informants of questionable credibility, and that the accused had not been allowed to cross-examine their accusers in any systematic fashion. "To any senator retaining a modicum of common sense it was clear that the hullabaloo was out of all proportion to the events."[50] A coterie of sympathizers had tried to mobilize support for their friend Catiline, but were they planning arson, murder, and revolution? If so, by what means? It was not with an invisible army of plebs and slaves, nor was it with Manlius and his veterans who petitioned the Roman proconsul only for land reform and relief from taxes and debts, nor with the Allobroges who were petitioning for grievances of their own and who gave no evidence of planning a Gallic invasion of Rome.

The following day, 4 December, as Sallust tells it, a certain Lucius Tarquinius was brought before the full Senate House. He claimed to have been on his way to join Catiline when he was arrested. Why the authorities thought he was suspect Sallust does not say. Told to speak by Cicero, Tarquinius readily related a story tailor-made to support Cicero's charges and strikingly similar to the one spun by Volturcius. But Tarquinius also claimed that he had been sent by Marcus Crassus to instruct Catiline to prepare his attack with all due haste. The mention of Crassus, an aristocrat possessed of immense wealth and prestige, had an unsettling effect on the Senate. It was one thing that Crassus may have supported Catiline for consul and bailed him out in an earlier extortion case, but something else to accuse him of plotting to overthrow the Roman government. Could the commander who had ruthlessly crushed Spartacus's slave rebellion in 71 now be leading a slave rebellion of his own? Could the richest landlord in Rome now want to torch his own properties?

Some senators found Tarquinius's statement beyond belief. Others thought it best not to provoke a powerful man like Crassus, regardless of how true or untrue the allegation against him. The full House swiftly declared the charges to be false, and decreed that Tarquinius be kept in custody until he revealed the name of the person who had put him up to such testimony. Some suspected that Tarquinius had been suborned by Cicero in an attempt to undermine Crassus, who had developed the habit of working with reform-minded leaders—including the popular Pompey (who at that moment was in Asia on a military campaign). Sallust writes, "At a later date, I actually heard Crassus declare with his own lips that this infamous accusation against him had been made by Cicero."[51]

Two leading optimates, Catulus and Piso, nursing political and personal grievances against Julius Caesar, urged Cicero to enlist informants to bear false witness against him.[52] But Cicero, perhaps mindful of how the charge against Crassus had redounded with ill effect, refused to risk it. Catulus and Piso then took matters into their own hands, circulating falsehoods that they pretended to have heard from Volturcius or the Allobroges, provoking enough feeling against Caesar to cause armed knights—strong partisans of Cicero's—to threaten him with their swords as he exited the Senate House.[53]

On 5 December 63, the Senate held a momentous session. Various senators now came forward with incriminating testimony against the five "Catiline conspirators." Consul-elect Silanus, a Cicero collaborator, declared that Cethegus had marked him and seven other high-ranking senators for death. Silanus offered no evidence to support this startling indictment, nor did he explain why he had waited until now to report it. Cethegus, Lentulus, and the other conspirators should suffer "the extremist fate," he demanded, a cry taken up by other senators.

With the conspirators' fate seemingly sealed, Julius Caesar took the floor. Still four years away from his first consulship, Caesar already was a leading figure in Roman politics, identified with the popular faction. Calmly he urged the senators upon a different course, reminding them of their constitutional duty. He could not countenance putting the accused to death without a trial. Instead he recommended keeping them in close custody until further investigation and adjudication. Surely, now was not the time to do something rash and irreversible—and certainly unconstitutional—something that might only generate a still graver crisis. Here Caesar was alluding to the possibility that the executions might rouse disturbances among the people, many of whom had taken to Catiline's late-blooming populism. Caesar's measured remarks, writes Plutarch, "wrought such change in the opinions of the Senate, which was in fear of the people" that even Silanus hastily announced that he too had not meant death when he called for "the extremist fate" but incarceration—which to a freedom-loving Roman was far worse than death.[54]

Catulus took the floor and sputtered in rage against the course urged by Caesar. He was followed by another optimate leader, the younger Cato, who angrily taxed Silanus for his recantation, then assailed Caesar for using the cover of humane words while "trying to subvert the state . . . seeking to frighten the Senate in a case in which he himself had much to fear." Here Cato was accusing Caesar of being secretly in league with Catiline. Why else would he essay to rescue enemies who had brought the country to the brink of ruin and whose deaths "would free the state from great slaughter and perils"?[55]

While Cato had the floor, it happened that a messenger delivered a note to Caesar. Seeing an opportunity to fix suspicion, Cato cried out that even now as he spoke, Caesar was communicating with enemies of the commonwealth. Cato bade him to read the missive aloud. Instead, Caesar rose and handed the sheaf to Cato who unhappily discovered it to be a billet-doux from his very own half sister Servilia (the mother of Brutus) who long had been engaged in a notorious liaison with Caesar. Plutarch describes her as being "madly in love" with him. In a distemper Cato threw the note back at Caesar, snapping "Keep it, you drunkard," an oddly inapposite epithet since Caesar was known to be a temperate imbiber, and the note pertained to a different sort of intoxication experienced by Servilia.[56]

Though his ploy against Caesar backfired, Cato turned the tide of opinion. The jittery senators voted to condemn the accused to death.[57] That same evening, under Cicero's direct supervision, Lentulus, Cethegus, Statilius, Gabinius, and Caeparius were taken to a prison, one by one lowered into a dank, foul chamber, and strangled to death.[58]

Other conspirators of lesser renown were rounded up in Rome and elsewhere in Italy. Under the law, now that his consulship had expired, Cicero held court in his home. Some of the accused were put to death on the testimony of an informer; others were acquitted. Some supposed to be guilty were allowed to escape. In a polemic sometimes attributed to Sallust, an anonymous critic notes that several among the accused who offered Cicero sumptuous gifts, including a house, a Tusculan villa, and a Pompeian villa, escaped retribution. But those who could not afford such favors were charged with plotting against the Senate, and Cicero was certain of their guilt.[59]

Some weeks later, Catiline and his poorly armed band in Etruria, beleaguered by Roman legions closing in from north and south of them, fought valiantly in what was essentially a defensive action. Catiline was killed and the Etrurian force was crushed. No prisoners were taken.

For the next twenty years Cicero tirelessly credited himself with "having preserved the state" and having "delivered the Senate House from massacre," describing his crusade against Catiline as "the grandest deed in the history of the human race." He had to admit that the only citizen the Republic "could not do without was myself."[60] In a letter to Lucius Lucceius, who was writing a history of Rome (lost to us), Cicero asked him to use his genius to eulogize the role that he, Cicero, had played in the city's history "with even more warmth than perhaps you feel, and in that respect to disregard the canons of history" by writing with a partiality that "enhances my merits even to exaggeration in your eyes . . . even a little more than may be allowed by truth." This would help bring "the vindication of my claims to everlasting renown." For "if a man has once transgressed the bounds of modesty, the best he can do is to be shameless out and out."[61]

Cicero's tireless rodomontade became the accepted opinion among intellectuals through the ages. Velleius Paterculus, Plutarch, Juvenal, Lucan, Dio Cassius, Florus, and other ancient writers praise him almost as much as he praised himself for having thwarted a pestiferous conspiracy against Rome and all its upstanding citizens.[62] Likewise, most modern-day historians accept Cicero's account of how he rescued the city from Catiline's clutches. They write of the "firm evidence" he produced, the "diligence" and "care" that "spared Rome from fire and sword," his "brilliant statecraft," "quick, decisive, and courageous" action, and "prompt countermeasures."[63]

For those of us less enamored with the great orator, troubling questions remain. Beginning with the more implausible charges:

- If the alleged conspirators sought to become the masters of Rome, why were they intent upon "wiping out the city and every single individual . . . menacing our country with annihilation," as Cicero claimed?[64] Why would they want to preside over a heap of corpses and burnt rubble?

- Catiline's secret band of confederates, according to Cicero, was composed of debtors, gamblers, layabouts, parricides, assassins, debauchers, effeminate degenerates, and louche characters of every sort.[65] How could the arch-villain hope to overthrow the Roman empire with such a raggle-taggle band of wastrels and misfits?

- Given Catiline's bloodthirsty designs, why were no murders committed? Assassination was hardly an unknown accomplishment in Roman politics, yet Catiline and his bumbling gang seemed never to get the hang of it. The two consuls-elect were supposedly targeted in the January 65 "murder plot," but nothing happened. As for the plot to kill hundreds of senators the following month, again nothing happened.

- There was the report, widely publicized by Cicero, of two Catiline conspirators who were appointed to kill him, but when denied entry into his house, they departed without a murmur and never bothered him again. Cicero claimed, "I had almost been murdered in my own home."[66] But why did he not have them arrested for conspiracy to commit murder? Why did he not produce them and his anonymous informant for public questioning?[67] Again, nothing developed. Commentators cannot even agree on the identity of these two lackadaisical perpetrators. Sallust is sure it was Cornelius and Vargunteius; Plutarch fingers Marcius and Cethegus; Appian accuses Lentulus and Cethegus; Dio gives no names; Suetonius and Velleius do not even mention the incident. And Cicero himself is oddly vague, saying only that it was "two Roman equestrians," which rules out most of the above.[68]

- Cicero refers to attempts against several other individuals, and an attempt to kill Catiline's competitors on the consular *comitia* of 63. Again, nothing happened. And what evidence was there that Catiline repeatedly assaulted Cicero with a dagger but apparently in so ungainly a fashion as to be thwarted by the consul's sidesteps? Why didn't Cicero have Catiline arrested for these attempts upon his life?

- Catiline and his accomplices were ignominious failures also when it came to arson attacks. If you can believe Sallust, Catiline enlisted a number of debauched society ladies to agitate among the city slaves and organize incendiary assaults. Again nothing came of it. It was said that Catiline planned to seize key points throughout the city with armed men. Again, no results.[69] The incendiaries were supposedly forestalled by Cicero's guards. This too is difficult to believe. Rome was a tinderbox; accidental fires were frequent and fierce. If bands of arsonists really intended to start a major conflagration, no number of guards could have prevented it.[70]

- What evidence did Cicero have to support his startling charge that Catiline's friend Lentulus sought a kingship over Rome? Lentulus was doubtless mindful of how kings were abominated by the Roman people. And he was sensibly aware that he himself, albeit a fine orator, laid claim to no strong following in the Forum, the Senate, or the military. How then could he have hoped to achieve such a grandiose goal? Without an army, how would he have hoped to resist a jealous Pompey who, hastening back to Rome with his legions, would have dispensed with any self-proclaimed king or, for that matter, any self-installed consul such as Catiline.

- Why would the five accused divulge their dangerously self-incriminating secrets in letters fixed with their personal seals to foreign envoys from Gaul with whom they had no previous connection? Cicero himself was aware that this incredible scenario craved explanation. His answer delivered before the Assembly on the afternoon of 3 December was that divine forces caused them to blunder! "Lentulus and the other traitors in our midst would never have been such madmen as to entrust these vital intrigues and communications to people who were both strangers and barbarians, unless the gods themselves had denuded their outrageous scheme of every shred of discretion." Before the Senate Cicero claimed, "Gentlemen, I feel conscious that the will and guidance of the immortal gods have been directly behind every single thing I have arranged."[71] This from a man who privately debunked the auspices and other religious beliefs.

- Given the supposedly massive dimensions of the plot, why was there no evidence other than the dubious testimony of several informants who simply reiterated the charges leveled in Cicero's invectives? Rewards were offered for information about the plot. For a slave, the prize was freedom and 100,000 sesterces (about ten years' earnings for the average laborer); for a free man, double that sum and a pardon for any share he had in the conspiracy.[72] Sallust notes that "not a man among all the conspirators was induced by the promise of reward to betray their plans."[73] As usual, Sallust does not question further, but we might ask, why did not one feckless turncoat issue forth with information in order to pocket the sumptuous reward and save his own skin?

Most probably the conspiracy was not betrayed because it did not exist, at least not to the phantasmal extent conjured by Cicero.

On 29 December, the last day of his consulship, Cicero attempted to make a farewell speech lauding his year in office. But the assembled crowd would not allow him to utter a word besides his oath. Instead they hooted him down for executing Roman citizens without a fair trial and without the consent of the people. In vehement protestation, the orator shouted back that the safety of the state and city "is due to my efforts alone," a boast that only succeeded in inciting still more anger from the crowd.[74]

Cicero had hoped that his renown as Rome's deliverer would prevail throughout the ages, and so it has among many classicists. But among the sensible commoners of Rome, his self-anointed glory endured for hardly a day.

6

The Face of Caesar

Caesar shall forth: the things that threaten'd me
Ne'er look'd but on my back; when they shall see
The face of Caesar, they are vanished.
— *JULIUS CAESAR* ACT II, SCENE 2

Rome's greatest *popularis* was Gaius Julius Caesar, known to his contemporaries as Gaius Caesar and to history as Julius Caesar. He was born in 100 B.C., the scion of an old patrician family. His uncle by marriage was Gaius Marius, the famous *popularis*, and his father-in-law was Marius's close ally Cornelius Cinna. Being Marius's nephew and Cinna's son-in-law during Sulla's reign of repression in 82 placed young Caesar on the defeated side and slated him for proscription. Sulla announced his willingness to spare Caesar's life if the youth would pledge himself to the reactionary cause. And to demonstrate the sincerity of his conversion, Caesar was expected to discard his wife Cornelia (Cinna's daughter) and marry someone chosen by Sulla.

Had Caesar been driven primarily by unprincipled ambition

and a lust for power, as Cicero claimed and many Ciceronian historians insist to this day, he would have eagerly accepted this chance to be catapulted into the highest circles as the tyrant's protégé. Instead, he spurned Sulla's offer though mindful of the ruinous consequences. Showing great displeasure, Sulla ordered his arrest and stripped him of his inheritance and his wife's dowry. Some historians report that Caesar saved himself by taking flight after bribing one of Sulla's captains with the considerable sum of two talents (approximately 100 pounds of gold or silver).[1] Others say he survived because Caesar's mother and conservative members of her family used their connections with well-placed Sullan partisans to prevail upon the tyrant to pardon the defiant youth. To those who advised Sulla against eliminating someone so young, he is quoted as saying, "Bear in mind that the man you are so eager to save will one day deal the death blow to the aristocracy, which you have joined me in upholding; for in this Caesar there is more than one Marius."[2]

For the next few years Caesar kept a healthy distance from Rome while Sulla's proscriptions were claiming thousands of victims. In 78, news of Sulla's death brought him hastily back to the city. The popular movement was surfacing anew, even seeming to threaten social revolution. With desperate energy the Senate aristocrats regrouped the Sullan forces and granted plenary power to Pompey to repress the disturbances. At this time Caesar refrained from entering the fray.[3]

In 75 Caesar journeyed abroad, most probably to claim a legacy from his deceased friend and former lover, King Nicomedes. On his way, the story goes, he was captured by pirates and held ransom for the huge sum of fifty talents. After weeks of effort, his envoys extracted this amount from the allied coastal municipalities. Many of the pirates were drawn from these same towns. Since the inhabitants often shared in the spoils, it was established that they should be required to make restoration. Upon being released, within the space of a day Caesar armed some ships and recruited a band of irregulars, who perhaps belonged to a clan that was a rival of his erstwhile captors. His makeshift force surprised the brigands that evening and captured some of their ships. Caesar executed his former captors and pocketed the immense ransom for himself, presumably after paying off his hirelings.[4]

Even at this point there still was nothing to prevent Julius Caesar from taking the well-paved path of an optimate career. He would have been welcomed into the oligarchic camp with open arms and ready rewards. Instead, he moved in the opposite direction, exhibiting a dedication to the popular cause that captured the people's affection. In 73, he supported a measure that would allow the return of pro-Marius political exiles banished during Sulla's reign. That same year, he sided with an interesting democratic leader and tribune, Licinius Macer, in a campaign to undo the Sullan decrees that had abrogated the powers of the people's tribunate.

It was Macer who helped create a democratic mode of public speaking (utilized by Caesar himself), arming his listeners with factual evidence and precise argument rather than rolling over them with the orotund periods and histrionic locution of classical oratory. Cicero describes Macer as being of unimpressive presence. His looks and manner detracted from the effect of his intellectual prowess, yet he was effective enough. "His language was not richly abundant but neither was it meager. His voice, gestures, and delivery were entirely lacking in charm. Yet his use of original material, and his arrangement of what he had to say, were so carefully thought out, as to be unsurpassed by anyone else in these respects."[5]

All we have of Macer's words is a speech preserved in the surviving fragments of Sallust's *History*. Living under the Sullan constitution in the late seventies, Macer was fully cognizant of the dangerous power wielded by the oligarchs. A tribune such as himself "alone and deficient in resources and with the mere empty semblance of office" could not hope to challenge them without mass support. "What an uproar they incite against myself," he remarked. Macer chastised the plebs for their lack of organized action and their willingness to lease themselves as clientele to aristocratic patrons. "You act like a tame herd, notwithstanding your great numbers, allowing yourselves to be possessed and fleeced by the few." By obeying the lordly commands of the consuls and the decrees of the Senate, the people fortified the very authority that oppressed them. If they did not struggle to regain their rights and defend their interests, they would only be subjected to still more severe injustices, he argued.

Under the pretense of conducting war, the nobles grab control of the treasury and the army, Macer went on. They trick the people into believing they are sovereign by waging raucous but vacuous political contests in which voters are allowed to select not their defenders but their masters. The populace, he argued, should not allow itself to be bribed with a meager grain disbursement

that was "not much more than prison rations." Even that paltry
handout was grudgingly granted only out of fear of social unrest.
Macer called upon the plebs to withdraw their empowering re-
sponses by resisting military conscription and refraining from
serving the rich: "I do not recommend armed violence or a secession but only that you should refuse to shed your blood in their
behalf. . . . [L]et those of us who have no share in the profits be
free also from dangers and toil."[6]

Macer's career illustrates how a popular leader can be immo-
bilized short of assassination. In 66, while serving as a provincial
governor, he was targeted by the optimates and charged with extortion. Presiding over his trial was Cicero himself, who gleefully
wrote to Atticus, "I gained more approval by his conviction than
I would have gained from his gratitude if he had been acquitted."[7]
Fully expecting to be found not guilty, Macer greeted the news
of his conviction with utter dismay, retiring to his home where
he either died of a heart attack or committed suicide.[8]

In 68, Julius Caesar delivered a public eulogy for his aunt Julia,
wife to Marius, at whose funeral he boldly displayed images of
Marius, something nobody had dared to do since the Sullan reaction. In the ensuing years, Caesar went on to win various public
offices. As aedile in 65, he used the money of rich associates to
organize festivals and spectacles of unprecedented extravagance.
And he won appreciation for the great care he gave to public
squares and buildings and for restoring the Appian Way. He also
ordered that under darkness images of Marius be placed in the

Capitol. The next day, as word of this spread, "Marius's party took courage, and it was incredible how numerous they were suddenly seen to be, and what a multitude of them appeared and came shouting into the capitol," many extolling Caesar as the one man "who was a relation worthy of Marius."[9]

In 64, when just thirty-six years old, Caesar presented himself as a candidate for high priest (*pontifex maximus*), a lifelong, prestigious position he occupied without benefit of any deep religious conviction. Plutarch reports that his election, won against two eminent older senators, "excited among the Senate and nobility great alarm lest he might now urge the people to every extreme of recklessness."[10]

Later that year Caesar and others put together a land reform bill that was designed to be moderate in method but comprehensive in scope. Allotments were to benefit both the landless poor and army veterans. The holdings would be acquired only from public lands and parcels purchased from landholders willing to sell. Land-rich nobles deeply in debt were guaranteed a good price despite depressed land values. Funds for the program would come from the sale of property and wealth confiscated from overseas dependencies, thereby costing the public treasury little, while finally providing a socially useful means for distributing war booty.[11]

On 1 January 63, the newly elected consul, Cicero, in his inaugural address before the Senate and in two subsequent orations in the Forum, threw the full weight of his office against the land reform bill, misrepresenting its moderate contents, and raising alarmist cries that the proposal was a "plot against liberty," "darkly engineered" and full of "secret purpose." Kahn notes that "Cicero was equating change with subversion," depicting any measure to mitigate material misery as a lunge toward revolution. The bill was either withdrawn or defeated in an Assembly vote.[12]

This setback must have taught Caesar something about the difficulties of peaceful reform within the existing system. Still, his own career moved forward. He was elected praetor in 62 and proconsul of Farther Spain in 61, where he engaged in a victorious military campaign against the Lusitani. It was during these years that he forged political friendships with Crassus and Pompey.

The ex-praetor Marcus Crassus, a former subordinate of Sulla (mentioned in the previous chapter as accused of participating in the Catiline plot), owed his celebrity to both money and military endeavor. He amassed vast amounts through investments, becoming a landowner and slumlord. His dubious claim to fame came in 71 B.C. when he headed the army that delivered the death blow to the great slave rebellion led by Spartacus. He hunted down and killed Spartacus and then crucified 6,000 of his men.

Pompey also had begun his military career as an ally of Sulla in 82, whom he served in outstanding fashion, winning the dictator's gratitude and admiration.[13] Summoned back from Spain to help quell Spartacus's rebellion, Pompey arrived in time to partake in the final bloodletting, which he and his associates trumpeted as a major military success eclipsing Crassus's endeavors.

Whatever clashes and feelings of rivalry they may have had, Crassus and Pompey managed to work together, getting themselves elected as consuls for 70 B.C. Pressured by popular agitation, they devoted their year in office to undoing some of Sulla's reactionary edicts. They encouraged the censors to expel sixty-four senators for gross corruption, and they supported a bill reducing senatorial membership on jury panels to one-third. Most important of all, a law proposed by Pompey lifted the restrictions Sulla had imposed upon the people's tribunes. These efforts won the applause of the people and the ire of the Senate, and qualified Pompey as a *popularis*, at least for a spell.

Through the sixties, Crassus associated himself with the popular cause, supporting Macer when he was hounded by the optimates in 66, then serving as Caesar's financial backer. By this time Pompey had won additional fame for his swift and successful campaign against the pirates who had been marauding the Mediterranean. In 60 B.C., Caesar invited Crassus and Pompey to join with him in what became known to modern historians as the First Triumvirate. Pompey had the prestige of a war hero and presumably the backing of his veterans, Crassus had the money, and Caesar had the support of the plebs. Together they challenged the optimates and emerged for a time as the dominant political force, able to undo some of the more reactionary features of the Sullan constitution, causing Cicero to denounce them privately as "three immoderate men."[14]

In the face of heavy optimate opposition, Caesar won the supreme office of consul, serving in 59. Early in his consulship he submitted another land reform bill, accepted by Pompey and Crassus, not unlike the one proposed in 63. Cicero was invited to serve on the land reform commission but refused. After the bill was filibustered to death in the Senate by Cato, Caesar applied the tactics of the Gracchi, dealing no further with the Senate and turning to the popular assemblies to get the law passed.[15] It was not long before Cicero was complaining that the land distribution program was "taking away our rents in Campania."[16]

Caesar's fellow consul Bibulus, the optimates' man, opposed Caesar's reformist measures and tried to paralyze proceedings within the assemblies by forever sighting bad omens. Whenever democratic sentiment gained sufficient momentum, it risked being thwarted by religious auspices (*auspicia*), that is, by divinations of the will of the gods. Auspices were conducted by the College of Augurs, an exclusive aristocratic preserve until the beginning of the first century B.C., after which notable equestrians were also inducted. By simply reporting unfavorable omens, the augurs could postpone action within the popular assemblies or invalidate the election of a pro-democratic official. It was customary to regard any sign from heaven as inauspicious and reason enough to suspend public proceedings.[17]

Divinations were issued after a ritualized study of the entrails of sacrificial animals, or after observing a sudden flight of birds, a thunderstorm, a streak of light in the celestial firmament, or some other "unusual" happening. The ruling circles appreciated the conservative veto offered by the auspices. Cicero was explicit on this point. While he privately dismissed augury as nothing more than just so much mummery, he was all for using it as a state weapon against "the frenzy of the tribunes" and "the unjust impetuosity of the people."[18]

A century before Cicero, Polybius commented on the political uses of religion: "[S]uperstition is actually the element that holds the Roman state together. . . . As the masses are always fickle, filled with lawless desires, unreasoning anger, and violent passions, they can only be restrained by mysterious terrors or other dramatizations. . . ."[19] Later on Gibbon wrote: "The various modes of worship which prevailed in the Roman world were all considered by the people as equally true; by the philosopher as equally false; and by the magistrate as equally useful."[20] One modern-day conservative historian acknowledges that religious auspices "helped to keep things going as they had always gone and to teach the lower classes to know their proper place."[21] So it came as no surprise that Bibulus, having shut himself up in his house through most of his co-consulship, would attempt to trump Caesar and the popular assemblies by repeatedly announcing inauspicious augurs, ploys that Caesar simply ignored, just as he must have disregarded Bibulus's vetoes.[22]

Whatever his popularity, Caesar still lacked the power and prestige of a military hero. Unlike Alexander, Hannibal, and Napoleon, he began his career as a politician rather than as a military leader. Originally intending, in the manner of Pericles and Gaius Gracchus, to attain his reforms without the use of force, he attended to the political arena for eighteen years. Then, at the age of forty, he became convinced that having an army at his back was a surer way when facing off against the death-dealing oligarchy.

By that time the Roman Republic ruled over a far-flung empire, extending across the entire Mediterranean basin from Spain to Asia Minor. Caesar added to its possessions and partook of its plunder and bloodletting.[23] In 58, he become proconsul (provincial governor) of Cisalpine Gaul (northern Italy) and Transalpine Gaul (France and Belgium). In a series of military campaigns that lasted for nine years, he brought all of Gaul under Roman suzerainty, along with portions of Germany. He continued as proconsul for five additional years under a law passed in 55 by Pompey and Crassus, who again were serving as consuls.

The alliance between Pompey and Caesar had been cemented by Pompey's marriage to Caesar's daughter Julia. But Julia died in 54, at a time when Pompey was becoming increasingly uneasy about Caesar's growing popularity and military strength. The following year, the Triumvirate came to an end when Crassus suffered a disastrous military defeat in his campaign against the Parthians in the east (present-day Iraq and northern Syria), and was then treacherously killed while attempting to negotiate with them. The Parthians knew something about Crassus. As Florus reports, they cut off his head, and poured molten gold into his mouth that he "whose mind had burned with desire of gold might when dead and inanimate be burned with gold itself."[24]

The death of Crassus not only brought the collapse of the Triumvirate but spelled the beginning of civil war. According to the Roman historian Lucan: "Caesar could no longer endure a superior, nor Pompey an equal."[25] Pompey was, according to Dio, greatly displeased by the general praise bestowed upon Caesar "whereby his own exploits were being overshadowed." He attempted to persuade the consuls not to make public Caesar's letters but to down-play his victories. He "reproached the populace for paying little heed to himself and going frantic over Caesar."[26]

Sensing Pompey's discontent, the optimates sought to enlist him to their cause. They feared Caesar as the shrewder and more dedicated *popularis* of the two. Although he was away on his Gallic campaign through most of the fifties, Caesar still managed to keep a hand in Roman politics, acting through surrogates or himself sometimes returning to Rome during the winter months.

Pompey proved receptive to the optimates' overtures. In 52, the senators designated him sole consul of Rome—in violation of constitutional practice that required two consuls to serve and both to be elected by the assemblies. About that time they extended his command in Spain for another five years. With Julia dead, Pompey rejected an offer to marry Caesar's great-niece and instead took the daughter of Metellus Scipio, a Senate optimate. He then selected his newly acquired father-in-law to serve alongside him as fellow consul for the remaining months of 52, another uncon-stitutional move that was perfectly acceptable to the senatorial constitutionalists. Highly influential aristocratic families such as the Metelli were willing to truck with Pompey at least until Cae-sar could be scotched.

In late December of 50, while Caesar was still in Gaul, the conflict between him and the optimates came to a boil. The Senate decided that a successor should be sent to replace him. The Senate's order was vetoed by Curio, a tribune sympathetic to Caesar. Caesar's counteroffer, put before the Senate by Curio, was that both he and Pompey resign their military commands. This proposal won enthusiastic support among the common people.[27] By a vote of 370–22, the senators readily approved this plan. Here was a chance to avert civil war and disarm both Caesar and Pompey.

But this was not good enough for the ultraconservative optimates hardened as they were against Caesar. They found a tribune who vetoed the mutual disarmament proposal. If Caesar resigned his command, they must have thought, this would not end his political appeal. In any case, there would be little to prevent him from calling up his veterans or levying new recruits at some future flashpoint. The following day one of the consuls, also of the conservative faction, called on Pompey to take command of two legions.

Negotiations continued into early January 49. Acting not at all like someone lusting for kingly power, Caesar again proposed that he and Pompey resign their commands. His message was put before the Senate by a tribune and political ally, Mark Antony, who had succeeded Curio. This time the senators angrily rejected it without debate. The optimates were now firmly gripping the senatorial reins, driving toward a showdown. With Pompey as their hired sword, they believed they could isolate and vanquish Caesar once and for all. The Senate passed a *senatus consultum ultimum* along with "resolutions of the harshest and most severe nature" to end Caesar's command and suppress "those distinguished officials, the tribunes of the people," as Caesar wrote.[28] Fearing for themselves, Mark Antony and another tribune fled Rome, making their way north to join Caesar.

Several days later, Caesar assembled his troops and recounted all the wrongs he believed had been perpetrated against him by the Senate oligarchs. They had seduced Pompey, played on his pride, and turned him against Caesar. They had used armed force to abrogate the power of the people's tribunes. They had passed a harsh *ultimum* that normally was reserved for suppressing mutiny or violence—of which there had been neither. They had ordered Caesar to disband his army while Pompey continued to levy troops. Despite Caesar's overtures, Pompey would make no promise to treat with him. Caesar reiterated his offer: "We shall both disband our armies; there shall be complete demobilization in Italy; the regime of terror shall cease; there shall be free elections and the Senate and the Roman people shall be in full control of the government. . . . By submitting our differences to mutual discussion, we shall settle them all."[29]

These proposals won the approval of his troops but were again summarily rejected by Pompey and the optimates. "Pompey," wrote Cicero approvingly, "is quite contemptuous of anything [Caesar] can do and confident in his own and the Republic's forces." For Cicero, a negotiated settlement with Caesar offered nothing more than "the dangers of a false peace."[30]

The choices Caesar now faced were attended with great danger. If he reentered Italy with his legionaries, he would spark a civil war the outcome of which loomed most uncertain. But were he to return without them, he would be powerless to pursue further reforms and risked being done in by the optimates' assassins. At the very least, he would be prosecuted for vote buying or treason or for having disregarded auspices and vetoes during his first consulship. The trial would be before a carefully selected jury, in a courtroom ringed by Pompey's soldiers, with a predictable outcome.[31]

Assured of the backing of his troops Caesar struck camp and prepared to march south. On 10 January 49 B.C., with only 300 cavalry and 5,000 infantry (the rest of his army was beyond the Alps), he crossed the Rubicon, a small river that separated Cisalpine Gaul from ancient Italy.[32] (To this day, as readers might recognize, "to cross the Rubicon" means to take an irrevocable step regarding an imposing issue.) By moving troops onto Italian soil without permission of the Senate, Caesar was committing an act of treason. Civil war between Pompey and him was now inevitable.

As Caesar made his way down the Italian peninsula, the local population began to swing over to his side. Writing a century after the events, Lucan, a sympathizer of the senatorial party, describes Caesar as "frantic for war . . . he would rather burst a city gate than find it open to admit him; he would rather ravage the land with fire and sword than overrun it without protest from the farmer."[33] This was hardly so. Caesar always preferred to make allies of former enemies. In January 49 he eagerly welcomed the allegiance of Italian towns and garrisons as they threw open their gates to him. He vowed to rule without the cruelty and repression that had marked Sulla's reign, declaring, "Let this be the new style of conquest, to make mercy and generosity our shield." He again called upon Pompey "to prefer my friendship to that of those

who have always been his and my bitter enemies, by whose mach-
inations the country has been brought to its present impasse."[34]
In mid-March 49, almost three months after he had entered
Italy—as Balbus reports to Cicero—Caesar was still eager to restore good relations with Pompey.[35]

Cicero himself would have none of it. He continued to wail
about Caesar's fiendish campaign "to plan debt cancellations, recall
[anti-Sullan] exiles, and a hundred other villainies. . . . I expect
nothing but atrocities from him."[36] The flowery hypocrisy that
Cicero long displayed toward Caesar came to full bloom by March
49. In a letter to Caesar he professed friendship and offered to
mediate the dispute with Pompey, and the very next day he wrote
to his friend Atticus of his distress regarding Caesar's impending
victory. Some time later, he bragged of his cunning, telling Atticus that a missive he sent to Caesar contained no other material
"except flattery," with not a word about what "I really believe."[37]

Most of the Italian countryside hailed Caesar. So too did the
Roman proletariat, in a far cry from the furiously hostile reception
they had accorded the troops of the reactionary Sulla decades earlier. Within weeks Caesar took Rome while Pompey and his forces
retreated to Greece where they anticipated greater support. With
both consuls and most of the Senate having fled, the people's
Tribal Assembly judged that the Republic needed a legally constituted authority. It passed a law giving the praetor, Lepidus, the
right to nominate a temporary dictator in place of the absent
consuls. As was expected by the people, Lepidus appointed Caesar.
Dio says that Caesar committed no act of terror while dictator.
Instead he recalled the descendants of Sulla's proscription, allow-

ing them to return to Rome with all their rights restored after over thirty years of exile. He also granted Roman citizenship to the Gauls who lived south of the Alps just beyond the Po.[38]

The rest is ancient history. Caesar resigns his dictatorship but now rules as consul. There follows more than four years of intermittent civil war, resulting in the defeat of Pompey's forces at Pharsalus (northern Greece) in 48. With Caesar in hot pursuit, a vanquished Pompey flees to Egypt. Ministers of young King Ptolemy, wanting neither Pompey as a master nor Caesar as an enemy, kill him. Caesar arrives in Egypt. When presented with Pompey's head, he turns away with sorrow and loathing. Upon receiving Pompey's seal ring, he bursts into tears. Then he puts two of Pompey's assassins to death.[39] Caesar occupies Alexandria with a small force and is besieged by the king's troops. Bolstered by reinforcements that arrive in March 47, the Romans prove victorious. Caesar installs Cleopatra and her younger brother as co-regents of Egypt, finding time to pursue a love affair with her that includes an extended cruise up the Nile. From 48 to 44, Caesar rules Rome, sometimes from afar, in a series of consulships that allows him to initiate wide-ranging reforms (discussed in Chapter Eight). After the defeat of Pompey's sons in Spain in March 45, peace is finally restored. Sometime in September or October 45, now at the height of his power, a triumphant Caesar returns to Rome where he is showered with extravagant honors including the title of *imperator perpetuus*. He has scarcely six months to live.

7

"You All Did Love Him Once"

You all did love him once, not without cause.
—*JULIUS CAESAR* ACT III, SCENE 2

Gaius Julius Caesar was a man of outstanding qualities, a commanding figure, uncommonly intelligent, attractive, and utterly charming when he cared to be. His associate Sallust testifies that he was esteemed "for the many kind services he rendered and for his lavish generosity."[1] An inspiring military leader, he was famously liked by his troops whom he led with a mixture of eloquent exhortation, bold example, iron discipline, and the rewards of plunder. Unlike most members of his class, he disdained luxury and excessive self-indulgence, though he was something of a dandy in his dress. Also unlike many members of his class, he usually refrained from excessive alcohol consumption. Even his enemies admitted that he was a temperate imbiber. As one of them remarked, "Caesar was the only sober man who ever tried to wreck the constitution."[2]

Caesar had no need to convince himself that he possessed exceptional qualities, but he strove to make it difficult for others to deny or devalue his abilities. His military exploits demonstrated his mastery over men and situations and promoted his own *dignitas* (reputation, authority, distinction), adding to his popular support and his ability to effect much needed reforms.

Highly regarded for the elegance and clarity of his writing, Caesar was thought to be one of Rome's greatest prose stylists.[3] His intellectual interests were impressively polymathic. He was a patron of arts and learning and had an expert interest in astronomy. Considered a superlative public speaker, he could stir crowds and touch hearts with his words. Even a renowned orator and bitter political rival like Cicero was obliged to admit that he knew of no one more eloquent, witty, lucid, and endowed with a more varied yet precise oratorical vocabulary than Gaius Caesar.[4]

Caesar also possessed some less than perfect traits, to say the least. He was known for his extravagant expenditures of borrowed money through much of his early career. Great sums passed through his hands, enabling him to buy elections, gather political influence, and raise armies. Suetonius observes that he was not particularly honest in his auriferous pursuits, pillaging shrines and temples, and sacking towns—especially ones with rich inhabitants. He stole 3,000 pounds of gold from the Capitol itself, replacing it with gilded bronze. And he extorted nearly 1.5 million gold pieces from King Ptolemy of Egypt.[5]

Far worse than that, like other military commanders of his day including many of the optimates, he was a despoiler of distant lands. It has been argued that his conquest of Gaul was a blessing in disguise. Deeply divided among themselves, the Gauls could not have withstood the impending onslaught of the Germanic tribes. In their subjugation to Rome they found peace and stability. Indeed, Gallic units did join Caesar's legions to fight against Ariovistus and other German invaders. But the "blessing" of Roman conquest offered no deliverance for the tens of thousands who were killed, bereaved, uprooted, enslaved, or otherwise made destitute during years of sanguinary contest.[6] Caesar himself owns to the worst atrocity his troops committed, in the siege of Avaricum when they slaughtered almost 40,000 inhabitants, "sparing neither those infirm with age nor women nor children."[7]

And how do we apologize for his treatment of Vercingetorix, a Gallic leader whose major crime was to wage a valiant campaign against Roman military domination in 52, in a last-ditch attempt to preserve the independence of his people.[8] When finally defeated, Vercingetorix was imprisoned by Caesar. He spent six years in chains only to be taken from his cell, marched through the streets during a triumphal procession honoring Caesar, and publicly executed.

As in every empire, the common people of the imperial nation itself also paid a price. From the dark soil of Spain to the hot sands of Egypt, the bones of Roman soldiers littered the empire. And of those who survived, what would be sufficient payment for their lost youth? Lucan has Caesar's weary legionaries complaining to him: "What limit of warfare do you seek? What will satisfy you if Rome is not enough? . . . We have lost the enjoyment of life, we have spent all our days in fighting."[9]

Caesar's sins also included those he shared with his era and his class. He was a slaveholder like all other leading Romans. And like many of them, he used slaves and women for his personal pleasure. Like other Roman leaders, he treated women as negotiable marital objects. He gave his daughter Julia in marriage to Pompey as a step toward cementing their early political alliance, even though Julia was betrothed to Caepio. To appease Caepio's wrath, Pompey promised him his own daughter although she in turn was already engaged to the late Sulla's son.

When Julia died in childbirth in 54 B.C., leaving Pompey a widower, Caesar sought to reverse the growing estrangement between them by offering Pompey his great-niece Octavia, unmindful that she already had a husband whom she would have to abandon. Caesar further asked leave to marry Pompey's daughter who was betrothed to Faustus Sulla. That Pompey declined both these proposals was likewise due to considerations more political than personal.[10]

Caesar was notorious for his sexual exploits involving, among others, the wives of numerous aristocrats and several queens, including Cleopatra. The poet Catullus, who despised Caesar's politics, inveighed against his escapades in the boudoir: "And shall that wretch with haughty gait / Exulting in his lofty state / Around our marriage couches move . . . ?" Caesar and his friend Mamurra, who was his chief of engineers in Gaul, were "Peers in adultery and greed / Rival mates among the nymphets . . . the shameless sods."[11]

Upon returning from a victorious campaign, Roman commanders were usually awarded a *triumphus* or "triumph." This consisted of an elaborate procession followed by feasts, entertainment, and the awarding of honorary privileges to the commander. Immediately after a triumph, it was customary for soldiers to gather before their general and subject him to scurrile jests. Such thrusts were intended to take him down a peg, thereby averting the jealousy of the gods. As Martial writes, after a triumph "no shame is it to a commander to be the subject of wit."[12] So during the celebrations of 46 B.C., Caesar's troops assembled before him and sang a ribald verse suggesting that he bedded women from across the social spectrum: "Home we bring our bald whoremonger / Romans lock your wives away / All the bags of gold you lent him / Went his Gallic tarts to pay."[13] These and a number of other jibes Caesar endured in good spirit.

In his younger days, Caesar served briefly as King Nicomedes's catamite. At his triumph, his troops sang a ribald verse about that too; it went in part: "Caesar conquered the Gauls, and Nicomedes conquered Caesar." He received this particular recitation with something less than good humor. And when he tried to deny it, he incurred the additional penalty of laughter.[14] Caesar's early dalliance in Nicomedes's court and several other homosexual encounters later in life left him open to taunts from political enemies including Cicero and Dolabella. Wishing to advertise Caesar's reputation for both adultery and sodomy, one opponent described him as "every woman's man and every man's woman."[15]

Contrary to the impression we might have, the Romans of the Late Republic were an odd mixture of profligacy and prudery. Many seemed to have indulged in same-sex liaisons. Caesar, Catiline, Mark Antony, Gabinius, Sallust, and Augustus are only a few of the better known. Still, homosexuality was not considered an acceptable practice. A century before Caesar, Polybius reported that any soldier in the Roman army "who in full manhood committed homosexual offenses" risked being flogged to death.[16] The *lex Scantinia*, a law of uncertain date, penalized homosexual acts committed with persons of free birth. To sodomize a fellow citizen was to rob him of his Roman manhood. Same-sex exploitation of slaves however carried no penalty. Since a male slave was not thought to possess a manhood, he could not be deprived of it.

A common form of political invective was to charge an opponent with effeminacy. Playing the passive role in a homosexual liaison, with either anal or oral submission, was considered the worst of perversions.[17] Cicero fixed upon this mode of attack in his vendetta against Catiline in 63. He spoke of "Catiline's praetorian guard of pansies," and charged that Catiline regularly seduced young men "in the most repulsive fashion; and he disgustingly allowed others to make love to himself." Cicero even saw homosexuality as a training ground for crime, exclaiming before the Senate, "[Catiline's] insidious seductions, that trapped one young man after another, have left them well equipped for a career of dreadful crime, or thoroughly stimulated to pursue a life of unrestrained sensuality." "These soft and pretty boys are experts at making love and having love made to them, and they know how to dance and sing; but they have also learned to wave daggers about and sprinkle poisons."[18]

The animus between the optimates and their prime adversary, Julius Caesar, could breathe a crude homophobia into their deliberations. As Suetonius tells it, a victorious Caesar once twitted a packed Senate House by announcing that he would triumphantly mount the heads of his opponents, an expression that carried a double meaning, the latter implying fellatio. When someone called out that such a feat would not be easy for a *woman*, Caesar attempted to parry the affront by observing that Semiramis had reigned as queen in Syria and the Amazons once held sway over much of Asia.[19]

Virulent homophobia retained a currency well into the imperial era, even while some emperors undisguisedly indulged in same-sex relations. Writing early in the second century A.D., no less a man of letters than Juvenal fulminates against the decadence of many upper-class males, the effeminate perfumed lads who painted their eyebrows, donned earrings and see-through dresses, flounced about with hand on hip, and married other men. These fluttering queens, he grouses, acted like no real queen such as "Semiramis bearing the quiver" or Cleopatra "on the deck of her Actian warship."[20] In Juvenal's mind, their effeminacy stood in pathetic contrast to the upright Roman warriors of an earlier epoch, the purveyors of an untainted *virtus*, whose feats of manly courage and sacrifice gave Rome its supposed grandeur.

*   *   *

Fuller's summation is doubtless the shared opinion among the many historians who reside in Cicero's camp: Caesar "was a supreme opportunist . . . Possessed of a magnetic personality and boundless egotism he lacked both fear and scruple . . . a man who would allow nothing to stand in his way."[21] In fact, Caesar's purpose seems to have been not to destroy republican liberty but to mobilize sufficient popular power to break the stranglehold of the senatorial aristocracy, reducing it to an advisory and administrative body.[22] He himself claimed his intent to be the people's champion rather than their master. To be sure, facile democratic professions have dripped from the lips of many an artful autocrat. Still, his words ought to be given some consideration, for they were often backed by actions.

In 49, after crossing the Rubicon, he proclaimed: "I merely want to protect myself against the slanders of my enemies, to restore to their rightful position the tribunes of the people who have been expelled because of their involvement in my cause and to reclaim for myself and for the Roman people independence from the domination of a small clique." Arriving in Rome some weeks later, he summoned together those senators who had not departed with Pompey, and said: "I was insulted and outraged by the interference with the rights of the tribunes. . . . My aim is to outdo others in justice and equity, as I have previously striven to outdo them in achievement."[23]

Some of the democrats sought a far-reaching social revolution with a cancellation of all debts and a division of wealth among poor Roman citizens (excluding slaves and foreigners). Caesar found their support useful, but he took care not to tread too hard upon moneylenders and big landowners.[24] Still, as we shall see in the next chapter, his policies were redistributive enough to cause consternation among the upper class. He "went far beyond his predecessors in providing for the masses," writes Yavetz, and this was "precisely what antagonized the senatorial aristocracy."[25] It was not Caesar's personal ambition that incurred the ire of the optimates. In their world, ambition was of common currency and perfectly acceptable. They loathed his *egalitarian* sympathies, his long-standing concern for the interests of the people.

To be sure, the conflict between *nobiles* and *proletarii* was not so neatly placed. There were some senators, not part of the optimate inner circle, who supported Caesar, and there were plebs, freedmen, and foreigners who, because of clientele enlistments and payoffs, ran with their aristocratic patrons. Still, if not perfectly then roughly, class lines were drawn in the fight between Caesar and the Senate oligarchs.

To this day, defenders of class privilege resort to ad hominem attacks, maligning any leader who pursues policies on behalf of the common people as a self-promoting demagogue, a panderer intent upon usurping power. To be sure, no popular leader can afford to be indifferent to considerations of popular power. Mass support is needed as a countervailing leverage to challenge entrenched ruling-class interests. In other words, the pursuit of power and the pursuit of egalitarian reform are not mutually exclusive but mutually imperative.

While leaders doubtless derive personal gratification from their

acquired renown, it would be a mistake to think they are motivated *only* by the pursuit of popularity and power, especially those
who align themselves with the powerless and the downtrodden.
As we have seen, in the Late Republic siding with the masses was
a perilous undertaking, not a promising career choice for ambitious leaders. Few *populares* enjoyed being snubbed and branded
as seditious agitators by their peers. None enjoyed being threatened with bodily harm. None anticipated that by courting the
support of unorganized masses they would win a smooth ride to
the pinnacle of power. Those like the Gracchi, Clodius, Caesar,
and others who ventured forth as champions of egalitarian causes
paid the supreme price for doing so, and were propelled by something more than—or in addition to—self-aggrandizement.

And what of the demagoguery of the optimates? Seldom do
scholars of the Late Republic raise any question about self-
interested duplicity and aggrandizement in regard to those privileged and powerful elites who advanced their interests by any
means necessary. Too many historians seem to share Cicero's glow-
ingly lyrical depiction of his elitist colleagues as men who ruled
for everyone's benefit, presiding over the helm of state "with all
their skill and devotion."[26]

Little is said about the misleading demagogic appeals made by
Cicero and his cohorts, pretending to be protectors of the people
while in fact operating as their expropriators. The optimates come
down to us through the filter of gentlemen's history as men of
the highest principles. Actually, they stuck only to those principles that fit their notion of the good life as they experienced it.
They opposed land reform, rent control, and debt cancellation.

More for the many meant less for the few. They opposed the secret ballot and all forms of popular input. Yet they were demagogic enough when running for public office to represent themselves as friends of the people.

A leading protagonist of the optimate faction was Marcus Porcius Cato (the younger), hailed throughout the ages as an unblemished keeper of republican rectitude. Plutarch lauds him for being devoted to the "rigid justice that will not bend a clemency or favor." Dio says that Cato was the only one of his generation who "partook of politics from pure motives without any individual desire of gain." Valerius refers to his "brave and unblemished life . . . his virtue complete on all counts." Valleius says that Cato "in every particular of his conduct, seemed more like the gods than mankind." And Sallust describes Cato as propelled only by righteous honesty.[27]

Modern historians are almost as effusive, extolling Cato as "the formidable high-principled conservative," "the redoubtable leader of the oligarchy," and of "high birth and character."[28] Even Theodore Mommsen, who once slipped and called Cato "a dogmatic fool," cannot on other occasions find enough good words for him: "honorable and steadfast," "earnest in purpose and in action," "full of attachment to his country and its hereditary constitution."[29]

Little attention has been accorded Cato's imperfections. Thus while he pronounced mightily against corruption and swore to prosecute bribery, he indulged in it himself, contributing to a slush fund on behalf of the conservative Bibulus (his son-in-law) when he stood for the consulship in 60, in what amounted to a spree of vote buying that elicited indignant comment even in that jaded era. The optimates were intent upon stopping Caesar, who was also spreading largesse among the voters. But when *Cato* indulged in vote buying it was no longer a matter of corruption but of high moral necessity, for "bribery under such circumstances was for the good of the commonwealth."[30]

In 51, Cicero was appointed governor of Cilicia (southeastern Turkey). He performed his duties competently and honestly, pocketing only the money that was regularly allotted to him, rather than plundering the province for all it was worth, as was frequently the practice. He also successfully engaged in military actions against brigands in the province. Upon his return in 50, he was awarded for his service with a public thanksgiving by the Senate. Cato voted against the thanksgiving. When asked by Cicero why he had done so, Cato explained not too clearly that, in effect, Cicero's provincial administration had been worthy of praise but not of a public thanksgiving, unless the thanksgiving be credited to the gods rather than to him. Immediately afterward, however, Cato voted for a thanksgiving for his son-in-law Bibulus, whose accomplishments were certainly no more notable than Cicero's. It seems the rigorously upright Cato could bend his standards for favored family members.[31]

Cato once urged that every candidate for tribune be required to deposit a huge sum of money in order to stand for office, a move that would have undermined the democratic mandate of the tribunate by turning it into a rich man's preserve.[32] In 52 B.C., he and Bibulus recommended that the Senate appoint Pompey to rule as sole consul, in default of elections and in violation of all constitutional practice.[33] Again in 49, even as other members of the hierarchy remained uneasy about the move, Cato urged the Senate to put the entire state command in Pompey's hands in order to suppress the people's movement mobilizing around Caesar.[34] A few years later, with the clouds of civil war gathering, one senator suggested that freedom should be granted to slaves in order that they might be used for military duty, a proposal that won support among the senators. But fixed in his property-loving principles, Cato argued that it was neither lawful nor right to deprive masters of their possessions.[35]

On at least two occasions he defended political murder. As described in Chapter Five, with a "vehemence of speech" (Plutarch's words) Cato swayed the Senate to uphold, on the basis of dubious testimony, the unlawful execution without trial of Lentulus and other political prisoners implicated in the "Catiline conspiracy" of 63. Eleven years later, when the optimates' gang leader Milo murdered the people's tribune Clodius, Cato again cast aside legal principles, urging that the murderer not only be freed but rewarded for services rendered to the state. Cato appeared in court for Milo and most probably voted for his acquittal.[36]

In a word, when popular leaders pursued policies on behalf of the people, Cato treated the obstacle-ridden procedures of the unwritten constitution as chiseled in stone. But when the optimates needed to bend or even suspend rules and basic rights—as their class interests might dictate—Cato was capable of infinite flexibility, treating the constitution as not only elastic but expendable. The law could be suspended to save the law, even if it meant setting free a murderer like Milo. As Cato saw it, Milo was not a murderer at all but a defender of the Republic. For Cato, anything done to safeguard the fixed concerns of his entitled coterie was ipso facto constitutional, for the interests of the aristocracy were seen by him as confluent with the well-being of the entire polity.

According to one of his modern-day admirers, Cato "never confused the personal and the political realms, and remained without animus . . . towards the person of Julius Caesar."[37] In fact, he hated Caesar, seeing him as representing everything he loathed: self-aggrandizement, contempt for the Republic, and betrayal of his class.[38] As we have seen, during a senatorial debate in 63, Cato delivered a snarling personal attack upon Caesar, addressing him without warrant as "you drunkard." Although he voiced disapproval of alcoholic overindulgence in others, Cato himself was known to tarry frequently in his cups until deeply inebriated.[39]

Dio claims that Cato "was a lover of the people as no other" but his love did not extend to seeing them decently situated. Ergo, he led the attack against Caesar's land reform.[40] Yet even the uncompromisingly conservative Cato could compromise when popular forces marshaled enough strength to force an issue. Thus, in 63, as proletarian restiveness seemed to be assuming menacing proportions, he became duly alarmed and persuaded the Senate to placate the urban multitude by including them in the grain distribution. Plutarch calls this an "act of humanity and kindness," though it appears more an act of grudging expediency designed to "successfully dissipate the threatening danger," as Plutarch himself writes.[41]

Cato was said to have been of impeccable character in his per-

sonal affairs. But even here one might raise an eyebrow. Aristocratic women were traded like so many game pieces in marriages
intended to advance family fortunes or political alliances. Cato was
no exception to the practice. First, he gave up his own wife, Marcia, to his very rich elderly friend Hortensius to marry. Hortensius
was seeking a community of children with Cato, so he said, and
Marcia was still young enough to bear offspring. Indeed, she was
said to be pregnant with Cato's child when she was passed off to
Hortensius. Some years later, when Hortensius died leaving Marcia
an immensely wealthy widow, Cato rekindled his interest and re-
married her. All this was enough for Caesar to accuse him of
trafficking in marriage: "For why should Cato give up his wife if
he wanted her, or why, if he did not want her, should he take her
back again? Unless it was true that the woman was first set as a
bait for Hortensius, and lent by Cato when she was young that
he might take her back when she was rich."[42]

Cato was devoted to the public, but "the public that counted
was Cato's own class, the hereditary nobility," Lilly Ross Taylor
reminds us. "Cato's cure for the ills of his day was apparently
much like Cicero's in the *Republic* and the *Laws*, a return to pre-
Gracchian days."[43] Today, the Cato Institute, a conservative think
tank, is named after the illustrious reactionary because he resisted
Caesar's rule and supposedly championed liberty. Needless to say,
the narrow class nature of that liberty remains unacknowledged
by Cato's admirers.

*   *   *

So too is Marcus Brutus hailed as acting only from upright motives. Brutus could not hide his distaste for Caesar's reforms, showing little sympathy for destitute petitioners and much concern for the brimming purses of the rich, especially his own. He was a leading conspirator in the assassination of a great popular leader, who had pardoned him and treated him well.

Shakespeare dubs Brutus "the noblest Roman of them all," and has him saying "I can raise no money by vile means / By heaven I had rather coin my heart / And drop my blood for drachmas, than to wring / From the hands of peasants their vile trash."[44] The reality is something else. Brutus was a usurer of the worst sort and a spoliator to boot. Having lent money at 48 percent interest (instead of the usual 12 percent, which was usurious enough), the noble Brutus then demanded that the Roman military help his agents collect the debt from the hapless Cypriot town of Salamis, in 50 B.C. At Brutus's insistence, the town council was besieged until five of the elders starved to death. Even Cicero was horrified by the terms of a loan that brought ruination to the Cypriot community. He was also put off by Brutus's arrogant and uncivil tone when dealing with the matter.[45]

Brutus once wrote to the people of Pergamum that if they gave money to Dolabella willingly, they must confess that they had wronged Brutus. But if they gave unwillingly, they can prove it by giving willingly to Brutus. On another occasion he wrote threateningly to the Samians because their contributions were "nonexistent."[46] Still, most classical historians have not an unkind word for Brutus, preferring to treat this money-grubbing assassin as a principled and unblemished defender of the Republic.

So there remains a double standard. Leaders who take up the popular standard are faulted as the power-hungry authors of their own unhappy fates, while their assassins are depicted as the disinterested stalwarts of republican virtue. As best we can tell, the Roman people themselves did not see it that way.

8

The Popularis

The evil that men do lives after them;
The good is oft interred with their bones.
—*JULIUS CAESAR* ACT III, SCENE 2

A s a *popularis*, Julius Caesar introduced "laws to better the condition of the poor," as Appian wrote.[1] During his last consulships, 46–44 B.C., he founded new settlements for veterans of his army and for 80,000 of Rome's plebs, distributing some of the best lands around Capua and elsewhere to 20,000 poor families that had three or more children. Plutarch writes that Caesar's reform law "provided that almost the whole of Campania be divided among the poor and needy."[2]

Caesar organized public entertainment and feasts, drafted a series of schemes to prevent the Tiber from flooding the city, and imposed new regulations for traffic flow and road maintenance.[3] He planned to drain marshes, using the newly gained land to employ many thousands in tillage.[4] He sent unemployed proletarians to repair ancient cities in the colonies or slated them for jobs on public works closer to home. He mandated that large landholders were to have no less than one-third of their laborers as freemen instead of slaves, a rule that would diminish unemployment, brigandage, and the landowners' inordinately high profits. He remitted a whole year of rent for low to moderate dwellings, affording much needed relief to poor tenants. And he deposited the wealth of vanquished foes in the state treasury to be distributed as gifts and benefits among the Roman citizenry, with each soldier receiving 5,000 denarii and every pleb 100 denarii.[5]

Under traditional Roman law, wealthy individuals who murdered a fellow citizen could be sentenced only to exile. Caesar added the punishment of seizure of property, for the opulent class a fate almost more frightening than death itself.[6] Following Gaius Gracchus and other *populares*, Caesar increased duties on luxury imports to encourage Italian domestic production and to make the rich pay something into the public treasury for their lavish lifestyle. He introduced sumptuary laws that placed strict limitations on ostentatious attire, funeral costs, and banquets. He attempted to impose honest administration in the provinces, where subject peoples had long endured the pitiless exactions of rapacious governors. He ejected from the Senate many of those associated with provincial despoliation. He put a cap on tributes in the more heavily taxed communities, and abolished the tithe in Asia and Sicily, substituting a land tax of a fixed amount, thus eliminating the much hated self-enriching tax assessors.[7]

Caesar reduced the numbers on the grain dole from 320,000

(almost the entire free male population) to 150,000, ridding the swollen lists of fraudulent recipients, including slaveholders who deliberately would "free" their workforce then present their slaves' food bill to the state for reimbursement.[8] Caesar prohibited the hoarding of huge sums of cash, and eased the desperate straits of a large debtor class by allowing people to repay their debts at lower prewar rates. He also imposed usury limits on creditors, at the same time forbidding them from suing for any arrears of interest that exceeded the sum of the original loan. He forbade proscriptions, property confiscation, and fines on debtors. He ordered all interest already paid to be deducted from the principal owed, and canceled the interest due since the beginning of the civil war. This last measure alone, Suetonius reckons, erased one-fourth of all outstanding debt.[9] It was a measure "for which the democrats had clamored so vehemently," grumbles Mommsen.[10] "Once again a serious loss had been inflicted on creditors," Grant comments, but adds with balance, "Yet they were obliged to admit that they would never have seen the rest of the money anyway—and that Caesar was not the destroyer of private property his enemies had made him out to be."[11]

There are two theories about why people fall deeply into debt. The first says that persons burdened with high rents, extortionate taxes, and low income are often unable to earn enough or keep enough of what they earn. So they are forced to borrow on their future labor, hoping that things will take a favorable turn. But the interested parties who underpay, overcharge, and overtax them today are just as relentless tomorrow. So debtors must borrow more, with an ever larger portion of their earnings going to interest payments, leaving even less for their needs and further increasing the pressure to borrow still more. This deepening cycle of debt eventually assumes ruinous proportions, forcing debtors to sell their small holdings and sometimes even themselves or their children into servitude. Such has been the plight of destitute populations through much of history even to this day. The creditor class is more than just a dependent variable in all this. Its monopolization of capital and labor markets, its squeeze on prices and wages, its gouging of rents are the very things that create penury and debt.

The second theory claims that people incur debts because they are spendthrift ne'er-do-wells. The roles of victim and victimizer are reversed: the creditor is now seen as the victim, and the debtor as the victimizer. This model actually does explain some forms of debt. But it should not be applied to the penurious lower classes. In fact, it better describes the improvident scions of socially esteemed families, *la jeunesse dorée,* the gilded youth (and not so youthful) who live in a grand style, cultivating the magical art of borrowing forever while paying back never, as did Caesar himself during his early career. Such seemingly limitless credit is more apt to be extended to persons of venerable heritage, since their career prospects are considered good. In a letter to Caesar, Sallust inveighs against the young men beset with self-consuming indulgences who squander not only their own patrimony but that of others, forever pursuing new fortunes to repair the ruins of the old. They treat fiscal temperance as tantamount to miserliness, and parade their profligacy as a generosity of spirit.[12]

Caesar's efforts at easing the oppressive entrapment of debt were designed to help the laboring masses, not the dissolute few. He took steps to limit the ascendancy of capital. According to Roman law, a debtor who could not meet his payments became a serf to his creditor. It was Caesar who gave insolvent individuals the right to cede their estates to the creditor, whether it sufficed or not, without having to surrender their personal freedom, a maxim upon which today's bankruptcy laws are based. A person's freedom was mandated to be inborn and unalienable, not bartered away like a piece of property—at least not if one were a free Roman citizen.[13]

Caesar was the first Roman ruler to grant the city's substantial Jewish population the right to practice Judaism, a religion that flabbergasted many polytheistic pagans because of its monotheism. As Dio Cassius remarked, Jews were distinguished "especially by the fact that they do not honor any of the usual gods, but reverence mightily one particular deity." Even more puzzling, they believed their god to be invisible and inexpressible yet omnipresent, and "they worship him in the most extravagant fashion on earth," dedicating to him "the day of Saturn [Saturday], on which, among many other most peculiar actions, they undertake no serious occupation."[14]

In an era when polity and religion were inextricably intertwined, Judaism took a position apart from the Roman state. Caesar was acquainted with the Jewish community in Rome including its poor tanners, dockers, and other laborers. In 47 B.C., untroubled by Judaism's singularities, he had the Senate ratify his treaties guaranteeing extraterritorial rights to Jewish settlements throughout the empire as "friends and allies of the Roman people."[15] That he had consorted with such a marginalized element as the Jewish proletariat must have been taken by the optimates as confirmation of their worst presentiments about his loathsome leveling tendencies.

Caesar granted citizenship to all medical practitioners and professors of liberal arts to encourage them to stay in Rome. He set about to provide Rome with "the finest possible public libraries."[16] In 47 he commissioned the prolific scholar and historian Marcus Terentius Varro to draw up plans for a grand new public library modeled after the great one in Alexandria, a project that was left uncompleted after Caesar's death three years later.

An enthusiastic supporter of libraries and learning, Julius Caesar has been falsely accused of having burned the library of Alexandria during his expedition to Egypt in 48–47, a charge tirelessly reiterated by regiments of writers from Plutarch and Dio Cassius down to modern-day biographers like Gelzer and Walter.[17]

Caesar did torch the Egyptian royal fleet in the harbor, and a stock of scrolls stored on the dock may have been destroyed. But the waterfront fire was a substantial distance from the library and did not cause a general conflagration in Alexandria, which would have been the only way the solidly built stone library could have ignited. Writing over two centuries after Caesar's death, Florus says nothing about the Alexandrian library going up in flames, noting only that the fire consumed "neighboring houses and dockyards."[18] And Lucan, who would not miss an opportunity to depict Caesar in the worst light, makes no mention of the famous library, writing only that the flames burned the fleet and some "houses near the sea."[19] No contemporary accounts allude to the library. Caesar himself says nothing about the fire spreading into town. What he describes is the destruction of vessels at port and in the dockyards.[20]

Furthermore, twenty years *after* Caesar's Alexandrian campaign, the Greek geographer Strabo worked in the two buildings that composed the Alexandrian library: the Serapeum, which was the temple and library annex, and the Museum, which was the main edifice. He describes them in some detail as perfectly intact.[21] Another overlooked source is Suetonius who reports that the Museum was thriving a hundred years after Caesar and was even adding a new wing to house some of Emperor Claudius's writings.[22] And Gibbon writes that "when Augustus was in Egypt [some fifteen years after Caesar's death], he revered the majesty of Serapis," which, far from being burned, stood undamaged in all its glory.[23]

Blaming Caesar for the great library's destruction takes the blame off the real culprits. The Serapeum—containing hundreds of thousands of scrolls and codices dealing with history, natural science, and literature—was in fact brought to ruination by a throng of Christ worshipers, led by the bishop Theophilus in A.D. 391. This was at a time when the ascendant Christian church was shutting down the ancient academies and destroying libraries and books throughout the empire as part of its totalistic war against pagan culture. "The burning of books," Luciano Canfora notes, "was part of the advent and imposition of Christianity."[24] As Gibbon describes it: "[Bishop] Theophilus proceeded to demolish the temple of Serapis. . . . The valuable library of Alexandria was pillaged or destroyed; and, near twenty years afterwards, the appearance of the empty shelves excited the regret and indignation of every spectator whose mind was not totally darkened by religious prejudice."[25]

The Christians also purged the Museum, the main library, over the next two centuries, so that by the time it was completely destroyed by Islamic invaders in A.D. 641, it housed mostly patristic writings.[26] Once Christianity gained ascendancy as the official religion under Emperor Constantine, Rome's twenty-eight public libraries "like tombs, were closed forever," laments the noted fourth-century pagan historian Ammianus Marcellinus.[27] In pagan times, the Romans boasted libraries of up to 500,000 volumes. But under Christian hegemony, laypersons were regularly forbidden access to books, the profession of copyist disappeared, and so did most secular writings. By the sixth century, the largest monastic libraries contained collections numbering a paltry 200 to 600 books, predominantly religious in content.[28]

Livy commented that "the writing of the history of the Roman people . . . is a time-honored task that many have undertaken."[29] Yet almost all of these many Roman histories are lost to us. Of course, the ravages of time and fortune take their toll, but so little of the prolific literature of the pagan era has survived thanks in good part to the systematic campaigns waged by the Jesus proselytes against library archives, secular learning, and literacy in general. Though depicted as an oasis of learning amidst the brutish ignorance of the Dark Ages, the Christian church actually was the major purveyor of that ignorance. Christianity's crusade to eradicate heathen culture and scholarship—a story not yet fully explored by latter-day scholars—was not only directed against historiography but carried over into the suppression of astronomy, biology, mathematics, medicine, anatomy, philosophy, literature, theater, music, and art.[30] Still, this factoid about Caesar's burning of the Alexandria library dies hard, as scores of historians, in their time-honored fashion, uncritically reiterate each other's misinformation without benefit of independent investigation.[31]

Plutarch faults Caesar for promulgating legislative proposals during his first consulship in 59 B.C. that were designed "simply to please the commonality."[32] Likewise, Dio Cassius maintains that during his first consulship Caesar "wished to court the favor of the entire multitude that he might make them his own to an even greater degree."[33] Neither Plutarch nor Dio allow that Caesar might have pursued reformist policies because he was responding to popular pressure and because he believed such reforms were just and beneficial to Rome and its people.

Nor does Cicero, who voiced the fears of his privileged class by equating redistributive reform with apocalyptic revolution: "I foresee a bloodbath . . . an onslaught on private property, the return of exiles and cancellation of debts." He believed Caesar would show no mercy in "killing off the nobility" and "plundering the well-to-do."[34]

Others have coupled Caesar with Sulla, the bloodletting autocrat. Thus Shackleton Bailey writes of "the autocratic regimes of Sulla and Julius Caesar."[35] Sir Ronald Syme goes further, implying that Caesar was even more self-aggrandizing than Sulla. "He had to curb the people's rights as Sulla had done," but Sulla resigned once he finished his "reforms," for unlike Caesar he had no desire to rule supreme and alone.[36]

The Roman plebs, although far less learned than our historians, were able to distinguish between the reactionary Sulla, whom they despised, and the reformist Caesar, whom they supported. Sulla imposed a retrogressive constitution. He suppressed any attempts at popular reform, stripped the people's tribunes of their ancient democratic authority, imposed a bloody terror upon popular forces, vested supreme power in the senatorial oligarchy, and abolished the grain dole. Caesar did much the opposite. He initiated popular reforms, restored the tribunes' authority, avoided the use of terror, made alliances with popular leaders, divested the senatorial oligarchy of much of its power, and maintained the grain dole. If he was criticized by some democrats of his day, it was not for his resemblance to Sulla but for not going far enough on debt abolition and other reforms, and for expending too much time and blood on foreign conquest.

Unlike Sulla, Caesar showed remarkable clemency toward his enemies after the civil war, in some instances not only sparing their lives and property but restoring them to honors and office. He removed the ban on the families of those who had warred against him, as even Dio admits, "granting them immunity with fair and equal terms . . . to the wives of the slain he restored their dowries, and to their children granted a share in the property, thus putting mightily to shame Sulla's blood-guiltiness."[37]

In 46, at the height of his fame as a military hero and domestic leader, he was showered with lavish awards and powers by the Senate, including the consulship for five consecutive years and the right to sit among the tribunes and exercise a veto. Appian reports that as consul Caesar began regularly to bypass the Senate and deal only with the people's Tribal Assembly.[38] Some gentlemen historians see this as evidence of his tyrannical disregard for the constitution. It might just as well be seen as a democratic move away from the oligarchic senatorial system.

John Dickinson charges that Caesar's moves to disempower the Senate were unaccompanied by any resolve to transfer power to popular institutions; his intent was to maintain a personal absolutism.[39] Actually, Caesar's rulings from his first consulship in 59 to his last years as *imperator* were regularly sanctioned by decrees from the Tribal Assembly.

It is not certain what Caesar would have done had he lived. His treatment of Athens suggests that he would have been receptive to democratic rule. During the time that Rome held imperial sway over Athens, the Athenian aristocrats, colluding with the Roman oligarchs, presided as a kind of comprador class over their own people. During the civil war, they naturally supported Pompey, the optimates' man. A victorious Julius Caesar pardoned the Athenian nobles but much to their disgust he allowed the city to adopt a democratic constitution, one that departed from a century of Roman-imposed aristocratic rule.[40] The common people of the other Greek cities that were ruled by Rome refused to stand against Caesar and openly resisted their Pompeian commanders. In some cases they threw open their gates or sent deputations to Caesar, pledging their allegiance.[41]

Caesar also enfranchised the population in Cisapline Gaul. After the Ides of March, Mark Antony published Caesar's plan to grant Roman franchise to Sicily. Cicero complained that Caesar had planned to confer "citizenship not merely on individuals but on entire nations and provinces."[42]

One of Caesar's first acts upon becoming consul was to have the proceedings of the Senate and Assembly publicly posted daily, making both bodies more accountable to the citizenry.[43] During his first consulship in 59, he regularly disregarded auspices. He updated and streamlined the voter registration rolls. And he decisively terminated Cicero's political witch-hunts against popular leaders, supporting Clodius in driving Cicero into exile in 58 for what proved to be only a brief period. During his later consulships he divested the senatorial oligarchy of its unaccountable executive powers including its control over the treasury, and secured the power of the people's tribunate to initiate legislation. Whether such moves are deemed despotic or democratic depends on the perspective from which they are viewed. He accumulated individual power in order to break the oligarchic stranglehold and thereby initiate popular reforms. Without too much overreaching, we might say his reign can be called a dictatorship of the *proletarii*, an instance of ruling autocratically against plutocracy on behalf of the citizenry's substantive interests.

Fully alive to the divisions that wracked Roman society, Caesar offered a forecast that would prove prophetic: "It is more important for Rome than for myself that I should survive. I have long been sated with power and glory; but should anything happen to me, Rome will enjoy no peace. A new civil war will break out under far worse conditions than the last."[44] How did Caesar hope to avoid another civil war? With reforms well short of revolution; he would rein in the plundering excesses and worst abuses of the rich while giving something more to the toiling multitude, including a greater role in governance.

The governing posts that demanded special confidence were filled by Caesar, as far as other considerations permitted, with "his slaves, freedmen, or followers of humble birth."[45] He promoted plebeians to the patriciate and increased the size of the Senate from 600 to 900, filling its ranks with equestrians and eminent provincials from Spain and Gaul. He even made senators of centurions, soldiers, scribes, and a small number of *libertini*, the latter being sons of liberated slaves who had risen to distinction on their own merit. He seemed to be following Sallust's surprisingly egalitarian advice: "Let no one be thought more qualified, on account of his wealth, to pronounce judgments on the lives and characters of his fellow-citizens; nor let anyone be chosen praetor or consul from regard to fortune but to merit."[46]

Needless to say, these newly created senators, men of humble antecedents, were snubbed by the senatorial blue bloods and moneybags.[47] In a letter to his rich friend Atticus, Cicero—unmindful of the slights he himself endured at the hands of the optimates, or perhaps compensating for them—complains of the newcomers: "Ye gods what a following! . . . what desperate gangs."[48] Centuries later, Gibbon describes Caesar's introduction of "soldiers, strangers and half-barbarians into the Senate" as an abuse of scandalous proportions.[49] In modern times, we have the estimable Sir Ronald Syme who dismisses the new senatorial appointees as nothing more than "a ghastly and disgusting rabble."[50]

The same nobles who supposedly were so protective of republican rule showed only hostility toward republican education. The first school for the study of Latin rhetoric, opened in Rome circa 95–93 B.C. by a supporter of Marius, was closed soon after by aristocratic censors who felt the schoolmaster was assigning politically unacceptable topics. The censors opposed all efforts at cultivating the oratorical gifts of youthful commoners who might incite democratic audiences and compete in courtrooms or election campaigns with the young bloods of aristocratic families. The oligarchs were determined that nobody but their own sons, and other well-placed class collaborators, should be armed with the weaponry of rhetoric and other such educational advantages. So they set about shutting down the unwelcome innovators.[51] Popular schools of Latin oratory were not reopened until the consulships of Julius Caesar. On this issue too it was not he but his enemies who sought to shut out Rome's citizenry from republican governance.

All this said, there are aspects of Caesar's career that suggest something other than popular rule. He was made Prefect of Morals (*praefectus moribus*), and arranged that half the magistrates be nominated by himself, again bypassing the Senate.[52] He could sit on the curule chair between the consuls at all meetings and speak first on all questions. His triumphal chariot was placed on the

Capitol opposite Jupiter's. Also on display was a bronze statue of him erected on a monument of the world, with an inscription—later removed on his orders—that in effect pronounced him a demigod.[53]

The Senate appointed him *imperator* for ten years. *Imperator* has been translated too often as "dictator." It is more akin to commander-in-chief, or supreme commander. In Latin, even *dictator* carries a rather different meaning from its present-day English usage. A *dictator* was a magistrate appointed in times of crisis and given absolute authority for a maximum six-month or one-year term. The senators heaped unprecedented and extravagant honors upon Caesar more in the spirit of bandwagon trepidation than genuine admiration. There also was the suspicion that some of them were seeking to compromise him in the eyes of his followers by stirring popular uneasiness about his accumulated power and glory, stoking the Roman people's historical hatred of kings.[54]

Although he knew the difference between flattery and goodwill, Caesar did not decline the lavish honors. While ostentatiously refusing the crown and avoiding the despised title of *king*, he took on the trappings of a monarch: he wore purple regal attire, put his image on coins, and filled the calendar with commemorations of his birthday and his military victories. In early 44, the last year of his life, he intended to occupy the office of consul for life with the new title of *imperator perpetuus*, thereby giving his enemies additional cause to cast themselves as righteous tyrannicides.

It is always assumed that a leader who so promotes himself is motivated only by vainglorious impulse. It may also be—or even primarily be—a way of strengthening his public image thereby maximizing his political clout. Caesar's concern was not to lord over the common people but to outdo a powerfully entrenched aristocratic oligarchy. By elevating himself above that plutocracy, he was more likely to attain success with his reform agenda.

It seems not the case that Caesar wanted to rule in the manner of a divine monarch as did the Roman emperors who came after him. Jane Gardner remains refreshingly out of step on this point, arguing that during the period of his dictatorship at Rome, "the myth that he wanted to make himself a king, or even a Hellenistic-type king worshipped with divine honors," was first propagated by his enemies. It has since been taken up "by historians and others in later generations who have shown themselves ready to accept the gossip put about by his detractors. . . ."[55]

Mommsen concludes that Caesar was a "democratic king" whose goal was the gradual equalization of the classes. Actually, Caesar never intended to level rich and poor, but he certainly did seek to roll back some of the worst class abuses perpetrated by the wealthy. He gave the poorest plebs and deracinated farmers a chance to own land of their own, and generally he expanded the opportunities for commoners to advance.

In 49 B.C., he attempted to enforce a law that limited private holdings at 15,000 drachmas in silver or gold, thereby leaving no one in possession of immeasurably large fortunes. The people were enthusiastic about this reform, and were prepared to go further. They urged that servants be rewarded for reporting masters who sequestered treasure beyond the allotted sum. But Caesar refused to add such a clause to the law, vowing that he would never trust a slave to testify against his master.[56] Even the great *popularis* had his class-bound limits.

One of Caesar's more lasting and uncontroversial reforms was his reconstruction of the Roman calendar. The Romans counted the years from their city's legendary origin, a method of reckoning that prevailed into the Christian era for a full five centuries. Thus Julius Caesar was assassinated in A.U.C. 710 (*ab urbe condita*, meaning "from the founding of the city"). It was sometime around A.U.C. 1277–1280 (or what later became known as A.D. 523–526), during the reign of Pope John I, that the monk and scholar Dionysius Exiguus devised the B.C.–A.D. mode of distinguishing the non-Christian and Christian eras. So today we say Caesar was killed in 44 B.C.

He met his fate on 15 March, the Ides of March. The Romans had an unwieldy way of keeping track of days. They divided a month into three sections: the Kalends (or Calends) was the first day of every month; the Nones, the seventh day of some months, and the fifth or ninth of others; and the Ides, the fifteenth of some months and the thirteenth of others. Dates were cited from these three fixed points.[57]

In Caesar's day the Roman lunar calendar was lagging almost three months behind the solar year, so that holidays were falling out of season, and estimates regarding harvests and planting were of little reliability. Caesar, who himself had a strong interest in astronomy, laid the problem before the best astronomers and mathematicians of his day. Drawing upon their efforts, he devised a system of his own that was more accurate than any other. It discarded the lunar method and matched solar movement and time. Beginning in 45 B.C., the Julian calendar served for more than 1,600 years.[58]

The new calendrical system however did miscalculate the solar year by eleven minutes, gradually falling out of synchronization with the annual solstices and equinoxes. Accordingly, in A.D. 1582 Pope Gregory XIII slightly modified the formula for leap years and set the date ahead ten full days.[59] Aside from these few adjustments, the calendar we use today is essentially the Julian version, owing far more to the efforts of Caesar and his astronomers than to Gregory and his. But given Christianity's dominion over the Western world, it comes down to us as the "Gregorian calendar," with no tribute rendered unto Caesar.

9

The Assassination

Cowards die many times before their deaths;
The valiant never taste of death but once.
—*Julius Caesar* Act II, scene 2

For Brutus is an honorable man;
So are they all, all honorable men—
—*Julius Caesar* Act III, scene 2

*T*he story of Caesar's assassination comes down to us as a mixture of fact and fiction, presented here with due caution for its less probable parts.[1] The conspirators were preparing to do away with Caesar even as they paid homage to him. As Dio writes, the honors they heaped on him were "all in excess, some as an act of extreme flattery toward him, and others as sarcastic ridicule . . . because they wished to make him envied and disliked as quickly as possible, that he might the sooner perish." So they strove "to embitter even his best friends against him" by calling him "king," a name often heard in their deliberations.[2]

The conspiracy was hatched, if we are to follow Plutarch, when

Gaius Cassius broached the subject with his brother-in-law Marcus Brutus, and prevailed upon him to join in the undertaking. Cassius and Brutus had fought under Pompey, only to be pardoned by Caesar after the war.[3] A surprise participant in the plot was Decimus Brutus (only distantly related to Marcus), one of Caesar's intimate associates and most competent officers in Gaul, who in the end felt a greater loyalty to his aristocratic class than to his commander's reform agenda.[4]

A long-standing legend has it that Caesar harbored a special fondness for Marcus Brutus because he was born at the time Caesar was having a protracted love affair with his mother, Servilia, and may have been Caesar's own son. This silly tale is as old as Plutarch and Appian and as recent as Will Durant. As historical myths go, it is of unimposing magnitude. Still it is curious how it survives to this day, given that Caesar was barely fifteen years old when Brutus was born in 85 B.C. By the time Caesar first slept with Servilia, her son must have been twenty years old or more.

It is reported that Caesar was much concerned for Marcus Brutus's safety at Pharsalus, issuing orders to his commanders that on no account must he be slain in the fighting. If Brutus surrendered, he was to be taken alive. If he resisted capture, they were to let him go without violence. But Caesar did this not because of a suspected paternity but for the sake of Brutus's mother, who was said to be one of the few real loves of his life.[5]

*   *   *

The conspirators numbered about sixty, according to Suetonius. Appian identifies fifteen by name. They included "many of the leading citizens of Rome, the men most prominent for their ancestry, their prestige, and their personal qualities," as Plutarch describes them. A paramount figure, Cicero, was not asked to participate even though Cassius and Brutus knew he would be well disposed to the deed. They feared that Cicero's inborn timidity—plus the caution that advanced age had put on him and his insistence on eliminating the smallest risk to any plan—might blunt their resolve at the very moment when decisive action was imperative.[6]

One strategy they considered was to wait for the consular elections when Caesar would situate himself on the wooden bridge used by voters walking to the poll. Some of the conspirators could topple him over the rail, while their confederates lurked below with daggers drawn. Another possibility was to attack him while he was en route to one of several public ceremonies.[7] It soon became known that Caesar was planning to leave the city on 18 March for a military campaign against the Getae and the Parthians, whom Roman leaders had long considered to be "threatening" in the east. Once embarked on that venture, he would be beyond the assassins' reach. So when it was announced that he was meeting with the Senate on 15 March in a hall adjacent to the theater of Pompey, in what probably would be his last public appearance before departing, the plotters fixed upon that occasion to strike.

A Senate session would provide a perfect cover for the large group of accomplices to muster their full strength without inviting unwanted attention. Their avowed purpose was tyrannicide, historically a most righteous act in Roman eyes, as with the Greeks. Their effort therefore would be greeted not as treason but as a highly principled feat performed on behalf of the common interest, or so they presumed.[8]

Few ancient or modern historians take note of the actual politico-economic interests underlying the assassination. So it is a pleasant surprise to come upon the following comment in such an unlikely place as Major General Fuller's biography of Caesar:

> The plotters were well aware that under Caesar's autocracy their opportunities for financial gain and political power would vanish, and the prestige of the Senate would be obliterated by further dilutions. In short, the way of life the senators had been following since the Second Punic War would end. Their struggle against reforms had opened with the murder of the Gracchi, and they fondly imagined that it could be closed by the murder of Caesar. Blinded by their arrogance and corrupted by their avarice, they overlooked the causes of the struggle, and persuaded themselves that were Caesar removed, the republican machinery would at once begin to function.[9]

Having agreed on a time and place for the deed, the conspirators still were divided over what specific course to pursue. Some also wanted to do away with Mark Antony, Caesar's coconsul, and Lepidus, his loyal cavalry commander. Both held great sway with the army. Antony had ruled frequently in Caesar's name when the latter was abroad, and had considerable influence among the plebs. But Brutus thought it impolitic to kill all three. Neither Antony nor Lepidus could be accused of aspiring to kingship. And Antony—suspected of having wavered at times in his loyalty to Caesar—might subsequently prove useful to the conspirators' cause. If they concentrated on Caesar alone, they would win glory for having done away with a king and tyrant. But if they also slew his associates, they would be accused of engineering a coup, acting out of partisan enmity as vengeful proselytes of the Pompey faction. This argument carried.[10]

This also might explain why they decided to do the dirty work themselves instead of delegating it to hired thugs, as was the less risky mode of aristocratic skulduggery. Caesar was no common magistrate to be dispatched by lowlife assassins, who in any case might have trouble getting close enough to him undetected or might prove to be of dubious reliability when confronting such an awesome prey. More than a mere political assassination, the deed was to be paraded as a glorious tyrannicide, a lesson for generations to come. To remove the usurper and save the Republic, only Rome's sterling leaders could qualify for such an upstanding historic mission.

On the penultimate day of his life, during the course of conversation while dining with Lepidus and a few other intimates, Caesar posed an unsettling question: What is the best sort of death? After his companions ventured various opinions, he himself commented that a sudden unexpected end was the one he would prefer.[11] That night, the story goes, his wife Calpurnia dreamed of seeing him lying in her lap with many wounds and streaming with blood. The next morning, much distraught, she implored Caesar not to stir from the house and to postpone the Senate session.[12] His wife's remonstrance gave him pause since she ordinarily was a composed and levelheaded individual, not given to "womanish superstitions," as Plutarch puts it.

Plutarch himself was richly freighted with superstitions, presumably male gendered. He tells us that just before Caesar's death, fire issued from the hand of a soldier's servant yet left him unburned. All the doors and windows of Caesar's house suddenly flew open of their own accord as he slept. And an animal sacrificed by Caesar was found to contain no heart, "a very bad omen because no living creature can subsist without a heart," the great historian reminds us.[13]

Suetonius and Dio also record portents: a herd of Caesar's horses displays a sudden repugnance for the pasture and sheds buckets of tears; a little kingbird flies into Pompey's Hall only to be torn to pieces by a swarm of other birds; and other such "unmistakable signs forewarning Caesar of his assassination."[14]

Omens aside, the political climate was disquieting enough. At least two years before his death, Caesar had his own misgivings about conspirators afoot. In a Senate speech in 46, Cicero sought to reassure him: "As for your own deeds, Gaius Caesar, no genius could be abundant enough, no pen or tongue sufficiently eloquent and fluent, to embellish them or even to describe them." As for Caesar's suspicions about some "sinister and treacherous conspiracy," they were "unfounded," for who would possibly want to harm

him? Surely not his former opponents, the defeated Pompey supporters like Cicero himself, who had been allowed to return to
Rome and the Senate with their properties intact, and who were
now his staunchest and most appreciative friends. "I think of you
day and night," cooed the great orator, who pledged to remain
eternally vigilant against would-be perpetrators. "Since you feel
there is some hidden danger to guard against, we [senators] promise you sentinels and bodyguards. And we swear we will protect
you ourselves with our own breasts and bodies."[15]

Such cloying reassurances failed to put Caesar at ease about his
newfound friends. Shortly before the Ides of March he voiced his
suspicion that Cassius was up to no good. Plutarch has him saying,
"What do you think Cassius is aiming at? I don't like him, he
looks so gaunt." Caesar said he "entertained no fear of such fat,
luxurious men" as Mark Antony and Dolabella, "but rather the
pale lean fellows such as Cassius and Brutus." (Thus did Plutarch
inspire Shakespeare's memorable lines: "Antonius! . . . Let me have
men about me that are fat; . . . Yond Cassius has a lean and hungry
look.")[16]

Now on the fateful morning of 15 March, uneasy about Calpurnia's dream, Caesar turned to Antony who had just arrived at his
house and instructed him to go postpone the Senate session. But
Decimus Brutus, one of the few to have regular access to his residence, entered as Antony was about to leave. On hearing of Caesar's decision, Decimus strongly urged a reconsideration. The
senators have been waiting in attendance for some time, having

been called into session by Caesar. Imagine their reaction if someone arrives and dismisses them until such time as Calpurnia
should chance to have more pleasant dreams. He must not give
his opponents further pretext for taking umbrage, fueling the
charge that his rule is insultingly arbitrary. Is it like Caesar to
hide behind a woman's fears or give such weight to superstition?
Even if he were strongly inclined to think the day unfavorable, it
would be more fitting if he went to the Senate and himself announced that he was postponing the meeting to a later occasion.
Caesar was persuaded. He allowed Decimus to walk him out of
the house to where his litter-bearers waited.

As the litter moved through the gathered crowd, Artemidorus,
a Greek teacher of logic and former tutor of Marcus Brutus, having
caught wind of the conspiracy, sought to warn Caesar. Accounts
vary; some have Artemidorus running to Caesar's house after his
departure, then failing to catch up to the litter-bearers. Others
have him reaching Caesar and urgently handing him a note out-
lining the plot, but given the press of petitioners Caesar had no
chance to read it. Others say it was someone else, perhaps a servant, who gave Caesar the note. All sources seem to agree that
some vain attempt was made to alert him.[17]

Before entering the hall, it is said that Caesar confronted Spurinna, the soothsayer, who previously had warned that a calamity
would befall him no later than the Ides of March. "The Ides of
March are come," he chided Spurinna, who responded, "Yes, they
are come but they are not yet past."[18] Forgoing further divinations
and pressed forward by enemies who pretended to be his friends,
he made his way into the Senate House, "for Caesar had

to suffer Caesar's fate," as Appian phrases it.[19] No personal guard accompanied him, for his *dignitas* forbade that he should betray apprehension especially before the very Senate that was pledged to guard his life. He is quoted as saying, "There is no worse fate than to be continuously protected, for that means you are in constant fear."[20]

The conspirators stationed a backup complement of gladiators in the adjoining theater who could rush to their assistance should senators loyal to Caesar give them trouble.[21] They were especially concerned about Mark Antony, a physically powerful man not easily routed. He would likely be situated close to Caesar. So they contrived to have Gaius Trebonius, Antony's acquaintance and one of the conspirators, detain him in conversation outside the hall.[22]

Upon Caesar's entrance, everyone rose to his feet. A group of senators quickly gathered about him in an apparently friendly manner. Caesar had scarcely occupied the ceremonial chair when one of them, Tillius Cimber, petitioned that his brother be allowed to return from exile. Caesar waved him aside. This was not the time for such a matter; they could pursue it on some other occasion. Others moved close, pretending to join in the request. Then suddenly Tillius laid hold of Caesar's robe, yanking it down from his shoulder, the signal for the assault.

The first blow came from behind, delivered by a trembling Publius Casca; it missed its mark, grazing Caesar about the shoulder. He whirled about, seizing his assailant by the arm and wounding him with the stylus he used for writing. Caesar then bolted forward only to be slashed in the face by Cassius. Desperately flaying at his attackers and issuing furious cries like a trapped beast, he took another blade into his side, then swift thrusts into his thigh, his back, and his groin, until he staggered and collapsed, some say, at the base of Pompey's statue. Even then the assailants continued savaging him with their daggers, some of them accidentally cutting each other in the mêlée. Suddenly all was quiet. Caesar lay motionless, bleeding to death from twenty-three stab wounds.[23]

At this point, Marcus Brutus turned to the Senate assembly to reassure them that all was well. He would now set forth the reasons behind this act of tyrannicide. Certainly, here was an apt venue for discoursing on the more unsavory imperatives of republican restoration. But the senators were in no mood for a civics lesson. Frozen in astonishment for the brief seconds of the onslaught, they began stampeding out of the hall, tripping over each other as they fled, some fearing they might be the next victims, others just wishing to distance themselves from the murder and all its frightful implications.

Brutus and his confederates followed them out, triumphantly brandishing their bloodstained weapons. Being still hot from their exploit, they marched as a body not like perpetrators who thought of taking flight but with an air of lordly assurance, calling to the people to reclaim their liberty and inviting persons of rank to join them. Some of the latter did enter their procession, acting now as if they too were authors of the bloody design and could claim a portion of its honor.[24]

In the empty meeting hall, Caesar's body lay crumpled in lonely silence throughout much of the day. Eventually three of his slaves ventured in and carted it away. Thus did Gaius Julius Caesar meet his sorry fate in his fifty-sixth year, on the Ides of March, 44 B.C.

Forty years earlier, on that very day, a graceful, handsome sixteen-year-old youth strode amidst a joyous gathering of family and friends who prayed that the divinity might fashion a brilliant destiny for him. It was a festival celebrating the threshold of spring on the Italian peninsula, when living things are touched by the sweet stirring of nature reborn, and people lift their hearts in the hope of better times to come.[25]

In the wake of Caesar's death, alarm spread throughout the city. A crowd gathered at the Forum to listen in uneasy silence to the assassins "who had much to say against Caesar and much in favor of the democracy."[26] They had killed him, they insisted, not to take power or any untoward advantage but so that all Romans might be governed rightly. The assassins with their sympathizers, paid clientele, and armed gladiators then repaired to the Capitoline where they offered sacrifices and remained through the night. Learning of what had happened, Lepidus occupied the Forum with his soldiers that same night. At dawn he delivered a fiery speech against the bloody deed. The angrily concurring shouts of the gathered crowd could not have escaped the assassins' ears since the Capitoline—as can be seen to this day—was hardly a hundred meters beyond the Forum.

How Caesar's legions were to be neutralized is a question that seems to have escaped the conspirators. Perhaps they assumed that an army bereft of its audacious commander would be unable to concert against the nobility. And what of the *plebs urbana* and *plebs rustica* who had benefited from Caesar's reforms? Would they not riotously contest a senatorial coup? If anything, the assassins expected the commoners of Rome to hail them as saviors of the Republic. For a brief spell after the assassination, Cicero himself remained convinced that "the whole population [is] inspired by craving for liberty and disgust for their long servitude," and "the whole citizen community" appreciates "having been freed of the tyrant."[27] To Decimus Brutus he wrote, "The people of Rome look to you to fulfill all their aspirations, and pin upon you all their hope of eventually recovering their freedom."[28]

Such a view of the people was not entirely hallucinatory. There certainly were citizens who feared that Caesar had aspired to monarchy. He had made a grand show of declining the diadem. However, "It was accordingly suspected that . . . he was anxious for the title but wished to be somehow compelled to take it, and the consequent hatred against him was intense."[29] Songs and posters expressed opposition both to the foreigners whom Caesar had appointed to the Senate and to his entire reign, which in the eyes of some had come to resemble that of a king in all but name. And probably some democrats were put off by his apparently monarchical pretensions and by what they saw as the halfway nature of his reforms. "Even the commons began to disapprove of how things were going," writes Suetonius, "and no longer hid their disgust at Caesar's tyrannical rule but openly demanded champions to protect their ancient liberties."[30]

Still, we might wonder whether these historians were not wishfully overstating the antagonism that the plebs nursed for their *imperator.* We might also wonder if the opposition songs and post-ers were not fashioned by the hired clientele of Caesar's enemies, being more an instigation than a symptom of popular disaffection. In any case, if Caesar was intensely hated as a usurper, it was not by most. While the plebs overwhelmingly opposed a kingship for him, they still supported much else he had done or was trying to do, including the very policies that moved the assassins toward their deed. As even Dio allows, Caesar enjoyed a great repute not alone for bravery in war, but for uprightness in peace.[31]

Early in the game, Cassius and his confederates convinced themselves that they were going to kill an isolated tyrant, a lone incubus who infected the body politic. In fact, they moved against a leader who enjoyed enthusiastic support among a large portion of the polity. The perpetrators correctly understood that the people were averse to monarchy. From this they incorrectly concluded that the people saw Caesar as the worst of kingly tyrants. Contrary to senatorial expectations, the assassination did not bring a quick restoration of the traditional Republic nor were the assassins hailed as saviors. Instead, as Caesar himself had predicted, his untimely death let slip the dogs of war.

The day after the assassination, the senators gathered afresh in the Senate House, situated on the hill just across from the Capitoline. Speaking with unusually deep intensity, Mark Antony addressed them: "Do you think men who served in Caesar's army will stand and watch while his body is dragged in the dust, and broken, and thrown aside unburied—for these are the penalties prescribed for tyrants by the law? . . . How will the populace here in Rome act? And the people of Italy? . . . I propose that we ratify all Caesar's acts and projects, and confer no praise of any kind on the law-breakers [assassins] . . . but spare their lives, if it be your wish, simply from pity, for the sake of their families and friends . . ."[32]

This seemed the most inviting course. The senators decided to retain Caesar's reforms in the hope of placating a seething populace and restive army. They also agreed to give Caesar a state funeral instead of defiling his body. And, as Antony advised, they voted to spare the lives of the assassins whom in any case they had neither the desire nor the means to apprehend.

The assassins must have become uncomfortably aware of the grim-faced legionaries who stood about in the Forum, fingering the hilts of their swords. Some of these veteran warriors doubtless were ready to march up to the Senate House and lay waste to every toga in sight. Others among them may have felt secretly relieved, thinking they were seeing an end to military campaigns now that Caesar was gone. Too many years away from home, too many wounds and lost comrades had they endured. But whatever their feelings, all of them were concerned that they might lose the modest land allotments and cash prizes their *imperator* had promised them.

The civilian population too was demanding guarantees that Caesar's reforms not be rolled back. With cries of "avenge Caesar" issuing from the public areas just below the Senate House, Brutus grudgingly reassured the demonstrators—after first sniping dis-approvingly at the whole practice of land redistribution—that they would retain what land they had been given, "and no man shall take it from you—not Brutus, not Cassius."[33] He and his confederates sent a letter to the Forum proclaiming that they would deprive no one of their promised allotment, and would not attempt to undo Caesar's laws. They offered these concessions to assure "a state of harmony, binding themselves by the strongest oaths that they would be honest in everything."[34]

Meanwhile, "the hired part of the crowd," as Appian describes those in league with the assassins, shouted for "peace for the city" in an attempt to drown out the cries for vengeance.[35] Cicero too on the day after the assassination played the great peacemaker— or perhaps the crafty tactician—calling for calm and unity in a splendid-sounding speech before the Senate. He argued that taking revenge for Caesar's death would only lead to further conflicts. He urged everyone to remember that they were all Romans, so to cleanse themselves of bitterness and ill spirit and show generous regard for one another. He also recommended that Caesar's reforms be retained if only to maintain peace and tranquillity.[36]

Privately, Cicero vented his outrage that Caesar's reforms remained in place. "Is it not lamentable that we should be upholding the very things that made us hate Caesar?" he wrote to Atticus.[37] And he could not contain his delight about the assassination, gushing forth about how "the Ides of March increased so much my love for [Marcus Brutus]."[38] To Brutus himself he wrote, "That memorable almost god-like deed of yours is proof against all criticisms; indeed it can never be adequately praised."[39] In a missive to Cassius, he referred to the assassination as "your noble enterprise" and wished that he himself had been its promoter.[40] Appian writes that Cicero hated Decimus Brutus while he served Caesar "but loved him once he turned assassin."[41]

When Caesar's body was brought to the Forum later that day, Antony delivered a funeral oration to the crowd (upon which Shakespeare based his famous "Friends, Romans, countrymen" speech). Antony dwelled upon the exceptional qualities of the fallen leader, the brilliance of his campaigns, and the generosity and justness of his rule. Caesar had received many honors from a grateful people. He had mercifully pardoned opponents and even assigned them honors, pursuing a policy of reconciliation rather than retribution. For the gods he was appointed *pontifex maximus*, for the people of Rome he governed as consul, to his troops he was *imperator*, and to his enemies he was *dictator*. It was Caesar who enacted special laws against murder. Yet this hero and father of Rome, whom none of the enemy abroad had been able to kill, now lay dead, ambushed within his own city, struck down in the very seat of the Senate in an act of vilest perfidy.[42]

Caesar was Rome's benefactor, Antony went on. Even in his death he remembered the people. In his will he allotted 75 denarii to every Roman adult male, and bequeathed them public use of his gardens beyond the Tiber. Antony then picked up Caesar's robe and displayed its bloodstained rents, pointing out each dagger gash and the number of wounds.[43] Overcome with anguish and fury, the assembled throng placed Caesar's body on a pyre and set fire to it. "Public grief," Suetonius writes, "was intensified by the crowds of foreigners lamenting in their own fashion, especially Jews, who came flocking to the Forum for several nights in succession."[44]

Many in the crowd denounced the Senate for witnessing the assassination without attempting to stop it. Even as the pyre burned, angry bands charged off to attack the houses of the murderers.[45] Cicero claims that "slaves and beggars were sent with firebrands to attack our homes."[46] Other disturbances erupted across the city, some of which were ruthlessly suppressed by the optimates' armed cadres. Still the situation was getting out of hand.

In his private correspondence, Cicero called for a violently vengeful policy that sharply contrasted with his high-sounding public pleas for harmony and reconciliation. He complained bitterly about the Senate's failure to undo Caesar's reformist laws, and urged "extreme measures" against the Caesarian forces.[47] A year after the assassination, we find him spurring Brutus on to sterner retribution, urging a final solution to the class conflict: "I do not admit your doctrine of mercy." There should be "a salutary severity," for "if we are going to be merciful, civil wars will never cease."[48] He praised one consul for massacring proletarian rioters and destroying a monument they had erected in the Forum in Caesar's honor.[49] Only the most thorough bloodletting would put an end to popular resistance, and he was all for it. Sometime later, however, upon finding himself on the losing side of the second civil war, Cicero once again was a temperate and conciliatory man. With his usual hypocrisy and poltroonery, he commended an acquaintance who sided with the Caesarian party for being "in favor of a moderate use of victory" for this was the only sensible and decent course.[50]

The assassins soon realized that the populace was not about to embrace them as heroes. Two days after the killing, with agitation and riot at an intense level, Decimus Brutus was writing to Marcus Brutus and Cassius urging that they all "clear out of Italy and emigrate to Rhodes or somewhere." If things got better, then they could return. If worse, then they could have recourse to armed conflict, a course they dared not pursue at present for lack of sufficient forces.[51] Cicero too now thought it better to depart, admitting that the city was "in the hands of traitors," and that neither Brutus nor Cassius could live there safely.[52] The two assassins departed Rome several weeks after the Ides of March.

In the Forum, Caesar's improvised funeral pyre burned through the night, fueled by the offerings of the crowd. The plebs tore up the platforms of the judges and flung them into the fire, along with boards, benches, and any other flammable materials they could find. Women threw in their ornaments and amulets; soldiers, their decorations and laurels. As the night wore on, the moaning wind sounded its requiem, lifting the flames upward. Not many in the assembled crowd understood that so too was their 500-year Republic going up in smoke.

Some years after Caesar's demise, when Augustus reigned supreme, there arose in the northern sky a comet. The elder Pliny writes that it was like a bright star "visible from all lands" for seven days. Privately Augustus happily interpreted the comet as having appeared in honor of himself. But Pliny has the emperor saying publicly: "The common people believed that this star signified the soul of Caesar received among the spirits of the immortal gods, and on this account the emblem of a star was added to the bust of Caesar."[53]

Today in modern Rome, amidst the ruins of the Forum there stands the Temple of Julius Caesar, reputedly built upon the very site where his earthly remains had been burned. Indeed, it seems centrally situated in the Forum, just where Caesar's body would most likely have been placed. The temple is a modest one-story structure composed of the dark narrow bricks that were the common building material of the Republic's public edifices. (Rome did not become a city of marble until Augustus.) It is said that the ashes of Caesar's pyre still rest somewhere beneath the structure. To this day, every year on 15 March, numerous bouquets of flowers are left at the temple entrance by persons unknown.

10

The Liberties of Power

Our reasons are so full of good regard.
—*JULIUS CAESAR* ACT III, SCENE 1

Some historians seem to think that Caesar's assassination was the outcome of a clash of egos. Being so overshadowed by this remarkable individual, the uneasy aristocrats decided to cut him down. As Dio asserts, they acted out of "jealousy of [Caesar's] onward progress and hatred of his being esteemed above others."[1] For Suetonius, what made them despise him so bitterly was his failure to rise to greet the Senate when it approached him with an imposing list of honors.[2] While exchanges between Caesar and his opponents were often caustic, such incidents hardly explain why the optimates opted for murder.

Suetonius himself acknowledges that Caesar went out of his way to cultivate amicable relations with members of the Senate including some bitter enemies.[3] In a private letter Cicero mentions "the notable and even greater than human generosity shown to my brother and myself by Caesar."[4] As late as August or September 46 B.C., he wrote that Caesar was daily becoming more conciliatory toward his opponents.[5] Yet, of course, Cicero enthusiastically sided with the assassins, finding his class interests far more compelling than Caesar's personal magnanimity.

Caesar had sympathizers in the Senate, including some of the eclipsed patrician families. He had active supporters among the equestrians, some of whom served as officers in his army. But the optimates, that highly conservative inner circle of wealthy and powerful aristocrats, shut him out coldly. All their instincts rose against him, for they understood, as Gelzer puts it, that "unlike themselves, he did not inevitably regard the conservation of their inherited supremacy in the state as the be-all and end-all of his life."[6]

Some writers argue that Caesar was assassinated because he usurped power and reduced the Republic to a shadow. Thus Appian states that Caesar's opponents acted "out of longing for the traditional constitution."[7] Ernst Mason, echoing Cicero, assures us that Caesar, "an ambitious, dangerous man [who] would do anything for power," was killed by "Romans loyal to the Republic."[8] Michael Grant maintains that the assassins carried out their deed because they "categorically refused to accept" one-man rule.[9] In fact, the senators willingly accepted one-man rule when it ruled in their favor, often casting about for a strongman who would roll back the popular cause. As Cicero admits in a private letter, "What we want is a leader, and a man of moral weight, and a sort of controller."[10]

The optimates had opposed Caesar well before he assumed dictatorial power, even before he first ran for consul in 60 B.C. They sought to thwart him during his proconsulship by attempting to confer on him a province from which he would have gleaned no advantage whatever.[11] They resisted his efforts to forge a way to high office because they detested everything he stood for. Caesar was not just another *popularis* who rallied the commonality—which would have been bad enough—but a brilliant charismatic one like Gaius Gracchus, who pursued a broad program of redistributive reform. Worse still, like Marius, he had an army at his back, and far beyond Marius, he had devilishly keen political instincts and a deep grasp of social policy. Furthermore, he was personally incorruptible. True, like other public figures he indulged shamelessly in the corrupt practice of buying influence and votes, but he himself could not be bought off or otherwise lured into an alliance with the optimates, as could reformers manqué such as Pompey.

Caesar treated erstwhile foes with unusual leniency. In 44, shortly before the Ides of March, he selected Aulus Hirtius and C. Vibius Pansa as consuls for 43, and Munatius Plancus and Decimus Brutus for 42. The latter was also assigned to rule Cisalpine Gaul. All four repaid him with their daggers. Caesar appointed Gaius Trebonius and Tillius Cimber to be governors of Asia and Bithynia respectively. They too participated in the assassination. And he appointed the leading protagonists of the plot, Marcus Brutus and Gaius Cassius, as *praetor urbanus* and *praetor peregrinus* respectively.[12] One opponent whom Caesar never had much opportunity to woo was Cato, who breathed only enmity toward him from the start. After the defeat of Pompeian forces in 46, Cato, seeing that the optimate cause was lost—and unwilling to submit to Caesar who was expressly ready to pardon him—committed suicide. Still Caesar refused to pursue a policy of retribution against his family, keeping Cato's patrimony intact for his children.[13]

Caesar's renowned clemency stemmed from neither lack of resolve nor reckless prepossession. Rather it was a conscious tactic borne of his strategy of reconciliation. His goal was to turn political enemies into allies. His modus operandi was cooptation rather than proscription. Harsh punitive measures, he believed, only created a toxic residue of enmity and vengeance. Rather than have the wealthy oligarchs skulking about in the shadows, harboring revenge in their hearts, he would give them responsibilities and places of honor in his administration.

He thought to box them in. Once they saw that he was the only one who could bring peace and stability, they would go along rather than resist, giving a little to the people in order to keep a lot for themselves. But history offers few if any examples of powerful classes becoming willing accomplices in the diminution of their own material privileges. What seems to have escaped Caesar's understanding, we can say with the benefit of hindsight, is that his generosity was insufficient recompense for oligarchs in high dudgeon. As long as his populist policies fed the unforgiving hatred so darkly nursed by the optimates, his leniency toward them could only work against him.[14]

It is a mistreatment of history to reduce this struggle to a factional or personal feud or even a purely constitutional issue devoid of social content. The oligarchs were less Caesar's personal rivals and ungrateful beneficiaries than his bitter politico-economic enemies. His power greatly alarmed them because he used it to work against, rather than for, their interests. Like other *populares*, he attempted to deal with unemployment, poverty, unfair taxes, excessive luxury consumption, land redistribution, rent gouging, usury, debt relief, and overall aristocratic avarice. Like every aristocratic reformer from Cleisthenes centuries before him in ancient Greece to Franklin Delano Roosevelt in twentieth-century United States, Caesar was branded a traitor to his class by members of that class. He had committed the unforgivable sin of trying to redistribute, albeit in modest portions, some of the wealth that the very rich tirelessly siphon from state coffers and from the labor of the many. It was unforgivable that he should tamper with the system of upward expropriation that they embraced as their birthright.

Caesar seems not to have comprehended that in the conflict between haves and have-nots, the haves are really the have-it-alls. The Roman aristocrats lambasted the palest reforms as the worst kind of thievery, the beginning of a calamitous revolutionary leveling, necessitating extreme countermeasures. And they presented their violent retaliation not as an ugly class expediency but as an honorable act on behalf of republican liberty.

Only a handful of historians have signed on to Badian's indictment of senatorial rule in the Late Republic: "No administration in history has ever devoted itself so wholeheartedly to fleecing its subjects for the private benefit of its ruling class as Rome of the last age of the Republic."[15] Such ruling-class rapacity rarely parades in naked form. Those ensconced at the social apex utilize every advantage in money, property, education, organization, and prestige to maintain their ideological hegemony over the rest of society. They marshal a variety of arguments to justify their privileged position, arguments that are all the more sincerely embraced for being so self-serving.

But ideology is not merely a promotion of class interest. The function of ideology is precisely to cloak narrowly selfish interests, wedding them to a more lofty and capacious view of society.[16] This helps explain why the optimates' ideology carries such a familiar ring today; it contains the standard mystifying tenets of all ruling propertied classes throughout the ages. These might be summarized as follows:

First and foremost, the oligarchic clique represents its own privileged special interests as tantamount to the general interest. Cicero laid the groundwork for future generations of elite propagandists when he argued that the well-being of the Republic and the entire society depended on the well-being of the prominent few who presided so wisely and resplendently over public affairs, and whose high station gave proof of a deserving excellence.

Second, ruling-class protagonists warn that such things as doles, rent caps, and debt cancellations undermine the moral fiber of those indigents who are the beneficiaries, pandering to their profligate ways at the expense of the more responsible and stable elements of society.

Third, the ruling elites maintain that redistributive social programs deliver ruinous costs upon the entire society. There is not enough land for small farmers to be resettled, not enough funds for grain doles or public projects that would employ hard-up plebs. No notice is taken that there is always money enough for war and massive public subsidies to the wealthiest stratum.

Fourth, when unable to openly attack popular reforms that bridle their own overweening greed, the oligarchs attack the reformers and their motives. They portray mass agitation not as a righteous resistance to economic injustice but as "class war," the work of unscrupulous, unstable, self-aggrandizing, power-lusting demagogues who, in Cicero's words, "inflame the passions of the unsophisticated multitude," but really do not have the people's interests at heart.[17]

Many latter-day historians are immersed in this age-old ruling ideological perspective. So they explain away Caesar's assassination in terms that are rather favorable to the assassins. They emphasize how Cicero and the other "constitutionalists" boasted of a republic founded on law and selfless virtue. But they take little notice of how these same "constitutionalists" swindled public lands from small farmers (in violation of the law), plundered the provinces like pirates, taxed colonized peoples into penury, imposed backbreaking rents on rural and urban tenants, lacerated debtors with usurious interest rates, expanded the use of slave labor at the expense of free labor, manipulated auspices to stymie popular decisions, resisted even the most modest reforms, bought elections, undermined courts and officeholders with endless bribery, and repeatedly suspended the constitution in order to engage in criminal acts of mass murder against democratic commoners and their leaders. Such were the steadfast republicans upon whom most classical historians gaze so admiringly.

As understood by the nobility, "republican liberty" was first and foremost liberty for the aristocracy, freedom to savor every class prerogative without restraint and with only the appearance of public devotion, to enjoy all the benefits of civil society while burdened by none of the costs, and to grow still richer at the expense of everyone else. Whatever its republican trappings, aristocratic liberty is essentially blue-blood plutocracy, the ruthless liberty of wealth that remains to this day inhospitable to any modicum of economic democracy.

Those who think that politics and history "are just all about power" might wish to reflect on the Late Republic. The wealthy class did not pursue power as an end in itself. Power was and still is an instrumental value; it enables the rich to secure and advance their opportunities to profit off human labor, exercise decisive control over disadvantaged groups, monopolize public resources and private markets, expand overseas holdings, and plunder government treasuries. Power enables them to preserve their precious privileges, their fabulous way of life, and the one thing that makes such a life possible, their immense wealth.

To be sure, ambitious individuals may pursue power as an end in itself, as a way to advance their unprincipled careers and cover themselves with glory. But to see personal ambitions and jealousies as the sum total of political conflict is to rule out larger interests. Then, what is called "politics" becomes nothing more than "the jockeying for wealth and power within a class that already holds a monopoly on wealth and power."[18] In fact, even a frenetic careerist like Cicero held views that were more than merely self-promotional, reflecting the genuine concerns of the wealthy owning class of which he was a part, and of the especially privileged and empowered coterie within that class, the senatorial oligarchs, whose matchless leader he dreamed of becoming.

Throughout history, in the name of "liberty," owning classes have opposed political leaders who have sought a more equitable distribution and use of wealth. And in the name of "stability" and "public safety," they have repeatedly surrendered some of their own power to autocratic leaders dedicated to preserving the privileged socioeconomic order. So it has been in just about every class society before and since the Late Republic. Power is not usually an end in itself; it is the precious means by which wealth is accumulated, preserved, and enjoyed. The climber who seeks above all else to promote himself becomes a ready tool of wealth. That career path is far less risky and more rewarding than the one trod by those who champion the cause of the dispossessed and powerless.

The same optimates who feared Julius Caesar's dictatorial power were able to hand dictatorial power to Pompey during the public disturbances of 52 B.C. In complete violation of constitutional practice, the senators appointed Pompey "consul without a colleague," so that he could exercise a one-man, veto-proof rule. They also granted him total control over the treasury and over the corn supply of the entire empire for five years. Both these moves also violated the constitution. By turning to Pompey in this manner, the senate oligarchs revealed their readiness to jettison republican principles when necessary.[19]

Consider other examples of senatorial extra-constitutionality. Some of Caesar's antagonists in the Senate inquired into the conduct of his Gallic campaign, going so far as to urge that he be handed over to the enemy. In 58 B.C., they attempted to promote a mutiny among his officers, and treasonously conspired with Ariovistus, a German leader and battlefield antagonist in Gaul, to assassinate Caesar. In a prebattle meeting, Ariovistus boasted to Caesar that many Roman nobles would richly reward him if he put Caesar to death—so messengers sent by the Senate optimates themselves had informed him.[20] In 51, Senate leaders collaborated with the Gauls in an attempt to undo Caesar, urging them to hold out for another year.[21] Such acts of criminal treachery and treason represented drastic departures from proper constitutional practice, yet they have evoked little critical comment from historians past or present.

The senatorial oligarchs openly demonstrated their intolerance of constitutional checks when they were the ones being checked. In 49, for example, the Senate passed a decree ordering Caesar to dismiss his army and surrender Gaul to Senate-picked generals, failing which he would be deemed a traitor. Serving as a people's tribune, Mark Antony issued a perfectly lawful veto of this decree. Yet he and another tribune were then forced to flee in order to save themselves from the optimates' potentially lethal wrath.

*　　*　　*

The death of Caesar did not bring the quiet restoration of a Senate-dominated Republic, as the assassins had hoped. With a civil war brewing, the optimates and their wealthy allies displayed an unwillingness to part with even a modest portion of their enormous fortunes to pay for an army strong enough to vanquish the Caesarians. "Our knottiest political problem is shortage of money," Cicero complained. The very rich "become more obdurate every day at the mention of a special levy. The proceeds of one percent, thanks to the scandalously low returns put in by the rich folk" proved thoroughly inadequate.[22] The rich may want power but they do not like paying for it with their own money.

At about this time there emerged upon the scene the relatively unknown youth Gaius Octavius, Caesar's great-nephew and adopted son, later known as Octavianus or Octavian. He was destined to become Rome's first emperor. Octavian initially allied himself with the senatorial party against Antony. In 43 B.C., when just nineteen years old, he led an army of Caesar's veterans, whose loyalty he nurtured, defeating Antony at Mutina. The Senate granted him the rank of senator. He marched on Rome and compelled a reluctant Senate to recognize him as Caesar's son and heir and nominate him consul for the remainder of 43.[23] The next year, however, Octavian formed a compact with Antony and Lepidus in what became known as the Second Triumvirate. The three leaders pushed through a law granting them dictatorial powers for five years. In 42, the triumvirs defeated the senatorial party in the battle of Philippi, at which time Brutus and Cassius committed suicide. Antony, Lepidus, and Octavian now ruled supreme.

The triumvirs recalled that Caesar had been killed by men

whom he had forgiven and favored with office and honors. These same men then had plotted against the triumvirs themselves and, judging from "the fate of Gaius Caesar," had demonstrated "that their evil nature cannot be tamed by kindness."[24] Hence the Triumvirate opted for proscriptions, hunting down and killing Caesar's assassins and their associates. Antony had already made a point of having Cicero tracked in 43. The story goes that, while trying to escape, Cicero leaned his head out of his litter to see who was approaching and was summarily decapitated by his pursuers.[25] So was silenced the golden voice of Rome's privileged coterie.

The Triumvirate itself eventually came apart. Lepidus was demoted by his two partners for supposedly collaborating with Pompey's son and for claiming Sicily as his own. In 36 B.C. Octavian put him under house arrest at Circeii. In 31, Octavian vanquished Antony at Actium (on the western coast of Greece), and now ruled supreme, dubbing his regime the Principate, literally "rule by the first man," or what amounted to rule by a kingship.

In 27 B.C., Octavian appeared before a Senate purged of his opponents and made a great show of offering up all his powers to that stately body and to the people. Having reached the ripe old age of thirty-five, he professed a desire to retire. As if on cue, the Senate showed itself overwhelmed by his selflessness and implored him to remain at the helm. Deeply touched by their entreaties, Octavian decided to remain in office for the rest of his life. The Senate immediately conferred upon him the title of "Augustus," by which he was henceforth known. It was a name applicable to all things godly and astral. Octavian embraced the illustrious title

along with the additionally exalted appellation of "Caesar," becoming the first of a long line of absolutist Roman rulers all of
whom were called "Caesar." *Imperator*, or emperor, became a title
monopolized by Octavian and his successors. As Augustus he was
never again visited by a self-effacing desire to retire. He reigned
for forty-five years, dying in A.D. 14.

All of Rome's emperors wielded substantially more power than
Julius Caesar. Yet the senators and the rich in general went along
with them, as Tacitus notes of their ready submission to Augustus,
"advancing in wealth and place in proportion to their servility,
and drawing profit out of the new order of affairs."[26] While Caesar
had opened the Senate to talented men of humble origin, Augustus kept the Senate as a preserve for the rich, even creating new
patrician members. As the elder Pliny reports, "Senators began to
be selected and judges appointed on the score of wealth, and
wealth became the sole adornment of magistrate and military commander. . . ."[27]

Augustus raised the property qualifications for senators from
8,000 to 12,000 gold pieces, and if any preferred member found
that his estate fell short of this, the young ruler made up the
difference from the Privy Purse.[28] He banned publication of Senate
proceedings, making that body less open to public criticism, undoing one of Julius Caesar's reforms. And he purged the Senate
of those who might prove less than friendly to the Principate.

It is not hard to divine why the nobility opposed the more
conciliatory Caesar but accepted the more autocratic Augustus and

his successors, showing no nostalgia for their beloved Republic. Unlike Caesar, Augustus promoted no economic agenda on behalf of the masses. He dissolved all worker guilds except long-standing ones that were conducting "legitimate business," doubtless sharing Suetonius's opinion that many *collegia* were "in reality organizations for committing every sort of crime."[29] Augustus manifested no interest in debt reduction or land allotments (except for his army veterans), and was indifferent to the well-being of the rural population in general.[30] The two taxes he initiated, a sales tax and death duties, were regressive, leaving aristocratic wealth untouched, all of which the nobility could not fail to appreciate.

Augustus did institute various reforms relating to marriage laws, administrative practice, and religious observances.[31] These did nothing to ease the plight of the plebs or diminish precipitous class inequities. Unlike Julius Caesar who turned to the popular assemblies, Augustus bypassed the assemblies and eradicated whatever limited functions they still possessed, moves that further pleased the affluent class.

In addition, Augustus sought to protect inherited wealth and the slavocracy by decreeing that slaveholders could not free more than a limited portion of their chattel. Freedom for slaves led to intermarriage with free citizens, and Augustus was concerned that native Roman stock not be "tainted" by foreign servile blood.[32] By freeing slaves, the owner could avoid feeding, clothing, and housing them in their less productive later years. But had manumission become too common it would have weakened the established order of slavery itself and created a realm unduly dependent upon free labor. Augustus's restriction on manumission illustrates how the state puts the overall interests of the owning class ahead of the immediate pocketbook interests of particular owners.

Augustus craftily downplayed the ostentatious trappings of power while husbanding its substance. He maintained an appearance of consultation vis-à-vis the Senate, delegating many responsibilities to that body but little decision-making power. He retained full control over the provinces and made certain to preserve his command over military forces, including a large body of guards in the heart of the capital. The "subtle tyrant," as Gibbon calls him, "crafted an absolute monarchy disguised by the forms of a commonwealth."[33]

After some five centuries, the Roman Republic with its limited but real popular liberties came to an end under Augustus's rule, though certain of its forms remained for some time. For generations, the senatorial class continued to play little more than a limited advisory role in civic institutions. The senators preferred "to ignore the fact that real power had migrated out of these institutions, into an imperial regime. . . . The self-respect of the senatorial classes depended on this denial."[34]

Augustus preserved the Senate's dignity but stole its independence, leaving it with the appearance of authority. More important to the senators, he fortified their privileged class position. Indeed, under his rule they grew still wealthier, though on occasion the emperor had to curb their cupidity so that the parasites might not destroy the very social organism upon which they battened. At the same time, the Senate House remained a prestigious place in which to dawdle and debate and exercise advisory responsibilities.

The point to be remembered is that the senators seemed untroubled by this loss of power and by the loss of their sacred republican institutions and traditions. No furious cabals in the Senate or in any other wealthy circles plotted to dispatch the usurper.

The ancient liberties of the Republic, such as they were, shrank away, and Rome under the emperors devolved into a military dictatorship. During the Republic, satirists and mimes readily directed their barbs and lampoons against leading political figures. So Cicero hoped to gauge popular reaction to Caesar's assassination from the skits put on by mimes.[35] Under the empire, however, mimes and satirists had no option but to range themselves on the side of the emperor, targeting those who were in bad odor at court, or sticking to trivial topics and avoiding politically touchy ones.[36]

Public debate became increasingly superficial in content and, by way of compensation, increasingly elaborate in style. In the repressive atmosphere of the imperial period, students of rhetoric were trained to make speeches that were politically safe but steeped in florid locutions and melodramatic histrionics. Tacitus—who was old enough to remember the finer level of debate of the Late Republic—complained, "[W]hat poor quality! And how incredible they are in content! The subject matter is far removed from reality. . . ."[37] It was the victory of style over substance, as dictated by the political circumstances of the day.

The loss of popular freedom also brought the systematic suppression of workers' guilds and other people's organizations. Consider the revealing correspondence early in the second century A.D. between Trajan and the younger Pliny who was serving abroad as governor of Bithynia. Having witnessed a widespread fire that destroyed many private homes and two public buildings, Pliny requested that he be allowed to organize a fire brigade limited to only 150 members all of whom would be genuine firemen, he assured the emperor. He added that "the privileges granted shall not be abused; it will not be difficult to keep such small numbers under observation." But Trajan would have none of it: "[W]e must remember that it is organizations like these that have been responsible for the political disturbances in your province, particularly in its towns. If people assemble for a common purpose, whatever name we give them and for whatever reason, they soon turn into a political club." Trajan suggested that fire-fighting equipment be made available to individual property owners, and that help could be marshaled ad hoc from the crowds that assemble during a blaze.[38] Clearly the emperor was less concerned about fighting house fires than preventing political ones.

Early in the realm of Augustus, opposition to one-man rule died out in the Senate, and over the next 400 years no serious attempt was ever made by the senators to restore the Republic. This or that emperor might act in a manner that incensed them, but their remedy was always to attempt to supplant him with another emperor rather than risk the popular challenge to their interests that democracy and an end to dictatorship might invite. Those senators who conspired against Caligula, Nero, and Domitian were ani-

mated by self-preservation rather than by a principled dedication
to republican liberty. They attacked the person of the despot but
never the despotic authority of the office.[39]

In sum, when their class interests were at stake, the senators
had no trouble choosing political dictatorship over the most ane-
mic traces of popular rule and egalitarian economic reform. They
seldom hesitated to depart from their own constitution when expediency dictated. Through the last eighty years of the Republic,
they repeatedly invoked the *senatus consultum ultimum*, suspending
all constitutional protections by *raison d'état*. So common was their
tendency to turn to one-man absolutism—even generations before
the *senatus consultum ultimum*—that Appian voices surprise about
one occasion when they did not. Commenting on their struggle
against Gaius Gracchus in 122–121, he writes, "I am amazed that
they never even thought of appointing a dictator, although they
had often in crises of this sort found salvation in absolute power,
[a] course of action which had proved most useful to their predecessors."[40] As we have seen, instead of appointing a dictator, the
optimates preserved their republican virtue by slaughtering Gaius
and his followers.

The description Aurelius Victor gave several centuries after
Caesar is worth recalling: the nobility "gloried in idleness and at
the same time trembled for their wealth, the use and the increase
of which they accounted greater than eternal life itself."[41] When
push came to shove, their vast holdings meant more to them than
state power—as long as state power was in the hands of someone
who protected their vast holdings.

11
Bread and Circuses

The rabblement hooted and clapped their chapped hands
and threw up their sweaty night-caps
and uttered such a deal of stinking breath
because Caesar refused the crown.
—*JULIUS CAESAR* ACT I, SCENE 2

*T*he critic who sees ancient Rome as riddled with class injustice is likely to be judged by today's Ciceronians as guilty of the sin of "presentism," in other words, guilty of anachronistically imposing modern-day values on a past society. But if we uncritically immerse ourselves in the context of a past society, seeing it only as it saw itself, then we are adopting the illusions it had of itself.[1] Thus when modern classical historians label Rome's popular leaders as "ambitious demagogues" they are not making an objective historical judgment but uncritically sharing the characterizations propagated by elitist commentators such as Cicero. Likewise, when they embrace the notion that Rome ruled for the benefit of its far-flung subjects, they are uncritically accepting the self-serving illusions that any imperialistic system has of itself. In short, those who insist that we perceive the past "purely on its own terms"—assuming that were even possible—often forget that this usually means seeing it through the eyes of its predominant class, the class that practically monopolized the recorded commentary of that day. In regard to the Late Republic, this means the wealthy oligarchs.

This "rule of contextual immersion," if I may call it that, is regularly violated by its proponents when it suits their own ideological proclivities. Hence, many historians make little effort to immerse themselves in the oppressive context that incited popular unrest, little effort to see the proletariat's struggle the way the proletariat saw it themselves. In regard to Rome, seldom is it asked: What were the human needs around which the plebs struggled? What were the actual conditions of misery and exploitation they faced? Were popular disturbances simply a manifestation of irrational, lowlife troublemaking, as claimed by optimate leaders, or a response to harshly unjust conditions?

Gentlemen historians have seldom thought well of the common people of history, when they bothered to think about them at all. Cicero was part of an already established tradition when he repeatedly described the *plebs urbana* as the "city dirt and filth" (*sordes urbis et faecem*), the "scum from out of the city" (*ex urbis faeces*), the "unruly and inferior," "a starving, contemptible rabble." (He acknowledges that they are starving, but sees it as their own fault.) And whenever the people mobilized against class injustice, they became in Cicero's mind that most odious of all creatures, the "mob."[2]

Long before Cicero, Polybius was asserting that "the masses are always fickle, filled with lawless desires, unreasoning anger and violent passions."[3] A century after the Late Republic, Plutarch described Caesar as "stirring up and attaching to himself the numerous diseased and corrupted elements in the polity."[4] Asconius referred to the supporters of Clodius as "a great crowd of slaves and rabble," an "ignorant mob."[5] Later on, Appian wrote of "the poor and hotheaded," and saw Caesar as "introducing laws to win the favor of the mob."[6]

The many classicists who follow Cicero's lead are no better. Yavetz records how nineteenth-century historians bemoaned the boundless appetite of the "Roman mob." He quotes Pohlmann: "The communist idea of sharing one another's victuals for these proletarians [became] second nature."[7] Various present-day writers refer to "the mob," "the idle city rabble," the "emotional masses" who were "no more than the tool of power," "the stupid . . . selfish, good-for-nothing mob," "the parasitic mob of the metropolis," "the worthless elements."[8]

Scullard sniffs at the "fickle" and "idle urban mob," as if their idleness were purely of their own choosing. Meanwhile, the parasitic, aristocratic idlers—who lived in obscene opulence off the labor of slaves and plebs—earn not a harsh word from him or most other writers.[9] Mommsen refers to "the lazy and hungry rabble"; for him the people's assemblies were agitated by "special passions, in which intelligence was totally lost." "That terrible urban proletariat" was "utterly demoralized . . . sometimes stupid and sometimes knavish."[10] And Christian Meier, agreeing with the Roman nobles who "referred to the urban mass as the bilge of the city," denounces "Rome's laborers, traders and artisans" for trying to assume a level of political participation "that was far beyond their capacity."[11]

Disapproving renditions of the Roman *proletarii* have enjoyed such widespread currency as to have influenced even dissenting egalitarian writers such as Karl Marx. He described the dispossessed peasants of the Late Republic who crowded into Rome as "a mob of do-nothings."[12] In more recent times, radical journalist-cum-classical historian I.F. Stone characterized the Roman plebs as "a rabble," comparing them unfavorably to Athens' "citizenry."[13] And the liberal Lewis Mumford referred to Rome's "parasitic mob."[14]

Juvenal writes scornfully of "the mob of Remus" and its preoccupation with "*panem et circenses*" (bread and circuses), a phrase that has echoed down through the ages, adding to the image of Rome's proletariat as a shiftless, volatile mass addicted to endless rounds of free victuals and free entertainment.[15] Scullard announces that "the city mob was far too irresponsible to exercise political power: rather it wanted '*panem et circenses*.' "[16] And Mumford sees only parasitism in "the dual handout of bread and circuses."[17]

Historians have been ever alert to the corrupting influence that state assistance might have upon the poor. Sallust speaks of "the populace who are now demoralized by largesse and the public

distribution of corn." Forced into idleness, they become "infected
with vicious principles" and need to "be prevented from disturbing the government."[18] Appian tells us that the corn ration at-
tracted "the idly destitute and hotheaded elements of the Italian
population to the capital," who contrast unfavorably with "those
who possessed property and good sense."[19]

Many centuries after Sallust and Appian, John Dickinson demonstrated that little has changed. He vents his disapproval of Roman welfare policy, denouncing Caesar for appealing to "the
cupidity and self-interest of those who desired to be supported at
the expense of the state" and for encouraging "the voters to act
from the baser motives of human nature."[20] Dickinson never explains why the impoverished plebs—many of them up from slavery or from families dispossessed by land-grabbing aristocrats—
were manifesting "baser motives" by struggling for subsidized
bread prices, land reform, public jobs, debt easement, and rent
control. Nor does he ever reproach the nobility for *their* "baser
motives," their self-indulgent plundering of the poorer classes and
the public treasure. In a similar spirit Scullard writes that Clodius's law to change the subsidized distribution of grain into a
completely free dole "hastened the demoralization of the people."
In contrast, Sulla's abolition of grain distribution is termed a "reform," and invites no critical comment for the hardship it must
have inflicted upon the poor.[21]

Contrary to the image propagated by past and present historians, dole recipients did not live like parasites off the "bread"
they received—actually a meager wheat or corn ration used for
making bread and gruel. Man (and woman) cannot live by bread

alone, not even at the simple physiological level. The plebs needed money for rent, clothing, cooking oil, and other necessities. Most of them had to find work, low-paying and irregular as it might be. The bread dole often was a necessary supplement, the difference between survival and starvation, but it was never a total sustenance that allowed people to idle away their days.

In any case, we might question why so many scholars have judged the Roman people as venal and degraded just because they demanded affordable bread and were concerned with having enough to feed themselves and their children.[22]

Alan Cameron is one of the few writers, along with Ste. Croix, who takes issue with the historical and somewhat hysterical image of the freeloading plebs: "That notorious idle mob of layabouts sponging off the state is little more than a figment of middle-class prejudice, ancient and modern alike." As with bread, so with circuses. Cameron remarks, "It was not the people's fault that public entertainments, being in origin religious festivals, were provided free."[23] At any one time, almost half the free adult population of Rome could be accommodated in its circuses, arenas, and theaters, Lewis Mumford calculates. Even in a provincial town like Pompeii, the amphitheater held 20,000, likely more than half the adult inhabitants. Mumford seems to think that attendance at the amphitheater became the proletariat's principle occupation. Lapsing into psychobabble, he asks us to believe that the commoners sought to escape their "own self-loathing" and "desire for death" by pursuing "a violent desire to impose a humiliating death on others" in the Roman arena.[24]

There is no denying that the games and races helped the poor to forget their grievances for awhile, acting as a popular distraction, not unlike mass sporting events today. The emperors seemed to be well aware of the diversionary social control function that the spectacles served, which was why they maintained them regardless of cost.[25]

Some writers forget that it was not the poor who pandered to the baser emotions by creating and financing the awful bloodletting of the amphitheater, nor were they the only ones to attend. Perowne writes that the circuses were the major sport of rich and poor alike.[26] Probably a higher proportion of wealthy nobles and equestrians frequented the games, seated in reserved front-row stalls that afforded them the best view. In the amphitheater, Juvenal reports, "All the best seats are reserved for the classes who have the most money."[27] Indeed, in the Colosseum the front rows were reserved for magistrates, foreign dignitaries, and senators. The rows directly behind them were set aside for the upper social classes, with additional seats for priests, military officers, and other special groups. Women were segregated, consigned to the worst seats in the house at the very top. And behind them was standing room for the poverty-stricken.[28]

Emperor Augustus himself admitted to enjoying the games.[29] And Emperor Tiberius's son eagerly presided over the gladiatorial contests, displaying an "inordinate delight . . . in the slaughter, though it be of men who mattered little."[30] The rich and well-born not only promoted and patronized the arena games but occasionally participated in them. Patrician children displayed their horsemanship. Young peers vied with one another in chariot races. Some knights and the son of an erstwhile praetor voluntarily engaged in displays of combat in a grand spectacle produced by Caesar. One senator desired to contend in full armor but refrained when Caesar voiced his acute displeasure at the idea.[31]

Portrayed as nothing more than a blood-lusting rabble, the plebs actually were sometimes critical of what they witnessed at arena spectacles. The ceremonies to dedicate Pompey's theater included a battle between a score of elephants and men armed with javelins. The event did not go as intended. The slaughter of the elephants proved more than the crowd could countenance. One giant creature, brought to its knees by the missiles, crawled about, ripping shields from its attackers and tossing them into the air. Another, pierced deeply through the eye with a javelin, fell dead with a horrifying crash. The elephants shrieked bitterly as their tormentors closed in. Some of them refused to fight, treading about frantically with trunks raised toward heaven, as if lamenting to the gods. In desperation, the beleaguered beasts tried to break through the iron palisade that corralled them. When they had lost all hope of escape, they turned to the spectators as if to beg for their assistance with heartbreaking gestures of entreaty, deploring their fate with a sort of wailing. Their pitiful shrieks moved the arena crowd to tears and brought them to their feet cursing Pompey. The audience was overcome by a feeling that these great mammals had something in common with humankind.[32]

Another instance might suffice. In 46, to celebrate his Gallic

triumph and his third consulship, Caesar produced a series of spectacles. Lions were hunted down and slaughtered in the Circus. A
naval battle was staged on a hollowed tract of the Campus Martius,
flooded for the occasion. And in a grand finale, two armies respectively composed of war captives and condemned criminals—
each side consisting of hundreds of foot soldiers, cavalry, and a
score of elephants—waged a battle to the death. But the plebs
were more distressed than enthralled by the bloody spectacle. As
Dio records, they criticized Caesar for the great number who were
slain, charging that "he had not himself become satiated with
slaughter and was further exhibiting to the populace symbols of
their own miseries." In addition, an outcry was raised because
Caesar had collected most of the funds unjustly and had squan-
dered them on such a wanton display.[33]

Who actually composed the Roman proletariat, this "heartless
mob" who wept for tormented elephants and sometimes deplored
the arena's dissipation of blood and treasure? Who might be this
"idle rabble" who organized into political clubs and workers'
guilds, and engaged in Forum meetings, demonstrations, and
street insurgencies?

The "mobs" of eighteenth- and nineteenth-century England and
France are described by upper-class critics of those times as composed of beggars, convicts, and other lowlife detritus. But records
reveal that rebel crowds consisted of farm laborers, masons, and
various other kinds of craftsmen, along with shopkeepers, wine
merchants, cooks, porters, domestic servants, miners, and urban

laborers, almost all of fixed abode, some temporarily unemployed, only a handful of whom were vagrants or had criminal records.[34]

The rebels of the Paris Commune of 1871, sentenced to death or imprisonment by the reactionary courts, consisted of carpenters, tin workers, watchmakers, bookbinders, teachers, housepainters, locksmiths, tailors, tanners, stonecutters, bricklayers, cobblers, dressmakers, and numerous other occupations. Still others listed themselves as medical student, accountant, cashier, man of letters, and head of primary school. About half the craftsmen and skilled workers of Paris disappeared in the summary mass executions of 1871.[35]

The long-standing stereotype of popular mobs as fickle, brutish, rootless, and mindlessly destructive was elaborated by Gustave Le Bon in his *La Foule*, translated into English in 1869 as *The Crowd*, a book that has been kept in print and assigned to generations of students for over 130 years. "Although Le Bon wrote in the relatively tranquil late nineteenth century," remarks Leonard Richards, "he managed to sound like an aristocrat dashing off a passionate indictment of the French Revolution several hours before it became his turn to meet the guillotine."[36] Challenging Le Bon, George Rudé shows that the "mobish actions" of the eighteenth century were not wanton irrational affairs but forms of social protest against unaffordable rents, food prices, and crushing taxes. The riots often were coordinated actions, targeting particular officials, merchants, granaries, landlords, and other culpable persons and places, depending on the issue. They agitated not only for bread but for decent wages, the security of their homes, and the right to dissent and organize unions. Rudé concludes that rioters did not consist of the lawless riffraff "imagined by those historians who have taken their cue from the prejudiced accounts of contemporary observers."[37]

So with ancient Rome. While Cicero characterized the activist elements among the plebs as "exiles, slaves, madmen," runaways, criminals, and "assassins from the jail," in fact, they were masons, carpenters, shopkeepers, scribes, glaziers, butchers, blacksmiths, coppersmiths, bakers, dyers, rope makers, weavers, fullers, tanners, metalworkers, scrap dealers, teamsters, dockers, porters, and various day jobbers—the toiling proletariat of Rome.[38]

This proletariat was quite capable of exercising critical judgment. For instance, in July 45, as Cicero himself records, the people showed their displeasure at Caesar's monarchical pretensions, refraining from applauding his statue when it was being carried with those of the gods in a procession. They retained enough historic memory and enough regard for their rights to nurse a deep loathing of would-be kings. Their disapproving silence pleased Cicero enough to cause him to enter a rare positive comment about the *plebs urbana*: "How splendidly the crowd behaved."[39] In this one instance, at least, they were not a foul rabble but a "crowd."

Many of Rome's proletarians were ex-slaves or the sons of slaves. Most were almost as poor as slaves. They sometimes worked alongside slaves, and were inclined to feel a common interest with the servile population on many basic issues. In parts of Sicily, free farmhands joined in common cause with slaves to rebel against big planters.[40]

An incident from Tacitus speaks volumes. In A.D. 61, the city prefect was murdered in his bedchamber by one or more of his slaves. By ancient custom, when a master was murdered by a slave all *servi* in the household had to be put to death. In this instance it meant the extermination of some 400 souls, including women and children. The possibility of such a mass execution caused a public outcry compelling the Senate to hold a formal debate on the issue. One of the senior members of the Senate spoke at length in support of the executions, maintaining that the slaveholder's interest demanded that there be no departure from ancient practice no matter how harsh the outcome. If all 400 slaves are not executed, who among us will be safe? he argued. There were a few uneasy outcries, but no senator took the floor to denounce the measure, which was passed without further debate.[41]

This mass execution however did evoke angry protests from the plebs, who assembled outside the Senate House armed with stones and torches. Nero had to bring out the troops to line the route over which the condemned passed. Of course, Tacitus refers to the protesters as "the mob" but he makes no critical reference to the lynch-mob mentality that prevailed *within* the Senate House among those who sanctioned this mass murder. The deep sense of moral outrage expressed by the protestors signaled a sympathetic bond between impoverished slaves and impoverished plebs.

For good reason, writes Plutarch, did Cato fear restiveness among the poorest citizens, for they "were always the first to kindle the flame among the people."[42] The Roman plebs played a creative democratic role by providing vital support to the various *populares*, including an exceptional leader like Caesar who was able to win their backing not because they were mesmerized by his "demagogic" ploys but because they strongly favored his reformist policies.

What sparse evidence we have of proletarian activism, as provided by Plutarch and a few others, is virtually ignored by modern-day classical historians. Regarding Tiberius Gracchus's agrarian reform, Plutarch writes, "It was above all the people themselves who did most to stoke Tiberius's energy and ambitions by inscribing slogans and appeals on porticoes, monuments, and the walls of houses, calling upon him to recover the public land for the poor." Also remember how the people directed their outrage at Tiberius's assassin, Nasica, causing him to flee Rome.[43]

And Gaius Gracchus, who left his home on the fashionable Palatine Hill to live among the poor near the Forum, was elected tribune for a second time "though he was not a candidate and did not canvass for the office; but the people were eager to have it so." After he put forth his reform legislation, "a great multitude began to gather in Rome from all parts of Italy to support him." Gaius won "the wholehearted devotion of the people, and they were prepared to do almost anything in the world to show their goodwill."[44]

After the Gracchi were assassinated, public acknowledgment of their existence was officially proscribed. The oligarchs were intent upon expurgating the collective historical memory. Yet the populace continued to commemorate the brothers. Plutarch offers a moving vignette:

The people were cowed and humiliated by the collapse of the democratic cause, but they soon showed how deeply they missed and longed for the Gracchi. Statues of the brothers were set up in a prominent part of the city, the places where they had fallen were declared to be holy ground, and the first-fruits of the season were offered up there throughout the year. Many people even sacrificed to the Gracchi every day, and worshipped their statues as though they were visiting the shrines of gods.[45]

Several years after Catiline's death, the plebs adorned his tomb "as formerly that of the Gracchi, with flowers and garlands."[46] *Nota bene*, the people never offered memorial tributes to Cicero, Cato, Sulla, Catulus, Milo, Brutus, Cassius, or any other prominent senatorial conservative.

In 88 B.C., more than thirty years after the Gracchi, when the reactionary Sulla marched his army into Rome in violation of a sacred constitutional prohibition against military units within the city limits, the plebs greeted the troops with barrages of missiles so intense as to make them waiver.[47] And in 67, when the optimate Catulus proposed that the people call for the appointment of a dictator for six months to deal with an emergency, the crowd hissed the hated name "Sulla."[48] On the eve of civil war, in February 49, Cicero assessed the bleak prospects of the optimate cause by noting that "the populace and the lower orders sympathize . . . with the other side and many [are] eager for revolution."[49] A few years later, the proletarians, still possessing enough historical memory of Sulla as the bloodletting champion of the aristocracy, pulled down his statue along with Pompey's.[50]

Early in his career, when Caesar delivered a funeral oration in the Forum in memory of his aunt Julia, he dared to laud the late *popularis* Marius, who had remained a taboo topic since the Sulla dictatorship. When some individuals began to raise a cry against Caesar, "the people answered with loud shouts and clapping in his favor, expressing their joyful surprise and satisfaction at his having, as it were, brought up again from the grave those honors of Marius, which for so long a time had been lost to the city."[51]

In 70 and again in 67, 66, and 64, radical tribunes packed the assemblies and launched demonstrations and electoral campaigns by mobilizing the *collegia*, those guilds of freedmen, slaves, and free poor. Such mass actions were enough to cause the Senate to pass a decree dissolving all but a few of the more innocuous *collegia*, depriving the popular movement of its key organizations.[52]

Popular support bolstered Caesar on more than one occasion. In 62 B.C., while serving as praetor, he and Caecilius Metellus, a tribune of the people, were suspended from office by senatorial decree for introducing what Suetonius describes only as "inflammatory bills" that "Caesar stubbornly championed" on the floor of the Senate. Threatened with force, Caesar hastened home, deciding to live in temporary retirement because, writes Suetonius, "the times allowed him no alternative. On the following day, however, the populace made a spontaneous move towards Caesar's house, riotously offering to put him back in his post; but he restrained their ardor." The Senate was so taken by "his unexpectedly correct attitude" that they showered him with warm praise and restored him to his praetorship.[53] One can suspect that the restoration was at least in part prompted by a desire to calm the popular agitation. Likewise, Caesar's later attempts at debt easement were not entirely of his own initiative but were propelled by democratic forces that struggled unsuccessfully for cancellation of all creditor claims against the poor.

More than once did the ordinary Romans put a check on Caesar himself. On one occasion, while he was seated in a golden chair at the Rostra to view a public ceremony, Antony entered the Forum and approached him with a diadem wreathed with laurel. There was a slight and scattered cheer, Plutarch records, "made by the few who were planted there for that purpose; but when Caesar refused it, there was universal applause." Caesar declined a second offer, again to enthusiastic approval.[54] There seems little doubt that his reluctance was much fortified by the strong popular sentiment against a kingship. The era of kings (753–509 B.C.) had been a time of special autocracy and repression for the common people, enough to sear their historical memory, leaving them still intolerant of royal pretenders over four centuries later.

In all, the proletariat played a crucial but much ignored role in the struggle for democratic policies. They showed themselves to be neither a mindless mob nor a shiftless rabble but a politically aware force capable of registering preferences in accordance with their needs, able to distinguish friend from foe. That their political efforts have been deemed worthy of little more than passing condemnation is but a further reflection of the class biases shared by both ancient and modern historians.

*   *   *

Lord Acton refers to "the convictions, errors, prejudices, and passions that urge the masses of mankind and sway their rulers." The image is a familiar one. The people are a great beast, irrational and prone to error, who "sway" rulers toward misadventure.[55] Seldom acknowledged is the converse, the numerous occasions when rulers have misled the people, the times when popular sentiment sought to restrain the potentates and deflect them from a damaging course. Also downplayed are the times when the people have pursued social betterment and more equitable and more democratic policies, only to face unforgiving opposition from those at the apex of the social pyramid.

To repeat, we hear that we must avoid imposing present values upon past experience, and we must immerse ourselves in the historic context under study. But few historians immerse themselves in the grim and embattled social experience of the Roman proletariat. If anything, they see the poor—especially the rebellious poor—through the prism of their own class bias, the same bias shared by ancient historians from Polybius and Cicero to Tacitus and Velleius. In the one-sided record that is called history, it has been a long-standing practice to damn popular agitation as the work of riffraff and demagogues. As far as the gentlemen historians can see, insurgency is not inspired by legitimate grievances but by the misplaced and manipulated impulses of the insurgents.[56]

The common people of ancient Rome had scant opportunity to leave a written record of their views and struggles. Among the surviving primary sources, there exists little information on how the *plebs urbana* organized their *collegia*, and how they felt about wages, prices, taxes, wars, land policy, or employment problems. Although we can draw certain inferences, history leaves us with only fragmentary impressions of their tribulations. Still, as I have tried to show, what we know of the common people tells us that they displayed a social consciousness and sense of justice that was usually superior to anything possessed by their would-be superiors.

In the highly skewed accounts of what is called history, Cicero, Brutus, Cato, and other oligarchs come down to us as the defenders of republican liberty; while Caesar—who tried to move against their power and privilege and do something for the poor—comes down to us as a tyrant and usurper.

And the people of Rome themselves, the anonymous masses upon whose shoulders the *populares* stood, come down to us hardly at all, or most usually as a disreputable mob. They who struggled against all odds with all the fear and courage of ordinary humans, whose names we shall never know, whose blood and tears we shall never see, whose cries of pain and hope we shall never hear, to them we are linked by a past that is never dead nor ever really past. And so, when the best pages of history are finally written, it will be not by princes, presidents, prime ministers, or pundits, nor even by professors, but by the people themselves. For all their faults and shortcomings, the people are all we have. Indeed, we are they.

Appendix: A Note on Pedantic Citations and Vexatious Names

My desire has been to make the classical sources used herein accessible to the lay reader. Most present-day historians of antiquity seem determined to make them *in*accessible, a fact that itself might be indicative of the pedantic and elitist nature of their training. In regard to ancient sources, they resort to a mode of Latin citation so severely abbreviated as to be identifiable only to select colleagues specially schooled in classical literature. So we encounter indecipherable references like "*B*.i.146" and "*De fin.*, V.65." To add to the difficulty, a key to such arcane abbreviations is rarely provided, thus ensuring that the interested layperson who wishes to delve into ancient sources, or at least fathom what they might be, is properly stymied.

Furthermore, the classicists make a point of not listing the ancient sources in their otherwise copious bibliographies, not even in the original Latin. With the help of lexicons and after a deep immersion in the literature, the persevering lay reader (including the non-classicist historian) eventually might be able to divine that "Sall. *Bell Iug* 71" is a reference to Sallust *Bellum Iugurthinum* and is available in English as Sallust's *The Jugurthine War*. Persistent lay readers might even be able to discover, as I did, that

"Plin. *NH* VII. 91–2" is a reference not to the younger Pliny but to Gaius Secundus Plinius (*maior*), *Naturalis Historia*, that is, the elder Pliny's *Natural History*. But what are the unanointed to do with "*Ad Q. fr.* II.iv.1" or "*Q.F.*I.i" (which happen to be *Ad Quintum Fratrem* or To [Cicero's] Brother Quintus)? Knowing enough Latin to guess that "*Ep. ad Caes*" (or sometimes it is just "*ad Caes*") is *Epistulae ad Caesarem*, one can conclude that someone had written a letter to Caesar; but when not even an abbreviation of the author's name is given, we would have to know enough on our own to guess that it was Sallust and not the more likely Cicero whose letters survive in such abundance.

This abstruse mode of citation is used even by progressive scholars such as Neal Wood and the incomparable G.E.M. de Ste. Croix, both of whom otherwise seem interested in communicating with audiences beyond the antiquarian priesthood. One of the few exceptions to such pedantry is Arthur D. Kahn, who in his *The Education of Julius Caesar* (1986) provides a listing of the ancient sources he used, both in English and Latin, as well as a key to their abbreviations—which is only one of several reasons for welcoming his book.

Herein, I give only English-language titles for ancient sources, and without abbreviation. Because some classical works come in so many editions, I use the classical text notation rather than the page number of a particular edition, for that is the more reliable way of locating the citation.

Some works in English translation present problems of their own, as when various editions and translations of the same volume have been published under different titles. Thus Lucan's epic poem used to be called *The Pharsalia*, and can still be found in library catalogues under that title, but the title given in ancient manuscripts is *De Bello Civili*. So I follow the English-language path taken by J.D. Duff in 1928 and probably by others before him and cite Lucan's work as *The Civil War*.

Another example: The very first English edition of the complete surviving works of Dio Cassius (1905) was entitled *Annals of Rome* by its translator, Herbert Baldwin Foster, who argues that the Romans would have called it *annales* and not *historiae*. That Dio was a Greek who wrote in Greek seems not to have troubled Foster, who decided—not implausibly—that Dio, who lived in Italy and was a Roman senator and praetor, was more Roman in his lifestyle than Greek (though the two lifestyles were much intermingled at times). I rely on Foster's translation, and possess all six volumes of that precious 1905 first edition of *Annals of Rome*, but I cite Dio's work as *Roman History* because that has long been the more commonly used title.

Even works originally written in English can present citation problems. Thus, it would be misleading to give a volume number when referencing Edward Gibbon's magnum opus since it comes in three-, six-, seven-, and eight-volume editions, and even in one-volume abridgments. Furthermore, the title itself has been changed. It was originally *A History of the Decline and Fall of the Roman Empire* but most editions printed over the past sixty years leave off the first three words of that title, as do I. The chapters of the various editions (except for some of the abridged ones) are numbered exactly as Gibbon had numbered them. Therefore, I cite the chapter number (as do most writers), asking the reader to keep in mind that I am relying on the Heritage Press (1946) volumes for page numbers.

Roman names can present a daunting challenge to both the writer and indexer who must wrestle with a tri-nomina web of *praenomen, nomen*, and *cognomen*. The *praenomen* is the given name, of which there were relatively few in use: Gaius, Lucius, Marcus, Quintus, Servius, Titus, Tiberius, and others. The *nomen* is the family or gens name, usually ending in *-ius*. And the *cognomen* is an adopted third name whose original function was to distinguish the individual from other males with the same first and family names. The *cognomen* usually was a nickname focusing on some physical characteristic or other idiosyncratic feature, sometimes humorous and not necessarily flattering; thus Ovid was Naso ("nose"), Licinius was Macer ("skinny"), Tullius was Cicero ("chickpea"). Over time, the *cognomen* was taken seriously enough, functioning as a kind of additional surname.

To further complicate things, some upper-class Roman males are regularly referred to by their *nomen*; thus Gaius Cassius Longinus is known to us as Cassius. Others are better known by their *cognomen*, as with Gaius Julius Caesar and Marcus Tullius Cicero. Only during the last days of the Republic did it become customary to call an individual by the gens name or *nomen*. So throughout his life Caesar was known as Gaius Caesar. Still, I cleave to the more common present-day usage, referring to him as Julius Caesar.

Adding further to the confusion, some writers will use the *nomen* and others the *cognomen* for the same person. In some books, C. Licinius Macer is Licinius, and in others he is Macer. Sometimes writers do not use enough names, referring only to, let us say, Cornelius Lentulus, leaving us to decide whether it be Cornelius Lentulus Crus, Cornelius Lentulus Marcellinus, Cornelius Lentulus Niger, or Cornelius Lentulus Spinther. In moments like that we might wish all available names were regularly used.

As if Roman names themselves are not sufficiently challenging, most classicist scholars—in keeping with their pedantry—take pleasure in indexing prominent people by their more obscure *nomen* rather than their better-known *cognomen*. My practice of choosing whatever names are most readily recognizable to the reader is at variance with the usual approach. Rarely can one find Sulla, Cato, Cicero, Gracchus, Brutus, or Caesar listed under their commonly recognized names in a book index. Instead, Cicero is indexed under Tullius, Caesar under Iulius or less frequently under Julius, and Brutus under Iunius. One of Rome's most prominent optimate families, the Mettelli, are not listed under Mettellus but under their rarely referred to *nomen*, Caecilius. In this way, readers who have not mastered the intractable web of Roman names are further deprived of ready access.

For well-known personages I resort to the Anglicized forms that are more familiar to the modern English-language reader. Hence, there was nobody in ancient Rome named Pompey or Mark Antony, but those are the names provided herein, instead of Gnaeus Pompeius Magnus and Marcus Antonius.

Spellings of Roman names can change. Thus Gaius is also Caius (I stay all the way with Gaius), Calgacus is sometimes Galgacus, and Gnaeus (or Cnaeus) can be Gneius (or Cneius). But in

abbreviation, the name reverts to the *C* form. Thus Gaius Julius
Caesar is always abbreviated as C. Julius Caesar (for Caius). Don't
ask why.

Names can change with one's destiny. Gaius Octavius took the
name C. Julius Caesar Octavianus when he became Julius Caesar's
heir. And, as noted in Chapter Ten, the Senate later voted him
the title of Augustus, which quickly became his name. So we
know him as Emperor Augustus or Caesar Augustus. Gnaeus
Pompeius became Pompeius Magnus (Pompey the Great), Magnus
being a self-promotional *cognomen* that Pompey adopted in imita-
tion of Alexander the Great.

Name choices also loom in regard to early historians. There are
still disputes about whether Gaius Sallustius Crispus should be
called Gaius Crispus Sallustius. I refer to him simply as Sallust,
as do present-day historians except for the more pedantic holdouts.
In the case of Cassius Dio Cocceianus we have someone with two
cognomina and no known *praenomen*—not unusual for a Greek. Some
writers, preferring the Roman style, call him Cassius Dio (*nomen*
and *cognomen*). Others, thinking that in Greek the *nomen* comes
after the *cognomen*, refer to him as Dio Cassius. To confuse us
further, there were Greeks who utilized the Roman style for their
own names, and Romans who preferred the Greek style. As far as
I can see, there is no compelling argument for selecting one over
the other. I use Dio Cassius simply because that seems to be the
more common form today.

Notes

Introduction: Tyrannicide or Treason?

1. In addition, one might consider Thornton Wilder's lesser-known and thoroughly fictional construction of Caesar in the last six months of his life: *The Ides of March* (New York: Harper & Brothers, 1948).
2. For a good overview of the literary commentary on Shakespeare's play, see Vivian Thomas, *Julius Caesar* (New York: Twayne Publishers, 1992).
3. Appian, *The Civil Wars* V.8. In about 41 B.C., Antony wrote to Octavian that he already had been intimate with Cleopatra nine years earlier, which would have been two years before Caesar set foot in Alexandria; see Suetonius, *Augustus* 69.2. See also, Victor Thaddeus, *Julius Caesar and the Grandeur that Was Rome* (London: Brentano's, 1928), 245.
4. Most historians do not give precise dates to designate the Late Republic era. Many leave the impression that it is the period sometime after Sulla to the downfall of Caesar, about 75–44 B.C. For some, 133 B.C. and the ensuing years of the late second century would be considered part of the Middle Republic.

1: Gentlemen's History: Empire, Class, and Patriarchy

1. Benedetto Croce, *History as the Story of Liberty* (London: George Allen and Unwin, 1941), 19; R. G. Collingwood, *The Idea of History* (New York: Oxford University Press, 1956, originally 1946), xii.
2. Edward Gibbon, *Memoirs of My Life* (London/New York: Penguin Books, 1984), 65, 75, 86, 128.
3. See my *History as Mystery* (San Francisco: City Lights, 1999), 171–176.
4. Gibbon, *Memoirs of My Life*, 157 and 175.
5. Gibbon, *Memoirs of My Life*, 173.

6. Gibbon, *The Decline and Fall of the Roman Empire*, II, 33 and III, 61.
7. For example, Valerius Maximus, *Memorable Deeds and Sayings* II.1.4–10 and II.3.1.
8. Sallust, *The Conspiracy of Catiline* 10.6. On Sallust's own corrupt ways while serving as proconsular governor of Africa Nova in 46 B.C., see Dio Cassius, *Roman History* XLIII.9; and Cicero *A Declaration Against Sallust* 7. It is believed by some that Cicero is not the author of this broadside.
9. Sallust, *Histories* book 4.
10. Tacitus, *Agricola* XXX–XXXI.
11. Dio Cassius, *Roman History* XXX–XXXV. fragment CVII. Peter Burke notes Tacitus's class bias. Unable to write the word "cook" to describe the one person who did not desert Emperor Vitellius in his last moments, Tacitus refers obliquely to "one of the meanest" in the emperor's household: Burke, "People's History or Total History," in Raphael Samuel, ed., *People's History and Socialist Theory* (London: Routledge & Kegan Paul, 1981), 4–5.
12. John G. Gager, *The Origins of Anti-Semitism: Attitudes Toward Judaism in Pagan and Christian Antiquity* (New York and Oxford: Oxford University Press, 1983), 266.
13. Juvenal, *Satires* VIII.88–90.
14. Joseph Schumpeter, "The Sociology of Imperialism," in *Two Essays by Joseph Schumpeter* (New York: Meridian Books, 1955), 51.
15. Cyril E. Robinson, *History of the Roman Republic* (New York: Thomas Y. Crowell, 1965), 146.
16. See Willson Whitman's introduction to Edward Gibbon, *The Decline and Fall of the Roman Empire*, condensed edition (New York: Wise & Co., 1943), ix–xi; and Gibbon's own self-exculpatory comments about the controversy in *Memoir of My Life*, 161–162.
17. Gibbon, *The Decline and Fall of the Roman Empire*, XV and XVI. For a detailed discussion of the historical myths relating to the rise of early Christianity, see my *History as Mystery*, chapters 2 and 3.
18. Gibbon, *The Decline and Fall of the Roman Empire*, I, 111.
19. Two notable exceptions are J.P.V.D. Balsdon, *Roman Women* (London: 1962); and the sympathetic essay by M.I. Finley, "The Silent Women of Rome" in his *Aspects of Antiquity*, 2d ed. (New York: Penguin Books, 1977), 124–136.
20. Keith Hopkins, "The Age of Roman Girls at Marriage," *Population Studies*, 18, 1965, 124–151.
21. Finley, "The Silent Women of Rome," 124–126.

22. Sarah B. Pomeroy, *Goddesses, Whores, Wives, and Slaves: Women in Classical Antiquity* (New York: Schocken Books, 1975), 199–201.

23. Pomeroy, *Goddesses, Whores, Wives, and Slaves,* 201.

24. There was Pompey's woeful Cornelia who willingly shared his grim fate at Pharsalus: Lucan, *The Civil War* VIII.87–108; and Brutus's Porcia who silently endured a self-inflicted wound to prove herself worthy of being her husband's confidante: Plutarch, *Brutus* XIII. See also the examples offered by Tacitus, *Annals* XV.71.7 and XVI.34.2; and Pliny the Younger, *Letters* VI.24.

25. Otto Kiefer, *Sexual Life in Ancient Rome* (London: Abbey Library, 1934), 52–54.

26. Appian, *The Civil Wars* IV.32–33. The wives of Mark Antony and Cicero both possessed large holdings. Carcopino makes the improbable claim that during the first and second centuries A.D., Roman women "enjoyed a dignity and an independence at least equal if not superior to those claimed by contemporary feminists": Jérôme Carcopino, *Daily Life in Ancient Rome* (New Haven: Yale University Press, 1940, 1968), 85.

27. Richard Bauman, *Women and Politics in Ancient Rome* (New York/London: Routledge, 1995); also, Judith Hallett, *Fathers and Daughters in Roman Society: Women and the Elite Family* (Princeton, N.J.: Princeton University Press, 1984), passim. Pomeroy is one of the very few who treats women of the lower classes as well as the Roman matron in her *Goddesses, Whores, Wives, and Slaves,* 150–204.

28. Sallust, *The Conspiracy of Catiline* 13.

29. Horace, *Odes* VI.iii.

30. Juvenal, *Satires* VI.

31. Robinson, *History of the Roman Republic,* 426.

32. Kiefer, *Sexual Life in Ancient Rome,* 7–63; and Pomeroy, *Goddesses, Whores, Wives, and Slaves,* 160.

33. Valerius Maximus, *Memorable Deeds and Sayings* VI.3.10–12.

34. Valerius Maximus, *Memorable Deeds and Sayings* VI.6.2–3; Pliny the Younger, *Letters* IV.19, IV.21, VII.5.

35. J.P.V.D. Balsdon, "Cicero the Man," in T. A. Dorey (ed.), *Cicero* (New York: Basic Books, 1965), 205.

36. Cicero, *Pro Flacco,* 1, 5, 12, and 67.

37. Theodore Mommsen, *The History of Rome,* a new edition by Dero A. Saunders and John H. Collins (Clinton, Mass.: Meridian Books, 1958), 49 and 327.

38. For these and other such unfortunate examples, see Robinson, *History of the Roman Republic*, 109, 177, 183, 213, 219, 288, and 301.
39. J.F.C. Fuller, *Julius Caesar: Man, Soldier, and Tyrant* (New York: Da Capo Press, 1965), 20.
40. Carcopino, *Daily Life in Ancient Rome*, 102.

2: Slaves, Proletarians, and Masters

1. A few historians estimate higher. Hopkins puts the slave population at 35–40 percent of the population of Italy: Keith Hopkins, *Conquerors and Slaves* (New York and Cambridge: Cambridge University Press, 1980), 9.
2. Keith R. Bradley, *Slavery and Rebellion in the Roman World, 140 B.C.–70 B.C.* (Bloomington and Indianapolis: Indiana University Press, 1989, 1998); Mommsen, *The History of Rome*, 25–30 and 93.
3. Carcopino, *Daily Life in Ancient Rome*, 23–44; Lionel Casson, *Everyday Life in Ancient Rome*, rev. ed. (Baltimore/London: Johns Hopkins University Press, 1998 [1975]), 37–38; Lewis Mumford, *The City in History* (New York: Harcourt, Brace & World, 1961), 221; and Arthur D. Kahn, *The Education of Julius Caesar* (New York: Schocken Books, 1986), 405.
4. Juvenal, *Satires* III.191–196.
5. Cicero, *To Atticus*, XIV.9, and XIV.11.2.
6. The poet Martial aimed a couple of his epigrams at the fuller's foul-smelling urine crocks: *Epigrams* VI.93, XII.48; see also Thaddeus, *Julius Caesar and the Grandeur that Was Rome*, 4; Carcopino, *Daily Life in Ancient Rome*, 42.
7. Casson, *Everyday Life in Ancient Rome*, 19 and 25.
8. Juvenal, *Satires* III.288–304; and Casson, *Everyday Life in Ancient Rome*, 45–46.
9. Casson, *Everyday Life in Ancient Rome*, 28.
10. Carcopino, *Daily Life in Ancient Rome*, 202; Mumford, *The City in History*, 219; Ernst Mason, *Tiberius* (New York: Ballantine Books, 1960), 29.
11. Carcopino, *Daily Life in Ancient Rome*, 66
12. Mentioned in Mommsen, *The History of Rome*, 543.
13. For a detailed study, see E. Badian, *Publicans and Sinners: Private Enterprise in the Service of the Roman Republic* (Ithaca, N.Y.: Cornell University Press, 1972).

14. P.A. Brunt, *Social Conflicts in the Roman Republic* (New York: W. W. Norton, 1971), 68–73.
15. H.H. Scullard, *From the Gracchi to Nero: A History of Rome from 133 B.C. to A.D. 68* (London: Methuen, 1959, 1963), 182; Mumford, *The City in History*, 219; Mommsen, *The History of Rome*, 543–544; Brunt, *Social Conflicts in the Roman Republic*, 34; Joseph Vogt, *The Decline of Rome* (New York: New American Library, 1965), 166.
16. Carcopino, *Daily Life in Ancient Rome*, 32–33.
17. Finley, *Aspects of Antiquity*, 127.
18. Juvenal, *Satires* III.137–147,159.
19. Gibbon, *The Decline and Fall of the Roman Empire* II, 31.
20. Carcopino, *Daily Life in Ancient Rome*, 56.
21. K.R. Bradley, *Slaves and Masters in the Roman Empire: A Study in Social Control* (New York: Oxford, 1987 [1984]), 19. On the ways that conservative ideology, especially anticommunism, has colored the scholarship on ancient slavery, see M.I. Finley, *Ancient Slavery and Modern Ideology* (London: Chatto & Windus, 1980), 61ff.
22. Casson, *Everyday Life in Ancient Rome*, 61.
23. Casson, *Everyday Life in Ancient Rome*, 64.
24. Kahn, *The Education of Julius Caesar*, 119.
25. Bradley, *Slaves and Masters in the Roman Empire*, 83, 107, 111.
26. Cicero, *On the Consular Provinces* 10; and Finley, *Ancient Slavery and Modern Ideology*, 177–178, n.99.
27. Lucius Annaeus Florus, *Epitome of Roman History* III.20.1.
28. Gibbon, *The Decline and Fall of the Roman Empire* II, 31–2.
29. Ronald Syme, *The Roman Revolution* (Oxford and New York: Oxford University Press, 1939, 1960), 446.
30. Columella, *Res Rusticae*, summarized and nicely discussed in Bradley, *Slaves and Masters in the Roman Empire*, 21–33.
31. Bradley, *Slaves and Masters in the Roman Empire*, 60 and 79.
32. Seneca, *On Mercy* I.18. On the fatal cruelty a household slave might face, see the incident Seneca relates in *On Anger* III.40.i.
33. Mason, *Tiberius*, 37; also see the incident in Tacitus, *Annals* XIV.42–43, treated in more detail in Chapter Eleven.
34. So it was with every case given by Valerius Maximus; see his *Memorable Deeds and Sayings* VI.5.5–7.

35. In some instances, runaways and criminal slaves were put to punishing toil in a specially cruel establishment called an *ergastulum*: Mason, *Tiberius*, 37.

36. M.I. Finley, *Ancient Slavery and Modern Ideology* (London: Chatto and Windus, 1980), 111.

37. Cicero, *To His Friends* V.9.2, V.10.1, V.11.3, XIII.77.3.

38. Finley, *Ancient Slavery and Modern Ideology*, 114–115.

39. Ammianus Marcellinus, *Histories* XXVIII.4.16

40. Seneca, *Epistle* 47.5–8.

41. Horace, *Satires* I.2.116–119.

42. Petronius, *Satyricon* 75.11

43. Martial, *Epigrams* I.84.

44. Martial, *Epigrams* VI.39, II.34, III.91, IV.66, VI.71, XI.70, XII.58.

45. Martial, *Epigrams* I.58 and I.90.

46. Bradley, *Slaves and Masters in the Roman Empire*, 115–116; and Martial, *Epigrams* IX.6.

47. Finley, *Ancient Slavery and Modern Ideology*, 105.

48. Cicero, *To Atticus* I.12.4.

49. Page Smith, *Trial by Fire*, vol. 5 of *A People's History of the Civil War and Reconstruction* (New York/London: Penguin, 1982), 657. For instances of the slave's "ingratitude," see Burke Davis, *Sherman's March* (New York: Vintage, 1988), 29, 166, 183–184, 191, 247; James M. McPherson, *The Negro's Civil War: How American Blacks Felt and Acted During the War for the Union* (New York: Ballantine Books, 1991) passim; Joseph T. Glatthaar, *Officers Forged in Battle: The Civil War Alliance of Black Soldiers and White* (New York: Meridian, 1990).

50. Valerius Maximus, *Memorable Deeds and Sayings* VI.8.1–7; and Appian, *The Civil War* IV.43–44.

51. Pliny the Younger, *Letters* III.14.

52. Finley, *Ancient Slavery and Modern Ideology*, 73–75, 96; Bradley, *Slaves and Masters in the Roman Empire*, 60.

53. The remarks of both Cato and Cicero are reported in Kiefer, *Sexual Life in Ancient Rome*, 88; see also Plutarch, *Cato the Elder* 13.

3: A Republic for the Few

1. Gibbon, *The Decline and Fall of the Roman Empire* III, 50.
2. Lucius Annaeus Florus, *Epitome of Roman History* I.25–26. The only remaining difference was that patricians were ineligible to hold both consulships in any one year and could not occupy the plebeian office of tribune nor the plebeian aedile. The plebian aediles, of which there were two serving at any one time, were magistrates who assisted the tribunes of the plebs in their duties, including guarding the rights of plebs. Along with the two curile aediles (of patrician origin), the plebeian aediles also were responsible for the care of Rome's streets, water supply, drains and sewers, traffic, public buildings, public games, and grain supply.
3. Florus, *Epitome of Roman History* II.6.
4. Plutarch, *Tiberius Gracchus* VIII.1–3.
5. Brunt, *Social Conflicts in the Roman Republic*, 36. See also C. Osborne Ward, *The Ancient Lowly*, vol. 1 (Chicago: Charles H. Kerr & Company, 1888), 246–247; and Max Weber, *The Agrarian Sociology of Ancient Civilization* (London: Humanities Press, 1976, originally published 1891).
6. Appian, *The Civil Wars* I.7–8.
7. Robinson, *History of the Roman Republic*, 139–141; Lily Ross Taylor, *Party Politics in the Age of Caesar* (Berkeley, Calif.: University of California Press, 1949), 5; Hopkins, *Conquerors and Slaves*, 11 and passim.
8. Pliny, *Natural History* II.63.158–64,159.
9. Pliny, *Natural History* II.68.174–69,176.
10. The people's Tribal Assembly did not win full legislative competence until the third century B.C. In addition there was the Plebeian Assembly (*concilium plebis*), a third legislative body, as it were. Through the fifth and fourth centuries B.C., it was without official standing within the Roman state, being merely an advisory organ that voiced the plebeian will. The Plebeian Assembly's resolutions (*plebiscita*) would be noted and sometimes accepted by the magistrates. However, in 287 B.C., a law (*lex Hortensia*) stipulated that all resolutions of the Plebeian Assembly were to have the force of law, binding upon the entire population. Yet we hear little about this assembly.
11. Praetors were second in magisterial rank after consuls; they dealt with the administration of justice. Third in rank were the aediles, discussed in note 1. Next in rank were the quaestors who were largely concerned with oversight of finance and treasury matters.

12. Taylor, *Party Politics in the Age of Caesar*, 5–6; Robinson, *History of the Roman Republic*, 44.

13. Robinson, *History of the Roman Republic*, 206; Mommsen, *The History of Rome*, 22–23; Brunt, *Social Conflicts in the Roman Republic*, 50–51.

14. Mary Beard and Michael Crawford, *Rome in the Late Republic* (Ithaca, N.Y.: Cornell University Press, 1985), 49–52. In the Roman Republic, "the oligarchic elements were in practice much stronger," writes G.E.M. de Ste. Croix in his treatment of Rome that is included in his remarkable opus: *The Class Struggle in the Ancient Greek World* (Ithaca, N.Y.: Cornell University Press, 1981), 340.

15. Robinson, *History of the Roman Republic*, 23.

16. Kahn, *The Education of Julius Caesar*, 140.

17. Michael Grant, Introduction to Cicero, *On Government* (London: Penguin Books, 1993), 5*fn*. For similar estimates, see S. A. Handford, Introduction to Sallust, *The Jurgurthine War/The Conspiracy of Catiline* (Middlesex, England: Penguin Books, 1963), 17; Scullard, *From the Gracchi to Nero*, 6; and Thomas Africa, *Rome of the Caesars* (New York: John Wiley & Sons, 1965), 22.

18. Sallust, *Epistles to Caesar* I.3. There has been controversy regarding the authorship of the two epistles to Caesar, usually ascribed to Sallust. It is well-discussed though inconclusively by Reverend Watson; see *Sallust, Florus, and Velleius Paterculus*, translated and noted by John Selby Watson (New York: Harper & Bros., 1872).

19. Weber, *The Agrarian Sociology of Ancient Civilization*, 281; also Casson, *Everyday Life in Ancient Rome*, 33.

20. Cicero, *Pro Sestio*, 97–98.

21. Asconius Pedianus, Exposition to his commentary on *Pro Cornelio*, in his *Orationum Ciceronis*.

22. Brunt, *Social Conflicts in the Roman Republic*, 140.

23. Tacitus, *Annals*, I.2.

24. St. Augustine, *The City of God*, III.30.

25. Gibbon, *The Decline and Fall of the Roman Empire*, I, 53.

26. John Dickinson, *Death of a Republic: Politics and Political Thought at Rome 59–44 B.C.* (New York: Macmillan, 1963), 257–323; Michael Grant, *History of Rome* (New York: Charles Scribner's Sons, 1978), 68; Grant also describes the Republic as "this once mighty institution"; see his introductory note to "In Defense of Titus Annius Milo" in Cicero, *Selected Political Speeches* (London: Penguin Books, 1989), 217; Robinson, *History of the Roman Republic*,

31, 103, 203; Scullard, *From the Gracchi to Nero*, 5, 8–9; see the general treatment in Andrew Lintott, *The Constitution of the Roman Republic* (New York: Clarendon Press, 1999). Like many others, Wilkinson approvingly refers to Caesar's aristocratic opponents as "the republicans" without qualifying the term. L. P. Wilkinson's notation in *Letters of Cicero* (New York: W.W. Norton, 1968), 185.

27. Polybius, *Histories* VI.3–5. In this same passage Polybius notes that "the process whereby the different forms of government are naturally transformed into one another has been discussed in the greatest detail by Plato and certain other philosophers." Plato made much of the "natural" transitions from one form to another but it is not my view that he favored a mixed constitution as we would understand the term: see Plato, *The Republic*, VIII.545–587 and passim. Plato was an aristocrat who tirelessly argued against Athenian democracy on behalf of government by those possessed of "expertise" and "excellence."

28. Cicero, *De Re Publica* I.54.

29. For one of the earliest statements on the mixed constitution, see Polybius, *Histories* VI.3–4; also Aristotle, *Politics* IV.6 and passim. On the framers of the U.S. Constitution, see my *Democracy for the Few*, 7th ed. (Belmont, Calif.: Wadsworth, 2002), Chapter Four. I have dealt with the limited and sometimes lethal democracy of capitalist Russia's executive-centered system; see my *Dirty Truths* (San Francisco: City Lights Books, 1996), 133–140 and *Blackshirts and Reds: Rational Fascism and the Overthrow of Communism* (San Francisco: City Lights Books, 1997), 87–96.

30. Mommsen, *The History of Rome*, 489–490.

4: "Demagogues" and Death Squads

1. Cicero *Pro Sestio* XLVI.99–100.

2. Brunt, *Social Conflicts in the Roman Republic*, 127; see also Saunders and Collins in their introduction to Mommsen, *The History of Rome*, 9; Scullard, *From the Gracchi to Nero*, 7–8; and Handford, Introduction to Sallust, *The Jurgurthine War/The Conspiracy of Catiline*, 16–17.

3. Appian, *The Civil Wars* I.9–10.

4. Plutarch, *Tiberius Gracchus* IX.1–3.

5. Plutarch, *Tiberius Gracchus* IX.4–5.

6. Plutarch, *Tiberius Gracchus* II.2 and XX.1–2.
7. Dio Cassius, *Roman History* XXIV fragment 83.1–3.
8. These quotations are respectively from Handford's introduction to Sallust, *The Jugurthine War/The Conspiracy of Catiline*, 20; Grant, *History of Rome* 170; Syme, *The Roman Revolution*, 60; Scullard, *From the Gracchi to Nero*, 27–28.
9. Even Cyril Robinson grants this point. See his *History of the Roman Republic*, 240.
10. Appian, *The Civil Wars* I.11–13; Plutarch, *Tiberius Gracchus* XV.1–3.
11. Plutarch, *Tiberius Gracchus* XVI.1–2.
12. Mommsen, *The History of Rome*, 50; and Handford, Introduction to Sallust, *The Jugurthine War/The Conspiracy of Catiline*, 21.
13. Quotations from Handford's Introduction to Sallust, *The Jugurthine War/The Conspiracy of Catiline*, 21; and Scullard, *From the Gracchi to Nero*, 28 and 30.
14. Plutarch, *Tiberius Gracchus* XIII.1–3, XV, and XIX.1.
15. Mommsen, *The History of Rome*, 48.
16. Plutarch, *Tiberius Gracchus* XXI.2–3.
17. Lucius Annaeus Florus, *Epitome of Roman History* III.12.8–9 and III.14.
18. Lintott, *Violence in Republican Rome*, 182.
19. Robinson, *History of the Roman Republic*, 239, 241.
20. Scullard, *From the Gracchi to Nero*, 30.
21. Plutarch, *Tiberius Gracchus* XX.1 and XXI.1.
22. Cornelius Nepos, *Fragments* I.2.
23. Sallust, *Epistles to Caesar* I.7.
24. Plutarch, *Gaius Gracchus* VI.3–4.
25. Plutarch, *Gaius Gracchus* XVII; Appian, *The Civil Wars* I.26.
26. Cicero, *On the State* (III) 41; and his *Against Catiline* I.4; and *Pro Milo* 14 and 68.
27. Dio Cassius, *Roman History* XXV. fragment 84.
28. Florus, *Epitome of Roman History* III.12.8–9 and III.14.
29. Valerius Maximus, *Memorable Deeds and Sayings* III.2.17, IV.7.1–2, V.3.2e–2f, IX.4.3, and VII.2.6b.
30. Velleius Paterculus, *Compendium of the History of Rome* II.3,6.
31. Saint Augustine, *The City of God* II.22.
32. Scullard, *From the Gracchi to Nero*, 38.
33. Christian Meier, *Caesar* (New York: Basic Books, 1982), 38.
34. Kiefer, *Sexual Life in Ancient Rome*, 26.

35. Brunt, *Social Conflicts in the Roman Republic*, 90. For a brief treatment of the occasions on which the *senatus consultum ultimum* was used, see Jane F. Gardner, "Appendix II: The Ultimate Decree" in Caesar, *The Civil War* (London: Penguin Books, 1967), 312–316.

36. Brunt notes that smallholders were vulnerable to the violence of the larger owners: *Social Conflicts in the Roman Republic,* 116; as does Mommsen, *The History of Rome*, 91.

37. Brunt, *Social Conflicts in the Roman Republic*, 91–92.

38. Even a conservative like Meier allows that the murders "clearly had the approval of the leading senators," *Caesar*, 159.

39. Appian, *The Civil Wars* I.34–36; Florus, *Epitome of Roman History* III.17; and Velleius Paterculus, *Compendium of the History of Rome* II.13.

40. Velleius Paterculus, *Compendium of the History of Rome* II.13.

41. Of the ancients, see for example Valerius Maximus, *Memorable Deeds and Sayings* VI.3; and Velleius Paterculus, *Compendium of the History of Rome* II.23.1c. Some modern examples include: Robinson, *History of the Roman Republic*, 278 and 280; John Hazel, *Who's Who in the Roman World* (London and New York: Routledge, 2001), 271; Erich Gruen, *The Last Generation of the Roman Republic* (Berkeley: University of California Press, 1974), 12. Meier downplays Drusus's murder, telling us that "the overheated atmosphere . . . cost Drusus his life": *Caesar*, 49.

42. See T.F. Carney, *A Biography of Gaius Marius* (Chicago: Argonaut, 1970).

43. On the knights' support of Cinna, see Asconius Pedianus, *In toga candida.*

44. Kahn, *The Education of Julius Caesar*, 44; see also Appian, *The Civil Wars*, I.64; and Mommsen, *The History of Rome*, 155.

45. Florus, *Epitome of Roman History* III.2, claims that Sulla butchered 4,000 in the Villa Publica alone. Sallust, *Letter to Caesar* II.4, refers to the massacre; Lucan, *The Civil War* II.139–222, gives an elaborately bloody account of the mass slaughter perpetrated by Sulla; Grant, *History of Rome*, 187, says that only forty senators but almost 10,000 opponents in all lost their lives in Sulla's proscriptions.

46. See Dio Cassius's account of the self-feeding savagery of Sulla's terror: *Roman History* XXX–XXXV. fragment CV.1–3.

47. Mommsen, *The History of Rome*, 198.

48. Matthias Gelzer, *Caesar: Politician and Statesman* (Cambridge, Mass.: Harvard University Press, 1968), 27–28; Robinson, *History of the Roman Republic,*

288–303; Grant, *History of Rome*, 188–189; Fuller, *Julius Caesar: Man, Soldier, and Tyrant*, 35.

49. Kahn, *The Education of Julius Caesar*, 94. Writing in the first century A.D., Velleius Paterculus tells us that "the best and most judicious flocked to Sulla's standard;" see his *Compendium of the History of Rome* II.25.

50. From a fragment of book III of Sallust's *Histories*.

51. Plutarch, *Sertorius* XXII.1.

52. Cicero, *To Atticus* XI.21.3.

53. Scullard, *From the Gracchi to Nero*, 83–84; Mommsen, *The History of Rome*, 157, 194; Meier, *Caesar*, 79–80; Arthur Keaveney, *Sulla: The Last Republican* (London: Croom Helm, 1982).

54. Kahn, *The Education of Julius Caesar*, 119–120.

55. Asconius Pedianus, commentary on *Pro Milo* (from his *Orationum Ciceronis*).

56. Velleius Paterculus, *Compendium of the History of Rome* II.45. See also Kahn, *The Education of Julius Caesar*, 295; Brunt, *Social Conflicts in the Roman Republic*, 134–135. Kahn and (for some reason) Brunt are among the very few historians who do not have a derogatory word about Clodius. The use of omens to block popular action is discussed in Chapter Six.

57. Cicero, *To Atticus* IV.3.2.

58. Plutarch, *Pompey* XLVI.4, *Cato the Younger* XIX.3, and *Mark Antony* II.4; Asconius Pedianus, commentary on *In Pisonem* from his *Orationum Ciceronis*; and Velleius Paterculus, *Compendium of the History of Rome* II.47.3–4.

59. For these and other quotations, see Mommsen, *The History of Rome*, 320, 329; Fuller, *Julius Caesar: Man, Soldier, and Tyrant*, 66; Robinson, *History of the Roman Republic*, 317 and 361; Grant in *Selected Political Speeches of Cicero*, 215 and 224fn; Dickinson, *Death of a Republic*, 328–329; D.R. Shackleton Bailey, comments in *Cicero's Letters to His Friends*, vol. 2 (Harmondsworth, Middlesex, and New York: Penguin, 1978); Meier, *Caesar*, 69.

60. Gelzer, *Caesar: Politician and Statesman*, 96; Lintott, *Violence in Republican Rome*, 82 and 196.

61. Cicero, *To Atticus* I.13.3 and I.16.9.

62. Kahn, *The Education of Julius Caesar*, 280.

63. Appian, *The Civil Wars* II.21–22.

64. Cicero, *Pro Milo* 4, 13, and passim.

65. Cicero, *To Atticus* IV.3.5.

66. Appian, *The Civil Wars* II.21.

67. Asconius, commentary on *Pro Milo.*
68. Asconius presents the testimony of Metellus Scipio and Aemilius Philemon, then dismisses it out of hand: commentary on *Pro Milo.*
69. Cicero, *Pro Milo* 53–54.
70. Kahn, *The Education of Julius Caesar*, 286.
71. Mommsen, *The History of Rome*, 142.

5: Cicero's Witch-hunt

1. Syme, *The Roman Revolution*, 4.
2. Quotations gleaned from Dickinson, *Death of a Republic*, 257–323; Grant, in Cicero, *On Government*, front page; Robinson, *History of the Roman Republic*, 342, 434; Scullard, *From the Gracchi to Nero*, 164–165.
3. Arthur D. Kahn, "Was There No Superstructure in Ancient Rome," *Monthly Review*, February 1990, 37. Theodore Mommsen and Wilhelm Drumann are also among the few prominent historians who do not share in the adulation of Cicero. And the writer Iain Boal informs me that the Latin schoolmasters and students of his day regarded Cicero as "a pompous windbag."
4. Quoted in Kahn, "Was There no superstructure in Ancient Rome?," 37.
5. Plutarch, *Cicero* VI.2.
6. Plutarch, *Cicero* VII.2.
7. *To Atticus* II.16.2.
8. Quoted in Grant's introduction to Cicero, *Selected Political Speeches*, 14.
9. *To Atticus* VI.1.7, XII.37.2., XII.14.4.
10. *To Atticus* IV.5.2–3.
11. Dio Cassius, *Roman History* XXXVIII.12.
12. Cicero, *First Philippic Against Marcus Antonius* 20.
13. Dio, *Roman History* XXXVI.42.
14. Cicero, *Laws* III.34–35.
15. *To Atticus* I.16 and VIII.3; and Cicero's *For Flaccus* 15–18, and *To His Friends* VII.1.
16. *To Atticus* I.19,4.
17. *To Atticus* II.6.
18. *To Atticus* IV.5.1.
19. Sallust, *The Conspiracy of Catiline* 20.12–23.3.
20. Sallust, *The Conspiracy of Catiline* 18.8.

21. Asconius reports that Crassus and Caesar supported Catiline but Crawford maintains that there is no hard evidence that they backed him at any time; see the discussion in Jane W. Crawford, *M. Tullius Cicero, The Fragmentary Speeches, An Edition with Commentary* (Atlanta, Georgia: Scholars Press, 1994).

22. Taylor, *Party Politics in the Age of Caesar*, 3.

23. Sallust, *The Jugurthine War* 63.6–7.

24. Quintus Cicero, *Handbook on Electioneering* 2.

25. Kahn, *The Education of Julius Caesar*, 135.

26. Dio, *Roman History* XXXVII.29.

27. Dio, *Roman History* XXXVII.25

28. Sallust, *The Conspiracy of Catiline* 33.1.

29. Kahn, *The Education of Julius Caesar*, 157–158.

30. Kahn, *The Education of Julius Caesar*, 158.

31. Dio, *Roman History* XXXVII.29,32.

32. Cicero, *Against Catiline* I.1–4, I.11, I.15, I.31–32, IV.2, and passim.

33. Cicero, *Against Catiline* I.15.

34. Cicero, *Pro Milo* 19.

35. *Against Catiline* I.4, I.ii.1–4; and *Pro Milo* 13–20.

36. Cicero, *Against Catiline* II.3. Even Dio, who uncritically embraces Cicero's wildest claims, observes that the Senate was reluctant to move against Catiline because Cicero was suspected of having uttered false charges: Dio Cassius, *Roman History* XXXVII.29.

37. Sallust, *The Conspiracy of Catiline* 35.1–5. Dio claims the Senate voted for Catiline to leave the city. But it is not clear why they would send out into Italy a person suspected of plotting revolution across Italy: *Roman History* XXXVII.33.

38. That Catiline departed initially without any intent of organizing an opposition in Italy is well argued by R. Seager, "Iusta Catilinae," *Historia* 22 (1973), 240–248.

39. Sallust, *The Conspiracy of Catiline* 36.1

40. Cicero, *Against Catiline* II.7–8.

41. K. H. Waters, "Cicero, Sallust and Catiline," *Historia* 19 (1970), 202–203.

42. Cicero, *Against Catiline* II.19 and III.vi. Cicero heaps praise upon himself throughout his attacks on Catiline; see his *Against Catiline* II.19; III.14–15,18; IV.18, and passim.

43. Sallust, *The Conspiracy of Catiline* 42.2.

44. Sallust, *The Conspiracy of Catiline* 45.1.

45. Four of the suspects, Lentulus, Cethegus, Statilius, and Gabinius, responded to Cicero's summons. A fifth, Caeparius, caught wind of the arrests and fled, but was later apprehended: see Sallust, *The Conspiracy of Catiline* 45.1–48.1.
46. Kahn, *The Education of Julius Caesar*, 167.
47. Cicero, *Against Catiline* III.11–12.
48. Cicero, *Against Catiline* III.10.
49. Cicero, *Against Catiline* III.11–12.
50. Kahn, *The Education of Julius Caesar*, 169, 172.
51. Sallust, *The Conspiracy of Catiline* 48.1–49.3.
52. On trial for extortion earlier in the year, Piso had been denounced by Caesar for unjustly executing a man in northern Italy. Defended by Cicero, Piso was acquitted. The ultraconservative Catulus disliked Caesar for his populist tendencies and for having defeated him in 64 for *pontifex maximus*, a prestigious post that would have capped Catulus's long and distinguished career.
53. Sallust, *The Conspiracy of Catiline* 49.3–4.
54. Plutarch, *Cato the Younger* XXII.1–3.
55. Plutarch, *Cato the Younger* XXIII.1–2.
56. Plutarch, *Brutus* V.2–3; and Plutarch, *Cato the Younger* XXIV.1–2.
57. Velleius Paterculus, *Compendium of Roman History* II.35.
58. Sallust, *The Conspiracy of Catiline* 55.6.
59. Sallust, *A Declamation Against Cicero* 2. If the charge is false, the writer goes on, then Cicero could demonstrate as much by listing what property he inherited from his father, and from what resources he was able to buy the house and villas.
60. Cicero, *To His Friends* I.9.13,16; V.1.1, V.2.8, and V.6.2.
61. Cicero, *To His Friends* V.7.2–3 and V.12.6.
62. Velleius Paterculus, *Compendium of Roman History* II.34; Plutarch, *Cicero* XVIII.1–2,4; XXII.5 and Plutarch, *Cato the Younger* XXII.1–3; Juvenal, *Satires* VIII.237–242; Lucan, *The Civil War* II.550–552. Dio writes that Catiline assembled the lowest characters, eager for cancellation of debts and land redistribution, to wage wholesale slaughter. And in preparation for revolution Catiline "sacrificed a boy" and tasted his innards while administering an unholy oath over the child's entrails: *Roman History* XXXVII.30,34.
63. Quotations by Gardner in Caesar, *The Civil War*, Appendix II, 314; Duane A. March, "Cicero and the 'Gang of Five,' " *The Classical World*, vol. 82, no. 4, 1989, 234; Frank O. Copley, introduction to Cicero, *On Old Age and On*

NOTES

Friendship (Ann Arbor: University of Michigan Press, 1967), x–xi; Copley accepts the existence of a conspiracy but notes that "the exact nature, extent, and importance of this conspiracy have been badly beclouded by Cicero himself"; Handford, introduction to Sallust, *The Conspiracy of Catiline*, 170; Brunt, *Social Conflicts in the Roman Republic*, 131; and Scullard, *From the Gracchi to Nero*, 114–115.

64. *Against Catiline* II.11–13.
65. Cicero, *Against Catiline* II.4,22.
66. Cicero, *Against Catiline* II.12.
67. Kahn, *The Education of Julius Caesar*, 160.
68. Sallust, *The Conspiracy of Catiline* 28.1; Plutarch, *Cicero* 16.1; Appian, *The Civil Wars* II.3; Cicero, *Catiline* I.9. In *Pro Sulla* 52, Cicero does belatedly name Cornelius; see the excellent discussion in Waters, "Cicero, Sallust and Catiline," 202–203.
69. Sallust, *The Conspiracy of Catiline* 24.4 and 27.1.
70. Waters, "Cicero, Sallust and Catiline," 204–205.
71. Cicero, *Against Catiline* III.*viii*.17–18, and 22–23.
72. Sallust, *The Conspiracy of Catiline* 31.3.
73. Sallust, *The Conspiracy of Catiline* 37.1–2.
74. Dio, *Roman History* XXXVII.38 and XXXVII.42; and Cicero to Metellus Celer, *To His Friends* V.2.

6: The Face of Caesar

1. For instance, Plutarch *Caesar* I.2–3.
2. Suetonius *Julius Caesar* 1. Plutarch notes a similar comment by Sulla: *Caesar* I.2–3.
3. During this period Caesar performed unsuccessfully as prosecutor in two high-profile cases of official corruption. One of these is mentioned in: Asconius Pedianus, commentary on *Pro Scavro* II.45 in his *Orationum Ciceronis*.
4. Velleius Paterculus, *Compendium of Roman History* II.42.
5. Cicero, *The Brutus* 238.
6. Sallust, *Histories* book 3.
7. Cicero, *To Atticus* I.4.2.
8. Plutarch, *Cicero* IX.
9. Plutarch, *Caesar* VI.1–4.

10. Plutarch, *Caesar* VII.1–3. Velleius notes that one of the two senators Caesar defeated, Quintus Catulus, was "universally esteemed as the first man of the Senate": Velleius Paterculus, *Compendium of Roman History* II.43.

11. See Kahn, *The Education of Julius Caesar*, 138–143, for a discussion of the land program and Cicero's role in defeating it.

12. Kahn, *The Education of Julius Caesar*, 141; also Cicero, *Contra Rullum* I, II, III.

13. Plutarch, *Pompey* VIII.1–4.

14. Cicero, *To Atticus* II.9.2.

15. Dio, *Roman History* XXXVIII.1 and 4; Velleius Paterculus, *Compendium of Roman History* II.45.3–4.

16. Cicero, *To Atticus* II.16.2.

17. In 56 B.C., Pompey claimed he heard thunder and used this as an excuse to dissolve the Assembly. Plutarch denounces his maneuver as a shamelessly deceptive ploy: *Cato the Younger* XLII.3–4.

18. Cicero, *Laws* III.27; *Pro Sestio* XLVI.98.

19. Polybius, *Histories* VI.56.

20. Gibbon, *The Decline and Fall of the Roman Empire*, II, 22.

21. Robinson, *History of the Roman Republic*, 226.

22. Dio, *Roman History* XXXVIII.4.

23. For a comprehensive study of Caesar's military skills and conquests, see Theodore Ayrault Dodge, *Caesar* (New York: Da Capo, 1997).

24. Lucius Annaeus Florus, *Epitome of Roman History* III.11.10.

25. Marcus Annaeus Lucanus (Lucan), *The Civil War* I.125–126.

26. Dio, *Roman History* XXXIX.25.

27. Plutarch, *Pompey* LVIII.2–3.

28. Caesar, *The Civil War* I.5.5.

29. Caesar, *The Civil War* I.7–1.13.

30. *To Atticus* VII.8. But a month later Cicero reports that Pompey was not happy with the forces at his disposal: *To Atticus* VII.14.1.

31. Suetonius, *Julius Caesar* 30.2.

32. Plutarch, *Pompey* LIX.1.

33. Marcus Annaeus Lucanus, *The Civil War* II.439–440.

34. Caesar to Oppius and Cornelius, *To Atticus* IX.7C.

35. Balbus to Cicero, *To Atticus* IX.7B.1.

36. Cicero, *To Atticus* VII.11.1 and VII.12.2.

37. Cicero, *To Atticus* IX.11A and 12, XII.51.2, and XIII.27.1.

38. Dio Cassius, *Roman History* XLI.36.
39. Plutarch, *Pompey* LXXVII.4 and LXXX.5.

7: "You All Did Love Him Once"

1. Sallust, *The Conspiracy of Catiline* 53.5.
2. The remark is ascribed to Cato: Suetonius, *Julius Caesar* 53; the same Cato who unjustly called Caesar a "drunkard" during the debate in 63; see Chapter Five.
3. For one of the better discussions of Caesar's writing endeavors, see F. E. Adcock, *Caesar as Man of Letters* (London/New York: Cambridge University Press, 1956), 6–18, 63–108.
4. Cicero, *The Brutus* 176–178, 260–263; Suetonius, *Julius Caesar* 55–57.
5. Suetonius, *Julius Caesar* 54.1–3.
6. Velleius estimates that Caesar slew some 400,000 people, and took prisoner a greater number during his campaigns in Gaul. Vehemently hostile toward Caesar, Velleius is apt to inflate the number; still it must have been a terrible toll: Velleius Paterculus, *Compendium of Roman History* II.47.1.
7. Julius Caesar, *Commentaries on the Gallic War* VII.29.
8. Caesar gives a detailed account of his campaign against Vercingetorix in his *Gallic War* VII.4–90.
9. Lucan, *The Civil War* V.273–276.
10. Suetonius, 27.1. Years earlier in 82, Sulla had offered and Pompey had accepted Sulla's stepdaughter in marriage, even though she was living with a husband and already was pregnant by him, and even though Pompey himself had to divorce the wife he had: Plutarch, *Pompey* IX.2–3.
11. Catullus, *Poems* XXIX. Catullus describes Mamurra as rapaciously corrupt and depleted by excessive sexual indulgence: *Poems* LVII.
12. Martial, *Epigrams* I.4.
13. Suetonius, *Julius Caesar* 50–52.
14. Dio Cassius, *Roman History* XLIII.43.20.
15. Quoted in Suetonius, *Julius Caesar* 49.1–3, 52.2.
16. Polybius, *The Rise of the Roman Empire* VI.37.2.
17. Anthony Corbeill, *Controlling Laughter: Political Humor in the Late Roman Republic* (Princeton, N.J.: Princeton University Press, 1996), 147–173 and passim; also Eva Cantarella, *Bisexuality in the Ancient World* (New Haven and London: Yale University Press, 1992).

18. Cicero, *Against Catiline* I.12, II.22–23.

19. Suetonius, *Julius Caesar* 22.2. Semiramis is described briefly in Herodotus, *The History* I.184.

20. Juvenal, *Satires* II.106–107 and passim.

21. Fuller, *Julius Caesar: Man, Soldier, and Tyrant*, 50.

22. Mommsen, *The History of Rome*, 495–508.

23. Caesar, *The Civil War* I.22 and I.32.

24. Alfred Duggan, *Julius Caesar* (London: Faber & Faber, 1955), 157; Kahn, *The Education of Julius Caesar*, 405.

25. Zwi Yavetz, *Julius Caesar and his Public Image* (London: Thames and Hudson, 1983), 136–137, 212.

26. Cicero, *Pro Sestio* XLVII.101; and *To His Friends* VI.1.3.

27. Plutarch, *Cato the Younger* IV.1 and IX.3–5; also Plutarch *Cicero* XXIII.2–3; Dio Cassius, *Roman History* XXXVII.22,57; Valerius Maximus, *Memorable Doings and Sayings* II.10.7–8; Velleius Paterculus, *Compendium of Roman History* II.35.1–2; Sallust, *The Conspiracy of Catiline* 53.5.

28. Michael Grant (ed.), *Selected Political Speeches of Cicero* (London: Penguin Books, 1989), 127; Syme, *The Roman Revolution*, 21; Brunt, *Social Conflicts in the Roman Republic*, 132. Albert Dragstedt explains away Cato's hostility to popular causes as due to his superior knowledgeability: "Cato defended the interests of the people—even against the people themselves": Albert Dragstedt, "Cato's *Politeuma*," A Γ Ω N, *Journal of Classical Studies,* no. 3, 1969, 69.

29. Mommsen, *The History of Rome*, 314, 265–266, 289, 320, 474. Marcus Porcius Cato is not to be confused with his great-grandfather, the identically named elder Cato (234–149B.C.); see Plutarch, *Cato the Elder*; and Livy, *History of Rome*, XXXIX.40.

30. The actual words quoted are Suetonius's, *Julius Caesar* 19.1, but they pretty much express Cato's view.

31. Cicero, *To His Friends* XV.6.1; *To Atticus* VII.2.7; and the discussion in Taylor, *Party Politics in the Age of Caesar*, 169.

32. Cicero, *To Atticus* IV.15.7; Plutarch, *Cato the Younger* XLIV.4.

33. Asconius, commentary on *Pro Milo*.

34. Plutarch, *Cato the Younger* XLVII.1.

35. Plutarch, *Cato the Younger* LX.2. Cato allowed that if slaveholders willingly gave up slaves, these could be enlisted into the military.

36. Cicero, *To His Friends* XV.4.12; Asconius, commentary on *Pro Milo*.

37. Dragstedt, "Cato's *Politeuma*," 72.

38. Hazel, *Who's Who in the Roman World*, 60.
39. As reported by Plutarch in his otherwise adulatory biography, *Cato the Younger* VI.1–2. Pliny the Younger also writes that Cato was known to have been publicly drunk on various occasions: *Letters* III.12.
40. Dio Cassius, *Roman History* XXXVII.22; Plutarch, *Cato the Younger* XXXIII.1.
41. Plutarch, *Cato the Younger* XXVI.1–2.
42. Caesar's comment is from his *Anti-Cato*, which is lost to us but is quoted by Plutarch, *Cato the Younger* XXV.1–5 and LII.2–3. A great admirer of Cato, Plutarch does not accept Caesar's accusation that Cato was capable of making the arrangement for material gain. Still he does squirm a bit: "But whether on other grounds, perhaps, the marriage was improper, was a matter for investigation."
43. Taylor, *Party Politics in the Age of Caesar*, 167–168.
44. *Julius Caesar* Act IV, scene 3.
45. Cicero, *To Atticus* V.1 and VII.21.
46. Both of these examples are from Plutarch, *Brutus* II.3–4

8: The *Popularis*

1. Appian, *The Civil Wars* (London: Penguin Books, 1996), II.11.
2. Plutarch, *Cato the Younger* XXXIII.1. According to Robinson, Caesar's plan for land reform was on a scale greatly exceeding anything the Gracchi had ventured: *History of the Roman Republic*, 343. Others like Yavetz saw Caesar's proposals as makeshift and improvised compared to Gaius Gracchus's program: *Julius Caesar and his Public Image*, 211–212 and passim.
3. Suetonius, *Julius Caesar* 56; Scullard, *From the Gracchi to Nero*, 148–149.
4. Plutarch, *Caesar* LVIII.4–5.
5. Appian, *The Civil Wars* II.48 and 101; see also Suetonius, *Julius Caesar* 40–44.
6. Suetonius, *Julius Caesar* 42.
7. Suetonius, *Julius Caesar* 40–44; W. Warde Fowler, *Julius Caesar and the Foundation of the Imperial System* (New York: G.P. Putnam's Sons, 1899), 344–345; James Anthony Froude, *Caesar* (New York: Charles Scribner's Sons, 1908), 490; Yavetz, *Julius Caesar and his Public Image*, 150–154; Gelzer, *Caesar: Politician and Statesman*, 246.

8. Dio Cassius says the dole list grew to such bloated proportions "not by lawful methods of increase": *Roman History* XLIII.21.
9. Suetonius, *Julius Caesar* 42. For discussions on Caesar's handling of the debt, see Fletcher Pratt, *Hail Caesar!* (London: Williams & Norgate, 1938), 295; Froude, *Caesar*, 488; Fowler, *Julius Caesar*, 342.
10. Mommsen, *The History of Rome*, 554.
11. Grant, *History of Rome*, 233–235.
12. Sallust, *Letter to Caesar* II.5.
13. Mommsen, *The History of Rome*, 555–557.
14. Dio, *Roman History*, XXXVII.17; also Casson, *Everyday Life in Ancient Rome*, 139.
15. Kahn, *The Education of Julius Caesar*, 370–371, 381, and 408; Gager, *The Origins of Anti-Semitism*, 98.
16. Suetonius, *Julius Caesar* 26, 42, 44; Carcopino, *Daily Life in Ancient Rome*, 193.
17. Plutarch, *Caesar* XLIX.6; Dio Cassius, *Roman History* XLII.38; Gelzer, *Caesar: Politician and Statesman*, 248; Gérard Walter, *Caesar, a Biography* (New York: Charles Scribner's Sons, 1952), 426.
18. Lucius Annaeus Florus, *Epitome of Roman History* IV.2.59.
19. Lucan, *The Civil War* X.488–505.
20. Caesar, *The Civil War* III.111.6–112.8.
21. Luciano Canfora, *The Vanished Library* (Berkeley: University of California Press, 1987), 81–82.
22. Suetonius, *Claudius* 42.5.
23. Gibbon, *The Decline and Fall of the Roman Empire* II, 25 n.9.
24. Canfora, *The Vanished Library*, 192. For a fuller discussion of Christianity's war against pagan literature and learning, see my *History as Mystery* (San Francisco: City Lights Books, 1999), 45–47, 95–103.
25. Edward Gibbon, *The Decline and Fall of the Roman Empire*, XXVIII, 891.
26. Canfora, *The Vanished Library*, 83–99 and passim.
27. Quoted in Thomas Cahill, *How the Irish Saved Civilization* (New York: Doubleday, 1995), 181–182. Cahill avoids mentioning that it was the Christians who turned the libraries into tombs, and systematically waged war on classical learning. Instead, he repeatedly blames the barbarians for the destruction of the libraries, offering not a single instance to support that misleading assertion; see my *History as Mystery*, 99–101.

28. J.W. Thompson, *The Medieval Library* (New York. Hafner, 1939).
29. Livy, *History of Rome*, preface.
30. Two examples from the world of art might suffice: The famous second century A.D. equestrian statue of Emperor Marcus Aurelius now stands in the Capitoline museum in Rome behind a specially built glass wall. The display sign notes that "the statue survived because it was falsely identified as being of Emperor Constantine." As such this coy comment makes no sense. At least one guidebook says it better: The equestrian statue of Marcus Aurelius "survived destruction only because the Christians believed it was really Constantine," the first Christian emperor: Dana Facaros and Michael Pauls, *Rome* (London: Cadogan Books, 1989), 80. Likewise, the beautiful Venus in the Capitoline museum, an excellent Roman copy of Praxiteles's Aphrodite of Cnidos, was discovered in the seventeenth century where its earlier owner, fearing the Christian axes, had carefully walled it up for safekeeping: Facaros and Pauls, *Rome*, 81.
31. Jane Gardner is one of the few modern-day historians who does not mouth the conventional opinion, noting it was "very doubtful" that "the great library was anywhere near the docks." If books burned they were more likely those "stored in warehouses by the docks"; see Caesar, *The Civil War*, translated and with an introduction by Gardner, 297, n.91.
32. Plutarch, *Caesar* XIV.1–2.
33. Dio Cassius, *Roman History* XXXVIII.1.
34. *To Atticus*, VII.7,5–7; and X.8,2.
35. Bailey, *Cicero's Letters to His Friends* vol.2, 449.
36. Syme, *The Roman Revolution*, 47 and 51.
37. Dio, *Roman History*, XLIII.50. One associate, Matius, reported that Caesar never discouraged him from socializing with whomever he pleased, even persons whom Caesar did not like: Matius to Cicero, *To His Friends* XI.28.
38. Appian, *The Civil Wars* II.13.
39. Dickinson, *Death of a Republic*, 326. Caesar's rule has been so thoroughly associated with autocracy as to make "Caesarism" a term of opprobrium coterminous with despotic power, especially in vogue during the nineteenth century. For an overview of nineteenth- and twentieth-century historiography on Caesar and Caesarism, see Yavetz, *Julius Caesar and his Popular Image*, 10–57.
40. Paul MacKendrick, *The Athenian Aristocracy, 399 to 31 B.C.* (Cambridge, Mass.: Harvard University Press, 1969), 49, 65.

41. Caesar, *The Civil War* III.11–12.

42. Cicero, *Marcus Claudius Marcellus* IX–X.

43. Suetonius, *Julius Caesar* 20. Grant believes that publication of Senate proceedings was intended by Caesar to discredit his conservative colleagues: Introduction to Cicero, *Selected Political Speeches*, 25.

44. Suetonius, *Julius Caesar* 86.

45. Mommsen, *The History of Rome*, 508.

46. Sallust, *Epistles to Caesar* I.7.

47. Froude, *Caesar*, 488; Yavetz, *Julius Caesar and his Public Image*, 126–127, 170.

48. *To Atticus* IX.18.

49. Gibbon, *The Decline and Fall of the Roman Empire*, III, 47.

50. Syme, *The Roman Revolution*, 78.

51. Kahn, *The Education of Julius Caesar*, 20; and Grant's introduction to Cicero, *Selected Political Speeches*, 17; Carcopino, *Daily Life in Ancient Rome*, 108.

52. Suetonius, *Julius Caesar* 41–42.

53. Dio, *Roman History* XLIII.14.6, 15.1–2, 21.1.

54. Plutarch notes that Caesar's monarchical desires were well advertised "and proved the most specious pretense to those who had been his secret enemies all along": *Caesar* LX.1.

55. Gardner, introduction to Caesar, *The Civil War*, 21.

56. Dio Cassius, *Roman History* XLI.38.

57. Thus March 30 was referred to as the third from the Kalends of April, March 31 was the second from the Kalends of April, and April 1 was the Kalends of April. March 13 was the third from the Ides of March; March 14 was the second from the Ides of March, and March 15 was the Ides of March. How the Romans settled upon this peculiarly cumbersome practice is not well understood. See Frank Parise (ed.), *The Book of Calendars* (New York: Facts on File, 1982), 62 and passim.

58. Plutarch, *Caesar* LIX.1–2; and Kahn, *The Education of Julius Caesar*, 408. Augustus made some adjustments to the calendar and renamed the month of Sextilis "August," after himself: Suetonius, *Augustus* 31.

59. October 5 through 14, 1582, were simply denied the opportunity of being enumerated into existence.

9: The Assassination

1. We have no surviving eyewitness reports of Caesar's assassination. The original sources—Plutarch, Suetonius, Appian, Dio Cassius, and a few others—all wrote generations after the event. In Appian's case it was more than a century later, and with Dio more than two centuries. But all of them had access to accounts that were closer to the time. Suetonius cites Cornelius Balbus, a close friend of Caesar's, as an eyewitness source: *Julius Caesar* 81. Appian and Suetonius both draw upon Asinius Pollio's lost histories. Pollio served as an officer under Caesar and was with him at the crossing of the Rubicon; see references to Pollio in Suetonius, *Julius Caesar* 55.4 and 56.3. In *Brutus* II.3, Plutarch had the benefit of "a brief but excellent account of the assassination" (lost to us) by the rhetorician Empylus, a friend of Brutus. Octavian, a prime actor in the last days of the Republic, and eventually the first emperor of Rome, wrote an autobiography that is lost to us but was read by Suetonius who refers to it in his own *Augustus* 2. Livy was Caesar's contemporary and wrote of his demise, but that portion of his history does not survive in its full text. These and other witnesses of the Late Republic were available to most of the ancient authors. Unfortunately, the ancients seldom cited their primary sources. One exception is Asconius Pedianus who is almost modern in his readiness to cite other writers, make cross-references, and even adjudicate between conflicting sources; see his *Commentaries on Five Speeches of Cicero*.
2. Dio Cassius, *Roman History* XLIV.7–9.
3. Plutarch, *Caesar* LVII.3–4.
4. Plutarch, *Caesar* LXIV.1; Appian, *The Civil Wars* II.111; Suetonius, *Julius Caesar* 83. Caesar so liked and trusted Decimus that he made him an heir in the second degree, that is, an inheritor if the primary heirs are unwilling or unable to claim the legacy.
5. Plutarch, *Brutus* V.1–2. In that same passage Plutarch lends credence to the myth about Brutus's Caesarian paternity; as does Appian, *The Civil Wars* II.112.
6. Plutarch, *Brutus* XII.1–2, XIII.1.
7. Suetonius, *Julius Caesar* 80.2.
8. Appian, *The Civil Wars* II.114.
9. Fuller, *Julius Caesar: Man, Soldier, and Tyrant*, 303–304.
10. Appian, *The Civil Wars* II.114. Antony later came to the same conclusion,

claiming he was spared "to make the act of tyrannicide look plausible and allow them to appear to be killing, not a number of men because they were enemies, but one man because he was a despot": Appian, *The Civil Wars* III.33.

11. Plutarch, *Caesar* XLIII.4.

12. Valerius cites Augustus as a source for the story of Calpurnia's precognitive dream: Valerius Maximus, *Memorable Doings and Sayings* I.7.2; see also Velleius Paterculus, *Compendium of Roman History* II.57.2.

13. Plutarch, *Caesar* LXIII.1–3,5.

14. Suetonius, *Julius Caesar* 81.1–2; Dio, *Roman History* XLIV.17. Appian accepts the validity of ill omens but says relatively little about them: *The Civil Wars* II.116.

15. Cicero, *Marcus Claudius Marcellus* I.1, VIII, and passim.

16. Plutarch, *Caesar* LXII.4; and William Shakespeare, *Julius Caesar*, Act I, scene 2.

17. Plutarch, *Caesar* LXV.1–2; Appian, *The Civil Wars* II.116; Suetonius, *Julius Caesar* 81.2; Velleius Paterculus, *Compendium of Roman History* II.57.2.

18. Valerius Maximus, *Memorable Deeds and Sayings* VIII.11.2; and of course both Plutarch, *Caesar* LXIII, and Suetonius, *Julius Caesar* 81.2–3, could not resist telling this anecdote.

19. Appian, *The Civil Wars* II.116; Dio Cassius, *Roman History* XLIV.18.

20. Appian, *The Civil Wars* II.109.

21. Dio, *Roman History* XLIV.16.

22. Appian, *The Civil Wars* II.117. Most biographers say it was Trebonius. Plutarch also names Trebonius in *Brutus* XVII.1–2, but contradicts himself in *Caesar* LXVI.3, claiming that Brutus Albinus delayed Antony.

23. The story goes that upon seeing Marcus Brutus attacking him, Caesar exclaimed in Greek *"kai su, teknon?"* (Thou too, my child?), to which Shakespeare gave his famous Latinized rendering: *"et tu Brute?" Julius Caesar,* Act III, scene 1. Dio notes that when Brutus struck him, Caesar uttered, "Thou, too, my child?": *Roman History* XLIV.19. Some accounts claim, according to Plutarch, *Caesar* LXVI.6–7, that Caesar ceased to struggle or defend himself when he saw Brutus's sword drawn, so disheartened was he. It is all more legend than fact. Caesar, as I have already noted, never thought of Brutus as his son. If he did register special dismay about a Brutus, it more likely would have been toward the traitorous Decimus Brutus, whom he trusted and loved as a comrade-in-arms.

24. Plutarch, *Caesar* LXVII.1–3.
25. Walter, *Caesar*, 530. According to Walter it was the festival of *Anna Perenna*.
26. Dio, *Roman History* XLIV.21.
27. Cicero, *To His Friends* XI.7,8 and XII.22.
28. Cicero, *To His Friends* XI.5.
29. Dio, *Roman History* XLIV.10–11.
30. Suetonius, *Julius Caesar* 80.
31. Dio, *Roman History* XLIII.50.
32. Appian, *The Civil Wars* II.134.
33. Appian, *The Civil Wars* II.131,141.
34. Dio, *Roman History* XLIV.34.
35. Appian, *The Civil Wars* II.131.
36. Dio, *Roman History* XLIV.23–33; Cicero, *First Philippic Against Marcus Antonius* VII.2–3 and VIII.
37. Cicero, *To Atticus* XIV.6.2
38. Cicero, *To His Friends* IX.14, also VI.15.
39. Cicero, *To Brutus* II.5.
40. Cicero, *To His Friends* XII.3; see also his letter to Atticus, *To Atticus* XIV.4.
41. Appian, *The Civil Wars* III.62.
42. Dio, *Roman History* XLIV.36–49.
43. Plutarch, *Caesar* LXVIII.1, and his *Brutus* XX.2–5. Suetonius gives a different account, saying that Antony said little, and that the crowd's pity and indignation carried its own momentum: *Julius Caesar* 84.
44. Suetonius, *Julius Caesar* 84.
45. It is said that one group of rioters chanced upon and killed C. Helvius Cinna, a tribune who was one of Caesar's devoted friends, mistaking him for Cornelius Cinna, one of the senatorial conspirators, who had publicly denounced Caesar immediately after the assassination: Plutarch, *Caesar* LXVIII.2–3; Suetonius, *Julius Caesar* 85.
46. Cicero, *To Atticus* XIV.10.1.
47. Cicero, *To His Friends* X.28 and XII.1.
48. Cicero, *To Brutus* VIII.2.1,2,5–6; also Cicero, *To His Friends* XII.4.I.
49. *To Atticus* XIV.15.
50. Cicero, *To His Friends* XI.27.
51. A copy of Decimus's letter is found in Cicero, *To His Friends* XI.1.
52. Cicero, *To Brutus* I.15.3–5.

53. Pliny, *Natural History* II.28.93–94. The same incident is mentioned in Suetonius, *Julius Caesar* 88.

10: The Liberties of Power

1. Dio Cassius, *Roman History* XLIV.1. Caesar himself notes that on the eve of the Civil War "those with old grudges against Caesar were mustered in the Senate": *Civil War* I.3.
2. Suetonius, *Julius Caesar* 78.
3. Suetonius, *Julius Caesar* 73. Suetonius offers several examples, including that of the poet Catullus, whom Caesar treated in a courteous manner even after being scurrilously attacked in his verses; see Catullus, *Poems* XXIX and LVII.
4. Cicero, *To His Friends* I.9.18.
5. Cicero, *To His Friends* VI.8.3.
6. Gelzer, *Caesar: Politician and Statesman*, 188.
7. Appian, *The Civil Wars* I. 4.
8. Mason, *Tiberius*, 8.
9. Grant, *History of Rome*, 241; and Grant's various comments in Cicero, *On Government*.
10. Cicero, *To His Friends* II.6.4.
11. Walter, *Caesar*, 121.
12. Plutarch, *Brutus* XI and passim; and Fuller, *Julius Caesar: Man, Soldier, and Tyrant*, 300. The *praetor urbanus* tried cases between Romans, and the *praetor peregrinus* handled cases between foreigners.
13. Valerius Maximus, *Memorable Deeds and Sayings* V.1.10.
14. As Gelzer comments, Caesar tried to complete his revolution without terror and without sufficient regard for his personal security; see his *Caesar: Politician and Statesman*, 331.
15. E. Badian, *Roman Imperialism in the Late Republic*, 2d ed. (Oxford: Blackwell, 1968), 87.
16. Peter Rose, "Cicero and the Rhetoric of Imperialism, Putting the Politics Back into Political Rhetoric," *Rhetorica*, vol. 13, no. 4 (Autumn 1995), 376n.
17. Quoted in Kahn, *The Education of Julius Caesar*, 144.
18. Rose, "Cicero and the Rhetoric of Imperialism," 361.
19. See Appian, *The Civil Wars* II.23,86; also Cicero, *To Atticus* IV.I,7; Fowler,

Julius Caesar and the Foundation of the Roman Imperial System, 246–254; and Yavetz, *Julius Caesar and his Public Image*, 209 and passim.

20. Caesar, *The Gallic War* I.40–44.
21. Caesar, *The Gallic War* VIII.39.
22. Cicero, *To Brutus* I.18.
23. Hazel, *Who's Who in the Roman World*, 28–29.
24. Appian, *The Civil Wars* IV.8.
25. Valerius Maximus, *Memorable Deeds and Sayings* V.3.4.
26. Tacitus, *Annals* I.2,1.
27. Pliny, *Natural History* XIV.1.5.
28. Suetonius, *Augustus* 41.1.
29. Suetonius, *Augustus* 32.
30. Brunt, *Social Conflicts in the Roman Republic*, 149.
31. Scullard, *From the Gracchi to Nero*, 238–244.
32. According to Suetonius, *Augustus* 40.3. On Augustus, see also Dio, *Roman History* LV.13; M.I. Finley, *Aspects of Antiquity*, 2d ed. (New York: Penguin Books, 1977), 150; Brunt, *Social Conflicts in the Roman Republic*, 154.
33. Gibbon, *The Decline and Fall of the Roman Empire*, III, 47–55.
34. Peter Dale Scott, *Deep Politics and the Death of JFK* (Berkeley: University of California Press, 1993), 313.
35. Cicero, *To Atticus* XIV.3.
36. Carcopino, *Daily Life in Ancient Rome*, 230.
37. See Jo-Ann Shelton's comments in her *As the Romans Did: A Sourcebook in Roman History*, 2d ed. (New York and Oxford: Oxford Univerity Press, 1998), 156, and excerpts therein from Tacitus, *A Dialogue on Orators* 34.1–6, favorably comparing rhetoricians from the earlier republican era to those of imperial times. As J.P. Sullivan comments, "Under the Empire political conditions reduced the importance of oratory enormously"; see his notes on Petronius, *The Satyricon and The Fragments* (Harmondsworth, Middlesex: Penguin Books, 1969), 182.
38. Pliny the Younger, *Letters* X.33–34.
39. Gibbon, *The Decline and Fall of the Roman Empire*, III, 55–56; and Ste. Croix, *The Class Struggle in the Ancient Greek World*, 380.
40. Appian, *The Civil Wars* I.16.
41. Quoted in Ste. Croix, *The Class Struggle in the Ancient Greek World*, 494. A similar point is made by Starr: the aristocracy's "primary function and activity after all was the supervision and maintenance of their wealth": Chester

Starr, *The Roman Empire, 27 BC to AD 476* (New York: Oxford University Press, 1982), 63.

11: Bread and Circuses

1. See the critical comment by Rose, "Cicero and the Rhetoric of Imperialism," 362n.
2. Cicero, *To Atticus* I.16,11 and I.19,4; *To His Friends*, XI.7.1; *Philippics*, II.116 and VIII.9.
3. Polybius, *Histories* VI.56
4. Plutarch, *Cato the Younger* XXVI.1–2.
5. Asconius Pedianus, commentary on Pro Milo, in his *Orationum Ciceronis*.
6. Appian, *The Civil Wars* I.59 and II.13.
7. Yavetz, *Julius Caesar and his Public Image*, 18.
8. For these and other such negative labeling, see Dickinson, *Death of a Republic*, 328–329 and passim; Brunt, *Social Conflicts in the Roman Republic*, 109, 139; Gelzer, *Caesar: Politician and Statesman*, 48 and passim; Saunders and Collins, in their glossary in Mommsen, *The History of Rome*, 589; Fuller, *Julius Caesar: Man, Soldier, and Tyrant*, 24, 53, 120n, 194, 284, and passim; and Robinson, *History of the Roman Republic*, 138, 222, and 344.
9. Scullard concludes that Clodius's democratic law to legalize popular guilds "was to have pernicious results" for these clubs organized "gangs of roughs" who "disrupted order and security." But when describing the optimates' gang that murdered Clodius, he applies a different vocabulary: a "rival band of supporters under the able leadership of [Milo]"; Scullard, *From the Gracchi to Nero*, 30, 32, 38, 120–121.
10. Mommsen, *The History of Rome*, 23, 48, 73–74.
11. Meier, *Caesar*, 41 and 151.
12. Marx quoted in Ste. Croix, *The Class Struggle in the Ancient Greek World*, 371.
13. In a talk before the Washington Press Club carried on National Public Radio in 1988. Stone had just authored *The Trial of Socrates* (Boston: Little, Brown, 1988).
14. Mumford, *The City in History*, 228–229.
15. Juvenal *Satires* X.77–81. *Panem et circenses* probably would more accurately translate as "bread and races," especially for the modern reader for whom "circus" conjures up misleading images of clowns and acrobats. *Circensis* is

an adjective pertaining to the racetrack. The masculine plural *circenses* means "races." The great circuses of Rome, such as the Circus Flamminius, Circus Maximus, and the Circus Gai, were immense oblong tracks constructed for chariot races.

16. Scullard, *From the Gracchi to Nero*, 235.

17. Mumford, *The City in History*, 229.

18. Sallust, *Epistle to Caesar* II.5,7.

19. Appian, *The Civil Wars* II.120; and I.59, respectively.

20. Dickinson, *Death of a Republic*, 331.

21. Scullard, *From the Gracchi to Nero*, 85 and 120.

22. Ste. Croix, *The Class Struggle in the Ancient Greek World*, 371.

23. Alan Cameron, "Bread and Circuses, The Roman Emperor and his People," Inaugural Lecture, King's College, 1973, quoted in Ste. Croix, *The Class Struggle in the Ancient Greek World*, 371. According to one early estimate, the Circus Maximus, rebuilt by Caesar and used mostly as a chariot racetrack, held as many as 385,000 spectators. The elder Pliny places it at 260,000, still a staggering figure; others offer a lower number: Pliny, *Natural History* XIV.139, and Carcopino, *Daily Life in Ancient Rome*, 214–215.

24. Mumford, *The City in History*, 229, 231, 233–234.

25. On the importance of the organized spectacles, see Roland August, *Cruelty and Civilization: The Roman Games* (New York: Routledge, 1994).

26. Stewart Perowne, *Caesars and Saints* (New York: W.W. Norton, 1962), 86.

27. Juvenal, *Satires* III.159, and Casson, *Everyday Life in Ancient Rome*, rev. ed., 100.

28. Casson, *Everyday Life in Ancient Rome*, 104.

29. Suetonius, *Augustus* 44.

30. Tacitus, *Annals* I.76.5.

31. Dio Cassius, *Roman History* XLIII.23.

32. Pliny, *Natural History* VIII.7.20–21; Dio Cassius, *Roman History* XXXIX.38; Cicero, *To His Friends* VII.1.

33. Dio Cassius, *Roman History* XLIII.24.

34. George Rudé, *The Crowd in History, 1730–1848* (New York: John Wiley & Sons, 1964), 199–201, 210.

35. P.-O Lissagary, *History of the Commune of 1871* (New York: International Publishing Co., 1898 [1876]), 382–465, 499–500; and Graham Robb, *Victor Hugo* (New York/London:W.W. Norton, 1997), 466–469.

36. Leonard L. Richards, *"Gentlemen of Property and Standing": Anti-Abolition Mobs*

in Jacksonian America (New York: Oxford University Press, 1970), 82–85 and passim.

37. Rudé, *The Crowd in History*, 30, 45, 55–56, 60–61, 68, 178, 189. Of course, not all crowd actions have been directed toward democratic goals; keep in mind lynchings, anti-immigrant riots, jingoist attacks on peace protesters, anti-Catholic riots, and anti-Semitic pogroms. Anti-abolition mob violence often was perpetrated by community leaders and other affluent individuals, see Richards, *"Gentlemen of Property and Standing": Anti-Abolition Mobs in Jacksonian America*, passim.

38. On the occupations of freedmen in ancient Rome, see Brunt, *Social Conflicts in the Roman Republic*, 137; Neal Wood, *Cicero's Social and Political Thought* (Berkeley: University of California Press, 1988), 19; and Carcopino *Daily Life in Ancient Rome*, 179–180. Cicero allows that there were shopkeepers among Clodius's followers, but he labels them "criminals."

39. Cicero, *To Atticus* XIII.44,1. When speaking before the popular assembly in the Forum, Cicero could pretend to admire the people; see his comments quoted in Ste. Croix, *The Class Struggle in the Ancient Greek World*, 624, n.14

40. Appian, *The Civil Wars* I.116.

41. Tacitus, *Annuls* XIV.42–45.

42. Plutarch, *Caesar* VIII.3–4. Also note Ste. Croix's comment in *The Class Struggle in the Ancient Greek World*, 353.

43. Discussed in Chapter Four; and see Plutarch, *Tiberius Gracchus* XXI.2–3. One exception might be Yavetz, who cites over fifty mass political actions known to have occurred during the Republican era: Zwi Yavetz, *Plebs and Princeps* (Oxford: Oxford University Press, 1969).

44. Plutarch, *Tiberius Gracchus* VIII.1–2,5; and *Gaius Gracchus* VIII.1–2, 5 and XII.1.

45. Plutarch, *Gaius Gracchus* XVIII.2. The people also erected a bronze statue to Cornelia, with the inscription: "Cornelia, mother of the Gracchi": *Gaius Gracchus* IV.2–4.

46. Mommsen, *The History of Rome*, 488.

47. Mommsen, *The History of Rome*, 145.

48. Kahn, *The Education of Julius Caesar*, 117.

49. Cicero, *To Atticus* VII.3.

50. Suetonius, Julius Caesar 75.

51. Plutarch, *Caesar* V.1–2.

52. Kahn, *The Education of Julius Caesar*, 134.

53. Suetonius, *Julius Caesar* 16.
54. Plutarch, *Caesar* LXI.3–4.
55. John Emerich Edward Dalberg-Acton, *Essays in the Study and Writing of History*, vol. 2 of *Selected Writings of Lord Acton*, edited by J. Rufus Fears (Indianapolis: Liberty Fund, 1986), 169.
56. For a valiant late-nineteenth-century attempt to redress this, see Ward, *The Ancient Lowly*, vols. 1 and 2.

Index

Acton, Lord, 221
Agrippina, 20–21
Ahenobarbus, Domitius, 76
Alexandria, library at, 154–57,
    249n27, 250n31
Ammianus Marcellinus, 38, 156
Antonius, 91–92
Antony, Mark
    Caesar's assassination and, 170–71,
        173, 175, 252n10
    Caesar's funeral oration, 182–83,
        254n43
    Cleopatra and, 6, 229n3
    and extra-constitutional senatorial
        decrees, 196
    fictional depictions of, 5, 6
    homosexuality of, 136
    murder of, 170–71, 252n10
    Second Triumvirate and, 197–98
    Senate address post-assassination,
        179–80
    Senate addresses on behalf of
        Caesar, 125, 160
    wife's property holdings, 231n26
Appian
    on Caesar as popularis, 149
    on Caesar's assassination, 169, 175,
        188, 252n1
    on "Catiline conspiracy," 108

on land reform of Tiberius
    Gracchus, 62
on Milo and murder of Clodius, 80
and myth of Caesar and Servilia,
    168
opinion of the common people, 48,
    207, 209
on post-assassination, 181, 182
and Senate struggle against Gaius
    Gracchus, 204
theme of "faithful slave," 42
Appian Way, 78, 80, 117
Appias, 17
Aptheker, Herbert, 10
Ariovistus, 133, 196
Aristotle, 35, 56
Artemidorus, 174
Asconius, 55, 77, 207, 241n68,
    242n21, 252n1
Atticus, 88, 117, 128, 161, 181
Augustine, St., 55, 69
Augustus, 199–204
    adultery codes of, 24
    attendance at games and public
        entertainment, 211
    becoming emperor, 198–99
    and Caesar's assassination, 252n1
    calendar and, 251n58
    daughters of, 21

Augustus (*cont.*)
  homosexuality of, 136
  loss of liberty and popular freedom
    under, 201–4
  protection of wealth by, 199–202
  Second Triumvirate and, 197–98
  undoing Caesar's reforms, 199–201
Aurelius Victor, Sextus, 204
auspices, religious, 121–22, 245n17

Badian, E., 191
Bailey, Shackleton, 157
Balsdon, J.P.V.D., 25
Bibulus, 121–22, 141–43
Boal, Iain, 241n3
Boyer, Richard, 10
Bradley, K.R., 33, 34
Brunt, P.A., 55, 59, 70, 240n56
Brutus, Decimus
  in Caesar's assassination plot, 168,
    173–74, 253n23
  as Caesar's trusted associate, 168,
    189, 252n4, 253n23
  post-assassination, 178, 182, 184
Brutus, Marcus
  in Caesar's assassination plot, 168,
    171, 176, 253n23
  Caesar's political appointment of,
    189–90
  Cicero and, 86–87, 146
  as corrupt usurer, 146
  "*et tu Brute?*", 253n23
  fictional depictions of, 5, 146
  historians' treatment of, 146
  and myth of Caesar and Servilia,
    168
  post-assassination, 180–81, 184

  wife Porcia, 231n24
Burke, Peter, 230n11

Caepio, 134
Caesar, Julius, 113–29
  calendar reform by, 165–66
  as candidate for high priest, 118,
    245n10
  and "Catiline conspiracy," 103–5,
    243n52
  consulship of, 120–23, 157–60,
    189
  debt reforms, 151–53, 220
  early dedication to popular cause,
    115–17
  early journeys abroad, 114–15
  early political career, 117–20
  egalitarian/redistributive policies, 3–
    4, 118–19, 138–41, 150–53,
    157–61, 164–65
  fictional depictions of, 4–9
  homophobic invective of, 135–37
  as *imperator*, 129, 163–64, 182
  infrastructural reforms, 149–50
  intellectual interests, 132
  Jewish population and, 153–54
  land reforms, 118–19, 120–21,
    144, 149, 150–51, 158, 248n2
  legislative proposals, 149–62
  loosening the oligarchy's grip on
    power, 3–4, 138–41
  military campaigns of, 122–29,
    133–34, 246n6
  monarchical pretensions and
    autocracy, 162–65, 178, 215,
    220, 250n39, 251n54
  as orator, 132

personal qualities of, 131–37
Pompey and, 119–20, 123–25,
    126, 127–28
popular displeasure with, 178,
    213, 215, 220
popular support for, 127–28, 177–
    81, 217, 219–20
post-assassination popular
    sympathy for, 177–81, 182–84
and proscription of Sulla, 113–14
Senate and, 3–4, 124–29, 138–41,
    159, 160, 161–62, 187–88,
    251n43
as Senate *popularis*, 55, 82, 113,
    149–53, 189, 191
sexual exploits of, 134–36
slaveholding by, 134
and Sulla's rule, 115–17, 158
as supporter of libraries and
    learning, 154, 162
treatment of his opponents, 157,
    187–88, 189–90, 250n37,
    255n3
treatment of women, 24–25, 134
writing of, 132
See also Caesar, Julius, assassination
    of
Caesar, Julius, assassination of, 167–85
ancient historians' accounts of,
    252n1
Antony and, 170–71, 173, 175,
    252n10
Antony's funeral oration, 182–83,
    254n43
assassination plot, 2, 169–71
attempt to alert Caesar, 174
avoiding appearance of coup, 171,
    252n10

Caesar's own suspicions about, 172–
    73
conspirators, 167–68, 169–70
date of, 165
described, 1–2, 173–77, 253n23
explaining Senate opponents'
    motives for, 2, 170, 187–91
fictional depictions of, 5
omens/auspices of, 171–72, 173–
    75
people's views of, 177–81, 185
post-assassination, 177 85, 254n45
strategies in, 169–71
and tradition of sympathy for
    assassins, 55
as turning point in history of
    Rome, 2
Caesar and Cleopatra (Shaw), 4, 5–8
"Caesarism," 7, 250n39
Cahill, Thomas, 249n27
calendar, Roman, 165–66, 251nn57,
    58, 59
Calgacus, 17
Caligula, 203
Calpurnia, dream of, 172, 173–74
Cameron, Alan, 210
Canfora, Luciano, 155
Carcopino, Jérôme, 26, 33, 231n26
Carthage, 46
Casca, Publius, 175
Cassius, Gaius
    in Caesar's assassination plot, 168,
        175, 179, 181–82
    Caesar's political appointment of,
        189–90
    Caesar's suspicion of, 173
    leaving Rome, 184
    suicide of, 197

Casson, Lionel, 33–34
Catiline, Lucius Sergius
  assassination of, 82, 106
  electoral campaigns of, 90–91, 92
  homosexuality of, 136
  popular commemoration of, 218
  as *popularis*, 88–89
  See also "Catiline conspiracy"
"Catiline conspiracy," 88–111
  Allobrogian delegation and, 99–
    100, 102, 110
  arrest of "conspirators," 99–102,
    243n45
  Caesar and, 103–5, 243n52
  Catiline's departure, 96–97,
    242nn37, 38
  Cato and, 105, 143
  Catulus and, 103–4, 105
  charges against Catiline, 89, 92, 94–
    95, 102–3, 108, 109, 136,
    243n62
  Cicero crediting himself with
    preserving the state from, 106–7,
    111
  and Cicero's acceptance of bribes,
    106, 243n59
  and Cicero's tenure as consul, 90–
    94
  and climate of fear, 93–96, 98,
    106
  demonizing of Catiline, 94–96, 97–
    98
  execution of "conspirators," 105–6,
    143
  historians' opinions of, 107, 243n63
  lack of evidence for, 98–99, 102,
    110–11

Lentulus and, 101, 104, 105–6,
    108–10, 143, 243n45
  original plot to kill consuls-elect,
    89–90, 108
  Senate session and charges against,
    94–96
  Senate session in which evidence
    was brought forth, 104–6
  senators' reluctancy to move against
    Catiline, 96, 242n36
  troubling questions and implausible
    charges of, 107–11
  Volturcius and, 99, 100, 101
Cato, Marcus Porcius, the younger
    141–45
  attack on Caesar's land reform, 144
  Caesar's fair treatment of, 190
  "Catiline conspiracy" and, 105,
    143
  corruption of, 141–44
  drunkenness of, 144, 248n39
  fear of restive poor, 216
  historians' admiration for, 141, 144,
    247n28
  Milo and, 143–44
  personal affairs of, 144–45
  personal attacks on Caesar, 105,
    131–32, 144, 246n2
  suicide of, 190
  as tribune, 51
Cato Institute, 145
Cato the elder, 43, 247n29
Catullus, Valerius, 134–35, 246n11,
    255n3
Catulus, Quintus, 97, 103–4, 105,
    218, 243n52, 245n10
Centurial Assembly, 50

Cethegus, 101, 104, 106, 108, 243n45
Christianity
  attack on learning and pagan culture, 155–57, 249n27, 250n30
  Gibbon's secular views of early, 20
Cicero, 85–111
  and "balanced" constitution, 56
  Brutus and, 86–87, 146
  and Caesar's assassination plot, 169, 172, 181–82
  Caesar's generosity toward, 187–88
  and Caesar's land reform bills, 118–19, 120–21
  on Caesar's legislative proposals, 157, 161
  on Caesar's lust for power, 114
  and Caesar's oratorical abilities, 132
  Cato and, 142
  Cleopatra and, 6
  Clodius and, 77, 78, 79–81, 95, 160
  and the common people, 87–88, 160, 206–7, 215, 221, 259n39
  early life and political career of, 86–87
  ethno-class bigotry of, 25
  First Triumvirate and, 120
  as gentleman historian, 17
  as governor of Cilicia, 142
  and Gracchi brothers, 69
  hatred of democracy, 87–88
  hatred of the populares, 59, 95
  historians' admiration for, 25, 85–86, 107, 193, 241n3
  on homosexuality, 136–37
  hypocrisy of, 88, 128
  love for himself, 87
  Macer and, 115, 117
  as member of equestrian officer class, 31
  as novus homo ("new man"), 90
  and omens/auspices, 121
  Pompey and, 126
  post-assassination, 178, 181–82, 183–84, 188, 197, 202
  on proletarian activism, 218
  and propaganda of Republic's well-being, 192
  Second Triumvirate and, 198
  on Senate optimates, 54–55, 140
  slavery and, 35, 38, 41, 43
  slum tenements of, 28–29
  Sulla's reign and, 75
  wife's property holdings, 52, 231n26
  See also "Catiline conspiracy"
Cimber, Tillius, 175, 189
Cinna, C. Helvius, 254n45
Cinna, Lucius Cornelius, 72–73, 82, 113, 254n45
Cisalpine Gaul, 123, 160, 189
city-dwellers (plebs urbana), 27–30, 215
class oppression, 26, 32, 191–94. See also slaves and slavery
Claudius, 20, 21, 155
Cleopatra
  Antony and, 6, 229n3
  Caesar and, 5–6, 25, 129, 134
  in Shaw's Caesar and Cleopatra, 5–8
clientela, 54, 76, 139

Clodius (Publius Clodius Pulcher), 76–81
and Caesar's wife, Pompeia, 78
egalitarian motivations of, 140
historians' views of, 77, 79–80, 240n56
Milo and the murder of, 78–81, 82, 143, 241n68, 257n9
reforms of, 76–77, 209, 257n9
supporters of, 207
Cnaeus, 6
College of Augurs, 121
collegia, 76, 200, 219, 222
Collingwood, R. G., 13
Columella, 36
common people
under Augustus's rule, 199–201
Caesar's egalitarian reforms to benefit, 3–4, 118–19, 138–41, 150–53, 160–61, 164–65
and Caesar's monarchical leanings, 178, 215, 220
Cicero and, 87–88, 160, 206–7, 215, 221, 259n39
city-dwellers (plebs urbana), 27–30, 215
and Clodius, 76–77, 207
composition of, 213–15
critical judgment exercised by, 213, 215
as ex-slaves/sons of slaves, 215
fictional depictions of, 5, 7, 8–9
guilds of, 76, 200, 202–3, 257n9
historians' views of, 3, 17–18, 25, 206–11, 221–22, 230n11, 257n9
Macer and, 116–17
mass political action by, 216–20

occupations of, 213–14, 215
"panem et circenses," 208–13, 257n15, 258n23
"people's history of," 10–11
post-assassination, 177–81, 182–85
propertyless proletariat, 27–30
public entertainment and, 210–13, 258n23
roles in democratic political system, 45–46, 50–51, 235n2
and social pyramid of Rome, 27–30, 50–51
stereotypes of popular mobs, 213–15, 216, 259n37
Sulla and, 218–19
support for Caesar, 127–28, 177–81, 217, 219–20
support for populares, 216–18, 259n45
welfare and public assistance, 192, 208–10
women's lives, 21–22
See also populares ("demagogues")
Constantine, 156
Copley, Frank O., 243n63
Cornelia (mother of the Gracchi), 259n45
Cornelia (wife of Caesar), 24–25, 113
Cornelia (wife of Pompey), 231n24
country dwellers (plebs rustica), 30, 48.
See also common people
Crassus, Marcus
Caesar's early friendship with, 119–20, 123
Catiline and, 90, 102–3, 242n21
death of, 123
military career and claim to fame, 119

Pompey and, 103, 119–20
Crawford, Jane W., 242n21
Croce, Benedetto, 13
The Crowd {La Foule} (Le Bon), 214
Curio, 124–25

debtor class
  Augustus's indifference to, 200
  Caesar's reforms regarding, 151–53,
    220
*The Decline and Fall of the Roman
  Empire* (Gibbon), 15
Dickinson, John, 55, 159, 209
Dio Cassius
  account of Caesar's assassination,
    167, 172, 187, 252n1, 253n23
  on Alexandria library burning, 154
  on assassination of Gaius Gracchus,
    69
  on Caesar as temporary dictator,
    128
  on Caesar's legislative proposals,
    157, 158
  on "Catiline conspiracy," 107, 108,
    242nn36, 37, 243n62
  on Cato, 141, 144
  on Cicero, 87, 107, 242n36
  as gentleman historian, 17, 18
  on Jewish faith and practice, 153
  on people's approval of Caesar, 179
  and plebs' criticism of circus animal
    slayings, 213
  on Pompey and Caesar, 123
Dionysius Exiguus, 165
Dolabella, Publius, 57, 135–36, 146
Domitian, 203
Douglass, Frederick, 36

Dragstedt, Albert, 247n28
Drumann, Wilhelm, 241n3
Drusus, Marcus Livius, 71, 82
Du Bois, W.E.B., 10
Durant, Will, 168

egalitarianism, *see* reforms, egalitarian
elites, *see* Senate; wealthy Romans
Empylus, 252n1
Engels, Friedrich, 86
Etruria (Tuscany), 92–93, 96–97, 106

fictional representations of ancient
  Rome, 4–9
Finley, M.I., 41
First Punic War, 46
First Triumvirate, 120, 123
Florus, Lucius Annaeus, 35, 65, 69,
  107, 123, 154
Foner, Philip, 10
freedmen, rights of, 76, 87
Fuller, J.F.C., 26, 138, 170
Fulvius Flaccus, 68, 69, 82

Gabinius, Aulus, 87, 136
Gager, John, 18
Gardner, Jane, 164, 250n31
Gaul
  Caesar's conquest of, 123, 133,
    246n6
  Caesar's enfranchising of, 160
  "Catiline conspiracy" and envoys
    from, 99–100, 102, 110
  Cisalpine Gaul, 123, 160, 189
  Transalpine Gaul, 123

Gelzer, Matthias, 77, 154, 188,
    255n14
gender biases of historians, 20–25. *See
    also* women
Gibbon, Edward
    on Augustus's rule, 201
    on Caesar's changes to Senate, 161–
        62
    on early Roman Christianity, 20
    gender bias of, 20
    as gentleman historian, 14–16, 18,
        20
    on library of Alexandria, 155–56
    on political uses of religion, 122
    on Roman slavery, 32–33, 35
    and sympathy for Senate oligarchs,
        55
Gladiator (film), 8–9
Glaucia, Gaius Servilus, 71, 72, 82
Gracchi brothers
    common people's support for, 217–
        18, 259n45
    egalitarian motivations, 140
Gracchus, Gaius, 67–70
    assassination of, 68–69, 82, 96,
        204
    Caesar and reform trends of, 150,
        189, 248n2
    people's support for, 217
    reforms of, 50, 67–70, 74, 189,
        248n2
    Senate struggle against, 204
Gracchus, Tiberius, 60–67
    assassination of, 65–66, 68, 69, 82,
        96, 217
    land reforms (*lex agraria*) of, 60–67,
        82, 217, 248n2
    as *popularis*, 60–67, 82

Grant, Michael, 55–56, 151, 188,
    236n26, 251n43
Greeks, 25–26, 159
Gregory XIII, Pope, 166
guilds, 76–77, 200, 202–3,
    257n9

Handford, S.A., 63
Hannibal, 46
Herodotus, 17
Hirtius, Aulus, 189
History (Sallust), 116
history and gentlemen historians, 13–
    26, 230n11
    admiration for Cicero, 25, 85–86,
        107, 193, 241n3
    and Alexandria library burning, 154–
        55, 157, 250n31
    alternative views, 16–17, 18–19,
        210–11, 241n3
    Caesar's redistributive proposals and,
        157–58, 159
    "Catiline conspiracy" and, 107,
        243n63
    Clodius and, 77, 79–80, 240n56
    common people, views of, 3, 17–
        18, 25, 206–11, 221–22,
        230n11, 257n9
    ethno-class bigotry and, 25–26
    feminist scholarship, 21, 231n27
    fictional representations of history, 4–
        9
    gender bias and, 20–25
    ignoring evidence of proletarian
        activism, 217
    and land reforms of Tiberius
        Gracchus, 60–61, 62–63, 64

and motives of Caesar's assassins, 2
as patrician literary genre, 17
on *populares*, 57, 59, 61, 63, 65–66,
    69–70, 77, 83, 95
and Republicanism, 7–8
risks of "presentism" or its opposite,
    205–6, 221
Roman imperialism and, 16–17, 18–
    20
Roman slavery and, 32–34, 35, 41
and Senate plutocracy and "mixed"
    constitution, 55–56, 57–58
socioeconomic status and class
    biases shaping, 7, 13–20, 18, 25–
    26, 193–94, 221
and views of idyllic earlier times,
    16, 24
wealthy oligarchs, views of, 55–56,
    57–58, 193–94, 205–6, 207,
    221, 257n9
See also names of individual historians
Homer, 17
homosexuality, 135–37
Hopkins, Keith, 232n1
Horace, 23, 33, 39
Hortensius, 145

John I, Pope, 165
Josephus, 17
Judaism, 153–54
Julia (Caesar's daughter), 123, 124,
    134
Julia Domna, 20
Julius Caesar (Shakespeare), 4–5
    Act I, Scene 2, 13, 59, 205
    Act I, Scene 3, 85
    Act II, Scene 2, 113, 167

Act III, Scene 1, 27, 45, 87,
    253n23
Act III, Scene 2, 1, 131, 149, 167
Brutus in, 146, 167, 253n23
Juvenal
    on Cicero and "Catiline conspiracy,"
        107
    homophobia of, 137
    misogyny of, 23–24
    opinion of the common people,
        208
    realistic picture of Roman
        imperialism, 18–19
    on Roman class supremacism,
        32
    on slum tenements, 28
    on street crime, 29–30
    on wealthy attendance at public
        entertainment, 211

Kahn, Arthur, 86, 119, 240n56
Keaveney, Arthur, 75
Kiefer, Otto, 70

land reform
    and Augustus's reign, 200
    Caesar and, 118–19, 120–21, 144,
        149, 150–51, 158, 248n2
    Clodius and, 209
    Gaius Gracchus and, 150, 248n2
    and Sulla's dictatorship, 74, 209
    Tiberius Gracchus and *lex agraria*,
        60–63, 66–67, 82, 217, 248n2
    wealthy landholders and publicly-
        owned lands, 47–49, 60–61, 64,
        66, 70, 82

Late Republic
  class supremacism in, 26, 32, 191–
    94
  dates of period, 9, 229n4
  power in, 194–96
  Roman imperialism and, 16–17, 18–
    20
latifundia (plantations), 27
Le Bon, Gustave, 214
Lemisch, Jesse, 10
Lentulus, 101, 104, 105–6, 108–10,
    143, 243n45
Lepidus, 128, 170, 171, 177, 197–98
lex agraria, 60–64, 66–67, 82, 217.
    See also land reform
lex Oppia, 22
libraries and learning
  Alexandria library and, 154–57,
    250n31
  Caesar's support for, 154, 162
  Republican education and, 162
Lintott, Andrew, 65, 77
Livy, 17, 156, 252n1
Lucan, 107, 123, 127, 133–34, 154–55
Lucceius, Lucius, 106–7
Lucius Septimus, 7

Macer, Licinius, 115–17, 120
Mamurra, 135, 246n11
Manilius, Gaius, 76, 87
Manlius, 93, 96–97
Marcia (wife of Cato), 145
Marcus Aurelius, 250n30
Marius, Gaius, 71–72, 82, 113, 117–
    18, 162, 189, 219
Martial, 39–40, 135, 232n6
Marx, Karl, 208

Mason, Ernst, 188
Mathiez, Albert, 10
Meier, Christian, 69–70, 75, 208,
    239n38
Messalina (wife of Claudius), 20
Metellus, Caecilius, 219
Metellus Nepos, 94
Metellus Scipio, 80–81, 86, 124,
    241n68
Milo, Titus Annius, 78–81, 143–44,
    257n9
Mithridates, King, 16
Mommsen, Theodore
  on Caesar as "democratic king,"
    164
  on Caesar's debt reforms, 151
  on Cato, 141
  on Cicero, 241n3
  disapproval for radical reformers,
    57, 75, 82
  opinion of common people, 25,
    207–8
  on Sulla, 75
  on Tiberius Gracchus, 63, 64
Morais, Herbert, 10
Morton, A.L., 10
Mumford, Lewis, 208, 210–11

Nasica, Publius, 64–65, 217
Nero, 20–21, 203, 216
Nicomedes, King, 114, 135
nobility, *see* Senate; wealthy Romans

Octavia (Caesar's niece), 134
Octavius, Gaius
  and Caesar's assassination, 252n1

daughters of, 21
Second Triumvirate and, 197–98
taking title of "Augustus," 198–99
See also Augustus
Octavius, Marcus, 62
oligarchy, see Senate; wealthy Romans
omens/auspices
of Caesar's assassination, 171–72
political uses of, 76–77, 121–22, 245n17
optimates ("best men"), 54–56. See also Senate; wealthy

"panem et circenses" (bread and circuses), 208–13
public entertainment, 210–13, 258n23
welfare, 208–10
Pansa, C. Vibius, 189
Paris Commune, 214
Parthians, 123
Pedius, 81
Pericles, 122
Perowne, Stewart, 211
Petronius, 39
Philemon, Aemilius, 80–81, 241n68
Piso, 103–4, 243n52
Plancus, Munatius, 189
Plato, 35, 57, 237n27
Plebeian Assembly, 235n10
Pliny the elder, 48–49, 184, 199, 258n23
Pliny the younger, 25, 42, 203, 248n39
Plutarch
on Caesar and library of Alexandria, 154

on Caesar's assassination, 167–68, 169, 172, 252n1, 253nn22, 23
on Caesar's candidacy for high priest, 118
on Caesar's legislative reforms, 157
on Caesar's monarchical desires, 251n54
on Caesar's suspicion of Cassius, 173
on "Catiline conspiracy," 104, 107, 108
on Cato, 141, 144, 248n42
on Gaius Gracchus, 68
as gentleman historian, 17
on law protecting smallholders, 47–48
opinion of the common people, 207
on political use of auspices, 245n17
populares and, 60–61, 62–63, 64, 68, 77
proletarian activism and, 216–18, 220
on Servilia and Caesar, 105, 168
and Shakespeare's Julius Caesar, 5
on Tiberius Gracchus, 60–61, 62–63, 64, 66–67
political structure of Rome, 45–58
"balanced"/"mixed" constitution and limited popular participation, 55–58, 237n27
Centurial Assembly, 50
democratic political structure, 49–52
election corruption, 52
founding of Rome and early rule, 45
imperialistic conquests and alliances, 46–47

political structure of Rome (*cont.*)
  legislative assemblies, 50–51
  magistrates, 51, 53, 235n11
  patrician-plebeian distinction, 45–
    46, 51, 235n2
  Plebeian Assembly, 235n10
  role of common people in, 45–46,
    49–50, 51, 235n2
  Tribal Assembly of the People, 50,
    62, 73, 74, 128, 159, 235n10
  Tribunate of the People, 51
  wealthy and, 47–49, 52–53, 82
  See also Senate
Pollio, Asinius, 252n1
Polybius, 17, 56, 121–22, 136, 207,
  221, 237n27
Pomeroy, Sarah B., 231n27
Pompeia, 78
Pompey
  as beneficiary of Cato's corruption,
    142–43
  Caesar's defeat of, 129
  Caesar's early friendship with, 119–
    20, 123
  "Catiline conspiracy" and, 110
  Crassus and, 103, 119–20
  murder of, 129, 231n24
  political use of auspices by, 245n17
  post-assassination, 195–96
  rejection of negotiated settlement
    with Caesar, 124–25, 126
  Sulla and, 119
  theater of, 212
  wives of, 123, 124, 134, 231n24,
    246n10
populares ("demagogues"), 55, 59–83
  assassinations of, 64–67, 68–72, 78–
    82

Caesar as, 55, 82, 113, 149–53,
  189, 191
Catiline as, 88–89
Clodius as, 76–81, 82
historians' disapproval of, 57, 59,
  61, 63, 69–70, 77, 83, 95,
  240n56
named and discussed, 70–72
reforms of, 60–72, 74, 76–77, 82
reforms of Gaius Gracchus, 67–70,
  74
reforms of Tiberius Gracchus, 60–
  67, 82
Senate oligarchs' attacks on, 64–
  67, 82–83
struggles against Sulla, 74–75, 120
Sulla's reactionary violence against,
  72–75, 120, 239n45, 240n49
See also land reform
Porcia, 231n24
propertyless proletariat (*proletarii*), 27–
  30. *See also* common people
proscriptions of Sulla, 73, 88, 113–
  14, 128–29, 239n45
Ptolemy, King of Egypt, 6, 129, 132

Quintus, 91

Ra, 7
reforms, egalitarian, 139–41
  Caesar's, 3–4, 118–19, 138–41,
    150–53, 157–61, 164–65
  necessity of popular leaders
    pursuing, 139–40
  and optimates' misleading appeals,
    140–47

Sulla's violent suppression of, 72–
75, 158, 239n45, 240n49
See also land reform
Reid, Whitelaw, 42
religion
auspices and omens, 121–22,
245n17
Christian attack on pagan culture,
155–57, 249n27, 250n30
Judaism, 153–54
Republicanism, 7–8
Richards, Leonard, 214
Robinson, Cyril, 19, 25–26, 56, 65,
248n2
Romulus, 45
Rudé, George, 10, 214–15
Rufus, in Shaw's *Caesar and Cleopatra*,
7
Rufus, Marcus Caelius, 57
ruling class. *See* wealthy Romans
Russia, present-day, 57

Salamis, 146
Sallust
on Caesar's personal qualities,
131
on "Catiline conspiracy," 89–90,
102, 103, 106, 108, 109, 111
on Cato, 141
egalitarian views, 152, 161
homosexuality of, 136
idyllic picture of earlier times, 16
as *novus homo* ("new man"), 90
opinion of common people, 208–9
on Senate governance, 54
on Sulla's order, 75
on upper-class women, 23

Saturninus, Lucius Appuleius, 70–71,
72, 82
Schumpeter, Joseph, 19
Scullard, H.H.
opinions of the common people,
207, 208, 209, 257n9
on Sulla's reforms, 75
sympathy for Senate oligarchs, 56,
65–66, 69, 75
Second Punic War, 22, 46
Second Triumvirate, 197–98
Semiramis, 137
Senate
and assassination of Tiberius
Gracchus, 64–67, 68, 69, 96
under Augustus's rule, 199–204
and "balanced"/"mixed"
constitution, 55–58, 237n27
Caesar as Senate *popularis*, 55, 82,
113, 149–53, 189, 191
Caesar breaking stranglehold of
senatorial aristocracy, 3–4, 138–
41, 160, 161–62, 188, 191,
251n43
Caesar's changes to make-up of,
160, 161–62
Caesar's exchanges and
relationships with, 124–29, 187–
88, 255nn1, 3
extra-constitutionality in interest of
elite power, 195–96
film depictions of, 8–9
inequalities within, 53–54
inner circle of nobles, 53–55
magistracy and, 51, 53
optimates ("best men"), 54–56
patricians and plebeians in, 46
patronage and, 54, 76

Senate (*cont.*)
and political structure of Rome, 51, 53–58
and *populares* reformers, 55, 59–83
post-assassination and Caesar's reforms, 179–82
as republic of the few (plutocracy), 55–58
Republicanism and oligarchic privilege, 8
under Sulla's rule, 73–74
and the Tribunate of the People, 51
See also Caesar, assassination; *populares* ("demagogues"); wealthy Romans
Seneca, 37, 38–39
Sertorius, Quintus, 75
Servilia, 25, 105, 168
Severus, 20
Shakespeare, William, 1, 4–5, 7, 146. *See also Julius Caesar* (Shakespeare)
Shaw, George Bernard, 4, 5–8
Sicinius, Cnaeus, 74–75
Silanus, 104, 105
slaves and slavery, 32–43
Augustus and slaveocracy, 200–201
Caesar's slaveholding, 134
Cato and slaveocracy, 143, 247n35
Cicero and, 35, 38, 41, 43
common people protesting retributive killing of, 215–16
ex-slaves in common population, 215
and exploitative class relations, 42–43
"faithful slave" theme, 42
fugitive slave problem, 37–38, 234n35

historians' treatment of, 32–34, 35, 41
lives of slaves, 38–41
manumission, 33, 34–35, 36, 200–201
racist ideology and, 35
relationship between master and slave, 35–38, 41–43
sexual exploitation of, 39–41, 136
slave class (*servi*), 27, 232n1
slave rebellions, 35, 38, 103, 119
slums and tenements, 28–29, 32
social pyramid of Rome, 27–43
city-dwellers (*plebs urbana*), 27–30
class supremacism, 26, 32, 191–94
country dwellers (*plebs rustica*), 30, 48
middle class, 30
propertyless proletariat (*proletarii*), 27–30
small farmers, 30, 47–48
wealthy officer class and nobility, 30–32
See also slaves and slavery
Spartacus slave rebellion, 35, 38, 103, 119
Spurinna, 174
Starr, Chester, 256n41
Ste. Croix, G.E.M. de, 10, 210
Stone, I.F., 208
Strabo, 155
street crime, 29–30
Suetonius
on Antony's funeral oration, 182–83, 254n43
and Caesar's assassination, 169, 172, 187, 252n1
on Caesar's debt reforms, 151

on Caesar's homophobic invective,
137
on Caesar's relations with his
opponents, 187, 255n3
on Caesar's spending and pillaging,
132
on "Catiline conspiracy," 108–9
on *collegia*, 200
as gentleman historian, 17
on library of Alexandria, 155
on popular views of Caesar, 178,
219
Sulla, Faustus, 134
Sulla, Lucius Cornelius, 72–75
Caesar and, 113–14, 115, 157–58
Caesar's rule as differing from, 158
Catiline and, 88
historians' approval of, 75
proscriptions of, 73, 88, 113–14,
128–29, 239n45
stepdaughter of, 246n10
violent suppression of egalitarian
reforms, 72–75, 120, 158,
239n45, 240n49
Sullivan, J.P., 256n37
Sulpicius Rufus, 71, 72, 82
Syme, Sir Ronald, 35, 85, 157–58,
162

Tacitus, 17, 55, 199, 202, 215–16,
230n11
Tarquinius, Lucius, 102–3
Taylor, Lilly Ross, 145
Temple of Julius Caesar, 185
Theophilus, bishop, 155–56
Thucydides, 17
Tiberius, 211

Trajan, 203
Transalpine Gaul, 123
Trebonius, Gaius, 175, 189, 253n22
Tribal Assembly of the People, 50,
62, 73, 74, 128, 159, 235n10

United States Constitution, 56–57

Valerius Maximus, 17, 24, 25, 42,
69, 141
Varro, Marcus Terentius, 154
Velleius Paterculus
on Caesar, 245n10, 246n6
on "Catiline conspiracy," 107, 108–
9
on Cato, 141
as gentleman historian, 17
opinion of the common people,
221
on *populares* and other reformers,
69, 71, 77
on Sulla's reforms, 240n49
Vercingetorix, 133
Vitellius, 230n11
Volturcius, Titus, 99, 100, 101

Walter, Gérard, 154
wealthy Romans
at arena games and public
entertainment, 211–13
Augustus's protection of, 199–204,
256n41
and Caesar's redistributive policies,
3–4, 118–19, 139–41, 150,
151, 152–53, 157–60, 164–65

wealthy Romans (*cont.*)
  fear and hatred of common people
    by, 3
  landholders and publicly owned
    fertile lands, 47–49, 60–61, 64,
    66, 70, 82
  officer class and Roman social
    pyramid, 30–32
  Roman political structure and, 47–
    49, 52–53
  ruling class ideology of, 26, 32,
    191–94
  women's lives, 22–25, 40, 231n26
  See also Senate
Weber, Max, 54
Wilder, Thornton, 229n1
women, Roman
  Caesar's treatment of, 24–25, 134

  feminist scholarship and research
    on, 21, 231n27
  gender biases of historians and, 20–
    25
  lives of common women, 21–22
  lives of upper-class matrons, 22–
    25, 40, 231n26
  property holdings of, 23, 52,
    231n26
  rebellion by, 22–23
  self-sacrifice of, 22, 231n24

Yavetz, Zwi, 139, 207, 248n2

Zinn, Howard, 10